THREE
CHANGES
OF
DESTINY

RAINBOW'S MEMORIES

PIERRETTE
FIRMIN-DIDOT

(ALIAS RAINBOW)

CONTENTS

PART TWO: ENGLAND

FOREWORD

I was tempted to begin by writing "once upon a time" but life is not a fairy tale. For a tiny moment in time mine may have started thus, but a fairy tale it was not. The only semi fictional pages of my narrative are in Chapter Two, "Sweet Dreams and Harsh Realities", otherwise the absolute truth, as I remember it, has been written without embellishment or exaggeration.

The story starts in 1930, then continues with the circumstances of my birth in poverty in June 1931. Followed by my being abducted at six months old by a nearby châtelaine, to be brought up on my father's estate as his daughter in "Le Petit Château", my home for twenty years.

From babyhood to early childhood my stepmother pampered and idealized me, her son aged fifteen, was amused but also resentful at the intrusion. My father made much of me, but immediately after my seventh birthday he died.

My stepmother had divulged that she was not my real mother. I was sexually abused by an estate worker. Nevertheless, this did not entirely mar my childhood, there were many joyous, memorable days too.

In July 1938, things changed. There began eleven years of an emotional and psychological dichotomous life. Up until then I had been secluded within the Estate. The Germans' occupation proved to be my own liberation. The Estate as one of their resting/training places for troops between there and the Front. Even Field Marshal Rommel visited. Originally we shared our home with the Officers, finally the entire Estate was requisitioned. My stepmother's and my rapport with the occupants remained amicable.

The English liberated Chandai in June, 1944. Afterwards my stepmother was arrested and put in prison and I was sent to a convent school in Paris.

I was never fully accepted or introduced to anyone. I was mostly ignored by all. Hopes and nightmares, great enjoyments and deep sadness were my life.

In 1951 a scheming clandestine meeting between my husband-to-be, my stepmother and cook was agreed, resulting in three hellish years of marriage. I left him in 1954 for Paris but was ill equipped to face city life.

After another rape and rheumatic fever I had a regular job, rented a bedsit and joined an ornithologist club from which sprang two life long friendships.

There were more adventures and misadventures, such as escaping from being sold to a Pasha, sharing a hospital ward with a woman who had a black-skinned foetus in her bag!!

Then a miracle happened in the shape of "My-Ellen". She and I became spiritual mother and daughter.

At twenty-eight years old I arrived in England as an "au pair", there sadness and happiness were about equal. I was made homeless and destitute twice, first when single, next literally "holding the baby"!

My one and only child, Erica, was the issue of a love affair, a love child and the second miracle in my life. My daughter was two years old when I met a Royal Navy Lieutenant whom I married. An uneventful, rather dull eight years union.

It took over half a century and much research before I located my real mother. No help came from the Red Cross or Salvation Army. I did it on my own. Seeing her became paramount. I first set eyes on her in Normandy when I was in my fifties, she was in her late seventies. I knew her not and vice versa. She was the mother of nine, most of them unknown to each other. Is it not unbelievable to relate that, important as it was, no one had shown the slightest interest in the matter; all in all 98% were living in a 25-kilometre radius!?

Soon I knew them all, except one. My daughter and I had been a blood-related unit of two, we were now part of a kinsfolk armada! Twenty-six years have elapsed, three are still in touch.

I have worked as a "lollipop lady", asparagus farm worker and nurse, of course, to name but a few. All had to be intermittent owing to recurring cardiac dysfunction which, by 1996, had taken ten years to control.

In 1997 I lost all my central vision and was registered blind with macular degeneration. I have, albeit rather poor, some peripheral sight. The writing of these pages was only made possible by using an electronic "mouse" which transferred, inch by inch, the written words from paper to screen. Without that invaluable help I can no longer read or write.

May the reading of this book be easier than its writing.

Rainbow
Sutton Benger 2009

PART ONE

FRANCE

Starting at her birth in a desolate and isolated cottage in Normandy, to her abduction when she was six months old, the authoress narrates her first twenty-eight years.
Twenty-one of them being of two folds. From baby's bottle to her majority. Now she was part of the domestics, now she was belonging to the squire's family whose residence was a château. The protagonist lived there at all times (except at some times during World War II, of course!) The reader will follow her dichotamous trials and tribulations, as well as "from riches to rags" and vice versa.
Times of incredible happiness, yet times of profound sorrow. In hope of better education, she opted to learn a foreign language… It was to be English.
Unbeknown to her it was not going to be an "au revoir" but Adieu la France…
A Change of Destiny…

THREE CHANGES OF DESTINY

Chapter One

CHANDAI

It was at the Gare du Nord on the damp and misty morning of January 29th 1959. A reluctant farewell was taking place.

On the platform a tall, thin, grey-haired woman stood alone. Through her spectacles her lavender blue eyes were focussing on a young woman: her "spiritual daughter" leaning out of the carriage window, both with hope in their thoughts and sadness in their hearts.

Their goodbyes were brief, resigned and irrevocable. A few blown kisses, the waving of hands, then the unknown.

As the train gathered speed, taking her away from her native France, the twenty-eight-year-old woman began to reflect on her past.

Thoughts flooded my mind! Names, places and questions, "la belle époque", about which I had heard so much so often and yet, had been too young to remember. Semi-somnolent I flicked through my adolescence, and then retraced my childhood in Normandy.

Ah! Normandy! Where camembert, brie and a wealth of different cheeses are still being made.

That region of France is also well known for its apple blossom, come spring, from the humble gardens with one or two trees contrasting with the hedged green acres of apple orchards. The blossom swaying gently in the breeze, sprinkles myriads of pink and white scented confetti into the air, carpeting the grass. Three kinds of cider are made, Gros Cidre (coarse cider), Cidre Doux (soft cider), Cidre Bouché (champagne cider). The renowned Calvados being made of distilled cider.

Rural Normandy is dotted with isolated cottages, hamlets and straggly villages. One of these, Chandai, is the starting point of my story.

Situated along one of France's main arteries, the Paris/Grandville Road, once the N24 now the N26. Many of its cottages fronted the main road between Verneuille-sur-Avre and L'Aigle, around 44km from Argentan.

That main road from east to west passes through a crossroads. The village slopes down to climb up again, passing over the river Iton to finish at the westward crossroad a short distance from L'Aigle Forest. Chandai has its own minor crossroad and to the north, on both sides of the unmade road called Le-Chemin de l'église. There were low cottages and a few larger dwellings all with their traditional geraniums cascading from the window boxes. The village bakery was also in Church Lane, so was the wet cooper's yard. Predictably at the end, on its small grassy hillock, stood the église. Alack! these craftsmen are no longer there and the church, though still in use, is kept locked.

Southward facing Church Lane is a similar dust road flanked on one side by the low walls and railings of a spacious house, whilst on the opposite side, a massive solid wooden double-door concealed a large cowshed and a long old barn, the winter quarters of a flock of sheep. Ahead, following the farm boundary wall, a gate revealed the beautiful brick farmhouse with its stables and dairy. Also a succession of low buildings where apples were kept and cider was made. The farm also had its animal trough and pump. Octogenarian chestnut trees half-shade the pond. The farm's name? La Grande Ferme of course!

Southward from the crossroad following the farm wall, lime and chestnut trees lined a ditch but on the right there was a sloping meadow that abuts the river. A hawthorn hedge separated the meadow from a large garden adjacent to a two-storey multipurpose building. This was attached to a small house called "la petite Maison".

Further ahead was visible a terrace of single-storey outer buildings, an imposing flour mill, opposite a spinney of splendid chestnut trees. Then an open space ended the last stretch of this dust road, which stopped short at six-foot walls and railings, together with a double wrought iron gate. The main entrance to Chandai Estate. There was nothing grandiose, ostentatious or conservative about the place. Every feature unconventional, from the gardener's house to the stables and large wooded area, all had the mark of individuality. It was lush, silent, heavenly and to that effect, for the purpose of my story, I shall call it the Lush Oasis.

Chapter Two

THE LUSH OASIS

Beyond the foreboding gate within the walled estate was the Squire's childhood residence (fig1), about thirty yards forth, on the bare ground the road forked. The Upper Drive curling to the left leaving the Lower drive to run straight between the foot of a small hill and the brow of the river Iton bank. Passing through another wrought iron gate leaving behind the laundry building and the Chapel (fig 2). Upon turning right it made its way across two lawns to arrive at the Grand Château's steps (fig 3); once the Squire's childhood home. The Upper Drive started with a climb then meandered across a semi-managed woodland area. Following to the west it became part of the tableland in front of the Petit Château (fig 4), the new family home.

The only lodge, a pretty little brick house, overlooked rough ground and, at the bottom of a slope, the river. Some of the railings to the entrance of the Lush Oasis were attached. Here the sole access, a narrow wrought iron door, also served as a tradesmen's way in. This entrance was approached by an outdoor short flight of steps leading to a tiny balcony. Its side wall was at ground level but unexpectedly, the back of the house looked as if it were hanging in space. Yet another longer set of steps led down to the cellar and the lavatory, opposite the steps and attached to the house at ground level there was an 8' deep pit about 18' long by 7' wide known as "le Saut de Loup", the wolf leap. Two rows of heavy metal chains attached to their thick round bollards were anchored around the top of the pit stretching from the Lodge wall to the stairs, presumably to prevent humans or beasts falling to their likely death. "Le Saut de Loup" was, indeed, a rather sinister landmark.

As already stated there was nothing grandiose, ostentatious or conservative about Chandai's Estate. Both drives were canopied by tall

Fig 1: The Lush Oasis, my father's estate. On the left, le Grand Château (fig 2); top right, le Petit Château (fig 3); top centre, la Chapelle fig 4); in the foreground le Manège, my childhood roundabout.

Fig 2: Le Grand Château, my anccestral home

Fig 3: Le Petit Château

Fig 4: La Chapelle du Château

trees. From le Grand Château's master bedroom, the greenhouses and stables to the park, all bore the mark of individuality. It was lush, silent, heavenly and to that effect, for the purpose of my story, remain being called "The Lush Oasis".

"Le Petit Château" had once been the Estate's Orangery and later converted into a dwelling with the rarely used name of "Pavillon St Hubert" (St. Hubert being the Patron Saint of Hunters).

To my knowledge "le Petit Château" had always been François Firmin-Didot's adult home. When it had been converted I never knew, neither do I know when he became the owner of the Chandai Estate. However, a rational assumption would be at his coming of age (twenty-one in those days) in 1914.

Monsieur and Madame Firmin-Didot enjoyed a delightful home, situated at the top of a long but gentle slope with an extensive view over the Iton as it snaked through pastures and flower meadows. La Chapelle, le Grand Château's left wing, the nearby manège and an historic large Lebanon cedar could also be seen.

Over several acres comprised the walled garden, where vegetables, soft fruits and flowers were surrounded with box borders, also an orchard and asparagus patch. All of this was worked by two gardeners and their assistant.

In the garden water-troughs, goldfish chased each other. In the park birds sang, whistled and called all day long. On the trees red squirrels frolicked. Nothing but peace and tranquillity reigned. This is exactly how I remembered it in my early childhood. Who then could have even contemplated the thought of a second world war? Alas, less than a decade had elapsed when in June 1940 German troops set foot on the Lush Oasis, leaving behind the scars of their destructive first assault. The Lush Oasis changed forever. Lush it remained but an Oasis it ceased to be.

Chapter Three

SWEET DREAMS AND
HARSH REALITIES

Before my existence in Chandai, village life was unfolding slowly and routinely, much as it had since the end of the Great War. Extraordinary happenings seldom occurred in Chandai and, like all villages, people thrived on news of weddings, births, deaths and gossip, more often superstitions both religious and pagan. They shaped their days to the pattern of old customs and above all, the Roman Catholic calendar. Far from anyone's mind was the thought of another war, let alone a German invasion.

For the few, summer holidays were spent away from home, for others the village fête was their highlight. Each autumn the shooting and hunting seasons would start. In one way or another most of Chandai's inhabitants would find themselves involved in those events.

All over France the gentry were sending each other invitations to sporting parties. Gamekeepers were organising groups of beaters. Sportsmen were busy making their own gun cartridges, polishing their game bags and preparing their guns. The people of Chandai were no exception.

In a nearby hamlet there was the Bureau family who lived in poverty, the wife Marthe, a plough woman with their three daughters under the age of five, bore the brunt of their poverty. Her husband Gabriel had many jobs, in turn as a mason, woodcutter and road sweeper. She worked on the land but, to make ends meet, she waited at various social occasions including the Gentry, where sometimes she would sing.

She was a handsome woman, tall with sparkling brown eyes, her long black hair and pale complexion gave her the look of a gypsy.

In September 1930, after a day's shoot on a neighbouring estate the usual meal was being served. It had been a prolific and amusing day for the guns. Wine flowed freely, food was in abundance, shared recollections and laughter reached hilarity.

Amidst the hullabaloo the intermittent silences were filled with Marthe's singing. Some songs fast and daring, others slow and sentimental, like "My heart is a violin". Amongst the guests François Firmin-Didot watched the singer. Their eyes met and lingered. Cigars, pipes and liqueurs brought on a soporific haze over the party and no one noticed when the singer stopped.

A short distance away, in the loft over the stable, rustling… much more rustling than the mice in residence made, could have been heard. Abandoned to the arms of Marthe, the plough woman, the Squire forgot about his origins and for a while ceased to be a gentleman. He had been married for only two years but this was a different pleasure of the flesh, intense, secret, forbidden. For the first time he learned to sing silently. Together they sang in harmony. Oops! I do believe I was conceived.

I must confess that it is the romantic streak in me that prompted these only fictional lines in my book, it is the truth that my mother-to-be did sing at parties and certain it is that, in September 1930, sometime, somewhere, somehow my mother and father knew each other. It cannot be denied that on June 30th 1931 a woman's cry was heard. It came from a candlelit cottage; my maternal grandmother (fig 5) had delivered my mother of yet another baby girl. I was born at 11.50 that night. There was already Solange, Marcelle and Louisette; now there was Pierrette. My Zodiac sign is the Crayfish! The Moon is my star!

Fig 5: My mother's mother by the candlelit cottage where I was born.

Chapter Four

EQUIVOCAL PATERNITY

Where, when or how François Firmin-Didot (fig 6) met his wife to be I was never told. However the year is more certain to have been around 1918.

He was twenty-six years, Madame Anne-Marie (fig 7), née "de la Brosse" was then Madame Margueritte, she was three years his junior. One of Paris' high society beauties, a divorcée who was bringing up on her own her three-year-old son Hubert, the survivor of her only two children from her first marriage.

After serving as a soldier in World War I (fig 8) François resumed his life of bachelor "gentleman farmer" at le Petit Château until 1929, when, ending a ten year courtship he and Anne-Marie became husband and wife (fig 9). The "now" Châtelaine took her role with great zeal in the running of the house with competent authority. She played the "good Samaritan", visiting the parish poor without much compassion but usually in an advisory manner.

Fig 6: My father, Francois Firmin-Didot.   *Fig 7: My stepmother-to-be.*

Fig 8: My father in uniform.   *Fig 9: Man and wife. 1929.*

A few weeks after my birth the Bureau family moved from their hamlet to dwell in a semi-derelict isolated barn. No water, no electricity, no food nothing but poverty. Then Monsieur Firmin-Didot allocated them a rent free cottage in the village.

Madame Didot, as she was commonly called by those whom she considered being of the "lower order", took very special interest in Pierrette, the plough woman's last born. First calling intermittently, followed by a daily visit to check on my welfare and to give me my bottle. Now and again she took me with her to Le Petit Château for the day. After a short while she collected me, and kept me all day and every day, except at night.

One frosty December morning my "Benefactress" found me screaming. To keep me warm my mother had, as it was usual by the poor, wrapped up a hot brick from the oven in paper and put it in my cot. Unfortunately owing to the covering becoming loose the top of my left hand suffered a third degree burn. Madame Didot burst into a fury bellowing that she, my mother, was unfit to look after me, threatening that the "welfare" would be informed. Snatching me from my mother's arms she stated that she would bring me back when I was fully recovered. Vouching secretly to herself never to do so. She left the cottage for the last time and carried me to the Lush Oasis where I lost all contact with my own mother. I was six months old. This indeed was to be my first change of destiny.

Following my abduction, my maternal grandmother called at le Petit Château from time to time to enquire about me. Could she see her granddaughter? And please, would it be alright to take her back? How was she? What about the hand? Once or twice her two older granddaughters, Solange, 7, and Marcelle aged 6 came with her. Half hidden in the folds of the old woman's long skirt, they bravely asked to hold their baby sister? All to no avail, the Châtelaine stood firm and so it went on. Each time my grandmother called, Madame Didot, standing high and imperiously upon the doorstep, reiterated her justifications to refuse such as: 'Pierrette was sleeping, Pierrette was unwell and not to be disturbed, Pierrette would be given a far better life if kept at le Petit Château, never needing for anything'' etc, etc.

Having lost all hope of retrieving me, my grandmother understood that the Firmin-Didots would honour their responsibilities and secure my future. Little did the poor woman know, she was never to set eyes on me again! My mother then left her other three children with her husband and disappeared. I was kept in ignorance of her existence until I was seven years of age.

Some months later my father was losing his legal battle to give me his name, no child and heir of his was to remain a bastard. There are two contradictory versions regarding my paternity. On the one hand, Madame Firmin-Didot's who always assured me that her husband, in spite of his perseverance, had been refused the legal right to adopt me. The law, she claimed, did not permit him to do so because he was under forty-five years of age. He was deeply saddened by this. On the other hand, the version from one of my sisters, and which came to the fore many decades later, said that she herself remembered vividly the day when Monsieur Firmin-Didot came to the Bureau's cottage and approached her father regarding his wish to adopt me. This gave rise to a furious debate between the two men and, when Monsieur Didot presented the adoption papers to be signed, Père Bureau refused categorically declaring that he would rather walk on his knees than to do that. The hectic discussion went on for some time and, although sensible reasons were put forward by the Squire, no papers were signed. Whether it is true or not, no man of any class, courage or creed, knowingly or unknowingly, would admit to being "cuckolded", let alone to his adversary.

As a young child, therefore, Anne-Marie was my Mama, François my Papa and I called them thus. He called me his "little girl" and signed holiday postcards to me "Your loving Papa". I never had the need to question whether or not he was my father and no reason to doubt it. I always have and always will consider him as such. As opposed to my own mother's husband who was known all around as "le Père Bureau", never my father. François Firmin-Didot was always referred to me as "your Papa", but never your father.

For my part I know which way my heart sways and always shall — towards Papa. The evident reasons will become obvious at a later date and throughout my narrative François Firmin-Didot is called Papa or my father, his wife is my Mama or my stepmother.

Fig 10: My father as a child.

Fig 11: Myself as a child.

Chapter Five

MY STEPMOTHER, SHE AND I

The Firmin-Didot decree of my being kept for life at the Château raised much curious speculation amongst the village people, let alone the staff. This was told decades later. Young Hubert was bemused if not resentful, the Châtelaine was exultant, the Squire victorious, but Pierrette, partially

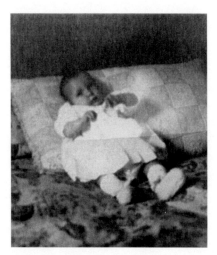

swaddled (fig 12) little thing that I was, was blissfully unaware of my new destiny.

My stepmother was an imposing woman, tightly corseted by whale-boned satin and cord-laced stays. Tall, bosomy she held her head high. She took great care of her appearance and usually wore close fitting three-quarter length skirts and blouses of sober colour. She had waist length blackish hair that she brushed meticulously twice a day. Her coiffure consisted of a bouffant that she beautified with waves made each morning using curling tongs previously heated on a

Fig 12: Myself, 6 months old on Madame Firmin-Didot's bed.

methylated spirit burner specially designed for the purpose. The remaining hair she plaited and made into a snailshell-like chignon. Stockings and low-heeled shoes, never sandals, were her usual footwear.

As one would have expected, Mama's make up was also completed as early as possible after getting up. Tastefully applied, cream, rouge, powder and lipstick but nothing near her eyes which, while piercingly blue, never seemed completely open. Her mouth was shapeless, her nose pointed, yet the vestige of her renowned beauty was still in evidence.

She was the second child of a family of ten. Their father, Monsieur de la Brosse, best friend of Monsieur Eiffel (as in the tower), was in charge of Nante's docks (I had always heard so). He had married a Fouquet du Lusigneul society girl who, having borne ten offspring, died in childbirth. After their mother's death my stepmother and her elder sister, Yvonne (Vonvon) helped with the care of their younger siblings. Later she and Yvonne were sent to a finishing school in Germany where both learnt the language fluently and had never forgotten it.

Later still, when as a divorcée my stepmother, then Madame Margueritte became engaged to François and for whom she had to wait ten years. She went to Rome and was requested to climb the steps of the Vatican on her knees, she complied. The Pope himself annulled her first marriage and gave her his blessing to re-marry in church.

This was one of my stepmother's frequent reminiscences. And so it came to pass that in the year of Our Lord 1929, Anne-Marie née de la Brosse, then Madame Margueritte, became Madame Firmin-Didot. Hubert, her son, retained his name of Margueritte.

The squire's mother did not altogether approve of her son's choice. A question of status and rank you understand! Two and a half years after legally becoming the châtelaine of Chandai Anne-Marie also acquired, by misappropriation, a baby, no less! Up until then she had been free to perfect the running of the house, socialising and keeping watch over her son Hubert's education given by Monsieur de Cikerzien, tutor in residence. Now she was to assume the permanent role of mother! (fig 13)

Fig 13: Anne-Marie became Mama.

Anne-Marie, my stepmother who became Mama, was distinguished and haughty, her speech, mannerisms, religious creed and judgement were rigid. She seldom raised her voice and even when her laughter reduced her to tears, it was done silently, yet she was authoritarian. Gesticulations were not done, arms akimbo were taboo. Crossed arms and hands were mostly used. When she reached her imaginary state of martyrdom, a frequent occurrence, she pulled out her handkerchief from under her waistband and could switch in one instant from being peevish to tearful. To her dying day, she exercised total control over Hubert and the defenceless, also over me, but not forever.

On looking back I now realise that Mama's method of caring for me was an odd mixture of love and cruelty. She was, in turn, possessive or dismissive and simultaneously charming yet disdainful.

My stepmother was indeed an enigma!

From early childhood to the time I began to assert my individuality and fight for my independence, our harmony was affectionate enough. She took me with her everywhere she went and watched me like a hawk; to what seemed to me, endless teas at her friends and relatives and to newly bereaved villagers. For each death in the village the Angelus "Ave bell", rang daily at 6.00 a.m., noon and 6.00 p.m., was replaced by the toll and still is. It rang thus for three days, the compulsory length of time between death and interment and during that time there was an uninterrupted wake. The devout called to view, bless the body and pay their respect to the mourners.

Mama never missed any dutiful visits and naturally I always went with her. It was usual on those occasions for the front door of the bereaved to be draped in black. Having entered we were ushered on tiptoe to the room where the wake was held. On the bedside table there were a crucifix, a burning candle and a scoop containing holy water and a small bunch of box leaves. Each caller, by making the sign of the cross in the air sprinkled the shroud with holy water; copying Mama and just tall enough to wave the magic bunch at bed level, I sprinkled the best I could!

Influenced by gruesome tales, a frequent subject of conversation at home, I used to wonder whether one of those lifeless creatures would one day be brought back to life by an ill-intended treasure hunter who would, as I had heard, cut their purple fingers off for the sake of gold rings. By the time I was a teenager, I had seen ample cadavers to prepare me for the horrors of the war to come and my future nursing career. As yet unknown!

However, the visits to Mama's family were slightly more agreeable. We often went to see her old aunt and uncle whose estate was six kilometres from Chandai. They lived in a delightful thatched manor. The old couple led separate lives. He spent most of his time in his library housed in a small outbuilding. He did join the company to take tea in the petit salon. If this was served in the grand salon, it was to listen to the baby grand being played. On these rare happenings, uncle would remain, otherwise he would retire to his books. Aunt

Fouquet, holding her walking stick, roamed up and down the corridors of the manor. I never made up my mind whether I did like her or not. Occasionally she spoke to me, a sentence or two, but mostly I was ignored by all. All except the uncle (fig 14) whom, when I grew older, I went to see secretly and with whom I held conversations about things concerning nature and books. From our common interests developed a close rapport. During the war I cycled to give him my ration of chocolate and we took tea together.

I would like to return to the "old" aunt who was often the subject of great amusement in our household. Not because she gave the impression of having stepped

Fig 14: My friend the old Uncle.

out of a novel written last century, neither because she wore long black clothes with pointed shoes turning up at the toes, but because of her habit of picking her nose! This she did skilfully and, having shaped fastidiously between her first finger and thumb the "pull-outs", she would casually dispose of them. Where pray? On her favourite radiator! This nauseous repository brought disgusted laughter to many faces and some called her Aunt Bogey!

My stepmother was my castigator, my comforter, my only guide. She could be my enemy or my ally but I never knew which it was going to be, she excelled in all the domestic skills, she made all my clothes, including overcoats, hats and handbags until I was eight and also supplied Papa, Hubert and myself with our long woollen socks (fig 15). She taught me to knit when I was four. Out of her own stock, she made me a five inch pair of knitting needles; they were blue with red sealing wax ends. Sitting on her lap leaning backwards against her ample bosom, her hands guided my small fingers while embraced in

Fig 15: She made all my clothes.

her arms, tongue out and holding my breath, I struggled with the wool. I felt so happy to be shown by her what she could do so well herself. There were so many gentle moments. In summer, we went to the flower garden and returned with our overflowing baskets. We would sometimes play butterfly-dominoes and cards.

Summers were summers then. Many consecutive weeks when frequent mellow whistling flocks of swifts undulated in the cloudless skies. The heat-scented breeze was carrying the soft sounds of the wild. Mama's flower-picking days were always beautiful. Immediately after breakfast she picked up our long, flat, brown wicker baskets from the floor by the front door. Down a short, bush-lined alley, Mama, basket and secateurs in hand, I with importance carrying my small basket with round-ended scissors on one side and my other hand holding Mama's trotted next to her. Flower arrangement was not the done thing, my stepmother assured me. Flowers in vases should look as if in their natural state. She never mixed any flowers but placed them in water to perfection. I too put mine in small vases.

Our autumn walks are also delightful memories, when we played buga-boo and hide-and-seek in the woods, knee-deep in the fallen leaves.

When I was very young, I used to spend the best part of the winter with Mama in both hers and Hubert's adjoining "en suite" bedrooms. There, in the seclusion of those quarters I whiled the time away nursing my dolls. They were always ill! Habitually I was told that I was too! I went down to the dining room for my midday meal but my supper, a sort of chocolate or vanilla custard pudding, I took upstairs; this my stepmother cooked for me on a small spirit burner that rested next to the marble washstand in our dressing room.

My intellect was fed on stories pointing out virtue and obedience to be praiseworthy, whilst individuality and initiative called for reprimand. Morality and religion, I was preached, were the panacea of perfection. Mama read fairy tales too, many fairy tales…. and then more fairy tales! I now find it interesting that Peter Rabbit, Brer Rabbit and the American Buster Brown also had their place on my shelf. Reading aloud was another of my stepmother's talents, she read to me all year round and at length. When she was in her reading mood there was no stopping her! It was not uncommon for her to read until her voice almost gave out!

Nevertheless, all was not happy and smooth as it might seem. By no means was I lying on a bed of roses. I had to endure my stepmother's change of mood and the principles she enforced to suit her peremptory self-interest. For example, all the while Mama read to me, I had to keep completely still and that proved quite difficult for a young child. Many a time I started, though timidly, to fidget, my goodness! I had broken Mama's flow!

"Don't you want me to read to you?" she would say crossly.

"Oh, yes please," I used to reply, wishing that the reading would stop.

"Well then, keep still! Here I am doing my best for you and all I get is ingratitude." She shouted, 'shall I continue? I thought you liked it." She insisted.

"Yes I do," I answered sitting rigidly. Perish the thought I should have said no! I remember how tears came to my eyes and how much my throat hurt to hold them back.

I recall with anger the two main procedures of getting ready for bed. Firstly, I had to soak for fifteen minutes seated in a bowl on top of the wash-stand. Those sittings, Mama maintained, would alleviate my eczema! How I disliked those performances, the practice of which continued well into my seventh year, and the feeling of humiliation when the dressing room door was kept open leaving me in full view of passing guests, usually males. Secondly, there was the religious routine. I had to rack my juvenile brain and confess to the Lord of the day's sins. Some evenings, having tried all day to be good, none came to mind. The problem was soon solved by the fact that thinking along these lines, I was committing a sin anyway! Pride, I was told, was one of the deadly sins!

After the purification of my soul, I was put to bed and left alone in semi- darkness whilst everyone else went to dine and spent the rest of the evening at the other end of the house. I was often petrified and calling in vain. The old furniture creaked, the wind howled eerily and my voice went nowhere. Rarely Mama came to me, but, if she did, it was to tell me that I was stupid and should behave. So I was better off hiding under the blankets!

It surprises me to know how many of my childhood memories are connected with my bed, presumably because I had to spend so much time in it, being, according to Mama, a delicate child. In later life I realised that, in order to fulfil my stepmother's excuse to pontificate and to gain her attention, the children under her care HAD to be delicate! This applied to her son, to me and later her grandson, but that is another story. It is a fact that before the removal of nasal polyps, I used to suffer from chronic sinusitis and frequent bronchitis, but I was by no means the invalid child that Mama would have everyone to believe.

I soon worked out that running a temperature was a sure way to justify all kinds of mischief. I had been known to carry a medical thermometer with me and by devious means, trying to increase its reading! Those proved useful.

I can think of two instances when my stepmother's nursing devotion changed my comfortable bed into a tiresome pen! I was six and kneeling on the arm of a chair watching Hubert doing a jigsaw. All of a sudden I lost my balance, fell on the edge of the windowsill and ended up head first in the wastepaper basket! Mama picked me up and carried me to her room. She cajoled me, everything would be fine, and she didn't think it was serious and so on. I suppose I was too shocked to cry, but when Mama laid me flat on her bed and blood gushed out of my head, my screams could have woken the dead! I had a two-inch cut on my scalp. Whilst the doctor sewed me up, without any anaesthetic, his "dear" wife held me firmly; poor woman, for years afterwards I hated her. How could I forget in a hurry such a painful experience? I was kept in bed for four days!

Five years later I was cycling along the lower drive when the handlebar snapped without warning, I fell flat on my face and this resulted in my nose being half severed. My tongue was lacerated and one of my front teeth was knocked out. What a mess! On that occasion I was in bed for a whole week! As soon as I was allowed out I went strolling over the scene of my accident. I caught sight of a small white object shining on the road. On investigation I could hardly believe my eyes! It was my tooth, intact, root and all.

Chapter Six

PAPA'S FAMILY

As opposed to Mama's relatives, of whom there were many including her aunt, uncle and others whom I saw frequently, I never saw much of Papa's family. Neither did Mama and Papa for that matter!

His family, on the other hand, consisted of his mother, sister and brother-in-law and their two children; the adults I addressed formally, whereas the two children by their first names.

There was also "Le Comte de L'Epée", Papa's uncle, a bachelor, who was the only adult whom I ever remember speaking to me personally and warmly and who allowed me to call him uncle. He never came to the Lush Oasis - why? I loved the beautiful surroundings of his country estate, St. Evroult Notre-Dame-des-Bois, where we visited him. Sometimes his other relatives too. I was fascinated with the small tunnel under the entrance steps leading to the front door of the Château and which to me, as a little girl, were great fun. Without him the visits there would have been more than tedious. He took great notice of me and taught me to play "pick-up sticks" from a beautifully carved ivory set. Sadly, and too soon, our great understanding came to an end when he died.

My father's mother had remarried when he was still a child. She wed the Marquis d'Hausen de Weidesheim, a man of Austrian origin whom I never met. She led a varied life, living sometimes in Paris, sometimes in Chandai and, of course, in Weidesheim. In my days in Chandai she only came for short visits. I last met her when I was about six years old, an occasion never to be forgotten! I was taken to Paris by motorcar and when we reached the centre it was as if I were being engulfed in a noisy labyrinth. The town house where the Marchioness lived, and who was bedridden at the time, reflected the epitome of silent austerity. A dusky sepulchre with whiffs of bees wax, lavender and camphor. Into the commodious, but snug bedroom I followed Mama. We were shown in by a solemn maid dressed in black and wearing a white frilly cap. The curtains were drawn but a red-shaded lamp threw a diffused glow onto a pell-mell of embroidered linen. Amongst the starched whiteness was a bony face with silky grey hair. The only sign of life in this ghostly tableau were the unyielding, but clear, blue eyes of that ageing lady. She suffered from rheumatoid arthritis and facial neuralgia and, to alleviate her pain, camphor compresses were used. We stayed the night. The house was intimidating, frightening even, but old as it was and unlike our home in Chandai, it had running water throughout whereas, in our house, we only had running water in the kitchen and bathroom. Before I went to bed I sat on a big blue and white decorated lavatory pan; I couldn't hold my balance and I wish someone had been there to help me for, at that point, I slipped backwards. Luckily there was a little platform half way down and I was most surprised, on pulling the chain, to see the result of my sitting being flushed away by a torrent of clean water!

I wore a special hair style then. Photographs show that I was given it when only a few months old and I had to bear with it until I was eight. It was an out-of-date style which Papa himself wore when he was little (as seen in figs 10 and 11). I never saw any other child with that hairdo. Ear length, both sides slightly curled inwards, whilst, from front to back on the top of the head, a tube-like curl stood tightly secured with grips. I hated that ridiculous contraption which necessitated hair pulling and scalp scorching by curling tongs used by Mama's rough and forceful hands. No exception was made on that unforgettable evening at Madame d'Hausen's. Two metal curlers were fastened to my head, then I was put into a string cot and left alone in a dark, strange room. I began listening to the thumping of my heart, in vain my eyes searched the dark for something to focus on. Then the dreaded "whatever it was" manifested itself!

All of a sudden I felt trapped! My hair was being pulled by someone very strong. No doubt some feral monster had got hold of me and would not let go. The harder I struggled the stronger the hold, the pain worse. I shrieked and yelled in panic but Mama didn't seem to hear me. Hysteria set in, I suspect now that it didn't last for very long, and ultimately Mama came through the door and put the light on. I was saved! She managed to convince me, eventually, that the culprit was not what I had imagined but simply the unfortunate combination of hair curlers and string cot.

Before the trip to Paris in 1937 I had only met my grandmother a few times when she came to stay with us. Our meetings were brief, only long enough for me to curtsy, take her extended hand and shyly murmur, 'Bonjour Madame'.

At the announcement of her visit our household got in a state of frenzy. Everyone behaved as if they had burning charcoal under their feet. Mama was constantly on at the cook and the maids, the butler and inspecting the kitchen. The softest sheets were taken out of their cupboard for my grandmother's bed, the hallmarked silver re-polished and the crystal glasses taken out of their storage trunk. Flower beds were carefully weeded and floral arrangements placed throughout the house. By mid afternoon on the day of the V.I.P's arrival we were all spick and span and waiting at the front door for the chauffeur driven grey Bentley. I do not know why, but my legs were a little shaky and my stomach seemed to shrink. The chauffeur opened the door and from the back of the motorcar the lady in grey detached herself and walked slowly towards us. She positively petrified me and yet, in a strange way, I liked the old dowager. I never spoke to her alone and there was no rapport between us, I was just Pierrette, a kind of ghost child, the "godchild" as I was known by some.

Before I had reached my eighth birthday she too, like her brother, had vanished into thin air. I vaguely remember Mama mentioning her demise, that is all, one person less in front of whom I would have to curtsy! Did she ever know, I always wondered, whether or not I was her granddaughter? She could not have failed to notice the striking resemblance between her son, when a child, and myself. Perhaps she couldn't resign herself to query or acknowledge the fact.

There was also Papa's sister, Madame de Pontalba, a calm and genteel woman who, with her husband and children, came to see us now and again. Aliette, the daughter, was a few years older than I and the memories of us playing together are pleasant but few. Our favourite game was "swimming". To that effect we lay, face down, on top of a small low table to practice the breast-stroke; there was much puffing, humphing and laughter as we tried to maintain our equilibrium whilst our arms and legs waved in the air, like those of two incapacitated frogs! We were convinced that we could launch ourselves into the river had we been permitted to do so.

Years later, when I was in my late teens, I realised how handsome Bernard, Aliette's brother, was. I began to feel attracted to him for I had noticed, once or twice, that he was not oblivious of my presence. One day I happened to mention it to Mama. She stopped breathing with shock! How dare I think that a young man of such calibre would set eyes on me, what a ridiculous idea that was. I might as well forget it at once. Men like "him" were not destined for "girls" like me! Little had I realised that he was, of course, my cousin.

I believed her once more and that was the end of another dream.

Chapter Seven

THE FATHER, THE CHILD AND THE GRANDFATHER CHAIR

My father was of medium height and dignified. He had a thin, neat moustache and straight dark hair; he rarely smiled but his facial expression looked slightly amused, yet assertive.

He was liked and respected by everyone in and out of his own circle. A busy man, he supervised the running of his land and forestry and attended to Chandai's mayoral duties.

I never remember him wearing anything other than knickerbockers and long hand-knitted socks, over which he used to fasten his highly polished leather gaiters.

When very young I knew nothing about his life and still know very little, but as I grew older, I managed to glean more. I gathered that at an early age he had lost his father and that he had been sent to a local agricultural boarding school (fig 16). Fifty years after the event I read, in his letters sent to his mother at that time, he had been lonely and unhappy there but trying his hardest to "do well" to please her and asking to see her or at least to hear from her. Later, on perusing his school exercise books, it was obvious to me that he had done

Fig 16: My father went to school at a very early age.

very well in natural history, drawing and essays, three subjects I am glad to say, he passed on to me.

Papa had been and still was Chandai's Master of the Hunt and hunted stags, wild boar and roebuck to the sound of the French hunting horn. He also had his own Shoot and was an expert angler. (fig 17)

Our home was cosy and beautifully furnished. Papa occupied the far left of the ground floor, Hubert and I were immediately above. I shared Mama's "en suite" bedroom to begin with and slept in a large brass cot which had small spherical brass nuts; I can still feel in my fingers the pleasure those gave me as I kept unscrewing and screwing them over and over again, to Mama's perpetual annoyance!

Fig 17: Papa was a keen fisherman (picture taken in 1933).

There were prints of hunting scenes and trophies on almost every wall and the stairways were covered with roebuck and stag's antlers and their mounted hooves. In my infancy each time I went downstairs I tried, on tiptoe, to smooth the silently snarling fox's mask which hung above the French window. On the wall facing the front door there was a ferocious looking wild boar's head surrounded by mounted tusks and trotters. In a recess by the entrance door hunting crops and tweed caps hung on antlers. On the floor, under the wrought iron coat rack, guns, game bags, boots and gaiters were always at the ready. What a struggle it was to retrieve my own coat and gumboots from amongst that manly chaos! On the vestibule's wall, facing the double glass-panelled sitting room door, there were two handsome ten-point stag's antlers, the resting place for my father's French hunting horns; they bring to mind one of the most cherished memories I have of Papa when I was not yet five and as a treat for having been a good little girl, he had promised to blow for me that evening. Kneeling on the window seat, against a specially made safety device, I waited. In the fading light the river valley stretched ahead, in the meadow beyond the mist was rising and I could see a herd of cattle looking like wooden toys niched in cotton wool. Then, magic upon magic, from the depth of the woods came the sound of the horn. To this day it still tugs at my heart and moistens my eyes.

Another dear occasion took place one winter evening in the snugness of the sitting room which was tastefully furnished in Louis XVI period furniture. A design of pink flowers and birds in the curtains was repeated in the wallpaper and loose covers. Mama was knitting on the chaise-longue beside the fire. Along the wall, between the door to the vestibule and the window, stood a chest of drawers on top of which rested a table lamp and a radio. Next to the window Papa was sitting in his grandfather chair smoking a pipe. Mama's knitting needles were clicking, the mantel clock was ticking, the fire was crackling. Papa and I were playing "hunt the thimble". I had been "a hunting" some time and papa had stopped saying, 'warm, cooler now, warmer', when, absorbed in my search, I inadvertently put my hand on an ashtray and Papa boomed, 'You are burning.' I jumped with fright and, forgetting all about the game, I ran crying to the safety of his arms. He consoled and cuddled me. Father and child perfectly fitting the contour of the old chair.

It was also from that chair that I watched the unforgettable sight of an "Aurora Borealis". Mama had fetched me out of bed to witness the scene, held on the back of the chair by Papa, and transfixed, looking through the window, I watched the phenomenon unfold. The familiar features were now silhouetted, all of them in black against the luminous raspberry pink light. Earth and sky merged, a glow of changing golden pink to fluorescent cerise, then to deep rose. Gradually the tableau faded. A misty purple replaced the pink hues and one by one the silhouettes vanished in the dark of the night. It had been an enchantment never to be forgotten.

The above anecdotes are the only distinct ones I can recall of my father and I being totally akin to each other but his intangible presence has never faded away. I loved him dearly, completely (fig 18).

Four years on, the last time I saw my Papa's chair being occupied was by a high ranking German officer in 1940.

Fig 18: Papa as I remember him.

Chapter Eight

TO LE GRAND CHÂTEAU, WITH OR WITHOUT MAMA

Back home, I returned to my dolls, nature "explorations" and continued to put my nose, so to speak, into everybody's business. Of all the things Mama and I did together, our sporadic visits to le Grand Château was one of my favourites.

Le Grand Château was a long, two-storey building, the centre part dating from the sixteenth century, built in attractive brickwork with taste and originality. It had high narrow windows and exterior grey wooden shutters and a colonnade stone balcony above the front door. At a later date extensions had been added to each end and the new walls were covered with lattices; later still, when towers and turrets came into fashion, a large extension symmetrically flanked by four two-storey towers were built to the right. I liked the towers with their three kinds of windows, high ones, small diamond-shaped ones and little top round ones. The similar red-tiled building was lined with eight dormer windows, also with brickwork surrounds and wooden shutters.

Le Grand Château was my fascination, situated on the flat at the end of the small slope which linked "La Terrace" to the greens and the river. There it stood, dormant, mysterious and to me, magnetic. I never knew how long it had been lifeless. Its keys, among many others, were kept in the vestibule table drawer. Should I detect Mama's hand nearing it? My controlled excitement started. It was better not to exteriorise my feelings too much for Mama might have told me not to be an imbecile or worse, she might have changed her mind about going, so I made sure I kept well behaved!

Keys in hand Mama and I walked down across the chapel's lawn and then along the dusty front of the old building. In bridled trepidation, my heart pumping fast, I watched the key turn in the lock, a twist of the white china knob, a small jerk and the heavily shuttered door swung inwards. A mishmash of smells hit my nostrils, those fusty, dusty whiffs were as of incense to me. As I followed Mama upstairs, along the corridors and from room to room those olfactory messages brought diverse emotions; the sense of knowledge and yet of the unknown, the feeling of love and yet of desertion, the sentiment of comfort and yet of fright.

The entrance hall was always cold. There was a white plaster mantelpiece and above it, also made of the same, keeping vigil was a ten-point stag's head. On the black centre star of the white mosaic floor stood an eight foot high, green marble sculpture, a fountain in fact, but without water. It was a museum piece. On the top of a low pedestal, there was a basin above three lovely swans, with smooth serpentine necks supporting a flat bowl. To the left of the front door there was a glass panelled double door, leading to both the petit and grand salons, then followed the reception room. Mama rarely went there. To the right, a door opened into a small hall at the bottom of the stairs, followed by the dining room and then the kitchens. Mama did not go that way either. Usually we went to the library, a large room whose four walls, from floor to ceiling, were covered with books and more on the table that took the rest of the space.

However, there was a chest of drawers too and it was the contents of these that attracted my stepmother's attention. Whilst she was busy fumbling elbow deep in the mahogany furniture I was browsing among the literary wealth. They were magnificent, all of them leather bound, many embossed in gold with the finest of steel engravings. They dealt with all subjects necessary to the education of royalty and others. François Ambroise Didot, one of my ancestors, was printer to King Louis XVI of France. There were books in Latin and Greek, some on travel, all the classics and many many more. I was always looking for those on natural history of course. Mama was never pleased at my fervent curiosity.

"There's no need for you to rummage like that. Those books are not suitable for you, you couldn't understand them anyway," she would say.

Too soon for my liking, Mama had found what she had been looking for and the shutters of the library were secured again. Generally we would check and make sure that things were as they had always been. There was a master bedroom with its balcony and between two wall cupboards in the recess was an imposing four-poster bed. We started there and went through two en-suite rooms. Of those three chambers I liked best the last one. Dark pink was the predominant colour scheme, going beautifully with a four poster, the chairs and dressing table all in "Period Empire" and my attention always focused on the particularly beautiful dressing table; comparatively, it was a small piece of furniture with a lift-up mirror. It had drawers with compartments full of treasures such as jewellery, snuff boxes and miniature powder boxes, mixed amongst ribbons and hat pins, each more appealing than the other things to my small fingers. Occasionally, my asking to take a treasure with me was granted. A miniature sewing box and an old gold Normand jewel were among the items that came from the hoard. I still have the latter and several others.

We left the room through its far door, climbed a few steps and pursued our inspection. Along the narrow corridor we peeped swiftly at half a dozen small bedrooms, entirely strewn with dead flies. On our way back we always stopped at the largest back room, the Bishop's Quarters. A short and dark passage led to it. In a turret to the right of the passage there was the one and only lavatory, a primitive affair, the seat was a plank with one hole! But the wooden lid fitted perfectly!

The Bishop's room was a very large one with a big alcove and washroom. What interested me most were the windows and I respectfully understood why those had to be special. Obviously "His Eminence" had been the most important visitor at le Grand Château and had to be accommodated comfortably. To that aim, the windows had external shutters, double windows and indoor shutters with thickly lined curtains. To be sure, there was no chance of "Monseigneur" feeling the draft!

Mama and I seldom went to the top floor and even less often at the back of the ground floor, but when I went to le Grand Château on my own, things were very different. I made countless and endless visits there. I preferred them to remain secret so sneakily taking keys, checking that no one had heard me, I ran all the way down. To me it was as if Sleeping Beauty had pricked her finger nearly a century ago and all these slumbering, inanimate objects were waiting for Prince Charming's arrival. At the door I glanced over my shoulder and full of agitation and awe, I passed the threshold of that forbidden, yet beloved sanctum. I quickly shut the door behind me, but did not lock it, too scary! Then there was no more running, on the contrary, tiptoeing was more the mode. Firstly because I was afraid to disturb the silence and secondly because I kept a keen ear on the ominous cracking of old wood, the rattling of shutters, the sensation of ethereal presences and the echo of my movements.

Facing the front door there was a cosy boudoir called the "Blue Salon". All the walls of this jewel of a room were covered with wood panelling. At each corner there were floor to ceiling corner cupboards. The lower part of the two were open fires, their surround was of blue delft tiles and had their cast iron grate. It had a subtle blue Persian carpet and the cupboards were full of glasses. I used to open one of the four windows overlooking the river. Surrounded by silver and blue curtains and cushions, I sat enjoying the sight of flowing water. I didn't sit for long for I was eager to open the door, which would take me a few steps nearer to the exciting aim of my being there. I walked purposefully through the billiard room, a large, dim and unwelcoming place whose far door opened into my "heaven"... The Museum of Natural History. Its length was that of both the salons and the reception room together. This gallery was all wood from floor, walls, shelves and ceiling. The two exterior walls instead were floor to ceiling windows. The smallest wall was entirely glazed with views of the river. Facing the windows there were asymmetric shelves of various sizes that hosted all sorts of stuffed animals. Owls, weasels, foxes, humming birds and flowers under glass domes.

Using a rickety tabouret I climbed up and down amongst the motionless creatures and at times thought they were live. I caressed the head of the marten and red squirrel's tail; I patted the fox's back and stroked softly the owl's chest. I spoke to them all and still think that sometimes they answered me! In the centre of the museum was a fully grown stag looking as if held at bay yet wayward, stood on its own base. Frequently I passed my fingertips over its smooth glass eyes, although I did so with some apprehension and at arm's length lest it should blink!

Having renewed acquaintance with my friends, I then turned to the most exciting thing of all. In a corner there was a tall mahogany chest of drawers and my delight was a collection of seashells that it contained. To handle, sniff and listen to! The large ones were easy, I merely buried myself head first into the bottom drawer! To reach the other specimens which ranged from medium size to minuscule was much more difficult. It is impossible to say how many hours I spent, perched on a wooden box on a chair for even on my toes, the three top drawers would have been inaccessible. Playing, reading Latin names, comparing from box to box these minute marvels of the sea. How long had they been there? Untouched, undisturbed, sleeping in their cotton wool beds? Now I have my own collection but it is in disarray, unlabelled but I do not have to stretch on a chair to see it!.

When I had had enough of the museum I used its far door to go to the reception room and where another kind of delight awaited. I opened one or two shutters slightly and from under a stage, I brought out the musical instruments. A mandolin, a violin and a zither. What a thrill it was when I managed to play a few notes of a known tune. I liked best the zither and many a metallic note flew across the dark, empty theatre. As for the piano, it was a joy. I drummed away and sang to my heart's content, filling the air with any tune that came to mind. Now and again I put some costumes on. I pulled open the heavy red curtains and lost myself in front of an invisible audience. I acted, applauded and sang, sang with all my heart the fairy tales that Rolande had taught me. My own fairy tale became live, I was the public and the artist but apart from the people in the two Rembrandt paintings, the animals dying from the plague and the anatomy lesson, I was alone, always alone. Once the shutters were fastened again, even the big crystal chandeliers had lost their glitter. When I returned to reality, the room was empty and I was alone.

Occasionally I would visit the kitchen with its larders and the old range. It also included the base of three of the towers, one was a marble shelved cool room, one totally filled with copper cooking utensils, the third one hosted the spiral stair case leading to the dining room and up to the domestics' rooms. The access to the remaining tower was from inside and it housed a double-seated wooden lavatory with lids.

It had been known that, in the course of my solitary spells in le Grand Château, an unfamiliar noise was heard. Panic stricken, abandoning all without another thought, dried mouth and looking straight ahead, I dashed outside and locked the door as quickly as I could.

Nevertheless, I have always had an immense affinity with the old building.

Chapter Nine

STRIFES AND VICTORIES

Although I was spending more time in the pursuit of discovery about plants, insects and birds, I still enjoyed being with Mama from time to time. I wanted to join and help her with all her activities but I could never predict whether or not she would accept or rebuke. For example, I recall a specific day when, as she was writing a letter, I had the urge to express my affection to her and, climbing at the back of her chair, I put my arms around her and gave her a kiss. Unkindly, she pushed me aside and, to quote, said 'Go away! You are like a bitch on heat!' The sensation of guilt and isolation that those words carried were hard to bear.

My stepmother was generous with her reprimands and slapping and I developed the habit of evading her whenever I passed within her reach. 'Don't' be such an imbecile!' Mama said. 'Take that! You are indeed too silly. One would think that you are being slapped nearly all the time!' Before I could avoid it the back of her hand, loaded with heavily jewelled rings, had fallen on my face. Ouch! 'If you expected to be slapped, so be it,' continued Mama, her words fading as I walked away. I have no recollection of ever being spanked. I should be grateful for small mercies! Slapping was Mama's way to discipline. She slapped the domestics, she slapped the dog, she slapped my governesses and me, of course! She did not punish but threatened me. 'How stupid you are! I will send you back to the gutter from where you came' or "I am going to send you to a reform school". Two statements I was to hear too often and for too many years... This used to reinforce my fantasies about my own mother who lived in the forest, as told by Mama in those "Shattering Revelations". I was far too young on that day to realise the full impact of that devastating conversation but I was old enough to know that, from then on, the mystery of my origin and the strong desire to know my real mother was a wish never to leave me.

I had begun building a fairy-tale, with my true mother being a "sorceress" and perhaps ill-treating her children. But she was also a "conjurer" and could make everything right. Her living in the forest added an attraction to the plot. My need to be comforted and understood induced me to believe that she would provide it all. I am not at all sure that it would have been the case. Nevertheless, I craved to pour out my heart to her.

More than four decades on, two old women in the village told me how, when I was a little girl, they had found me at the Estate's gate trying to get out and crying, 'I want to go and see my Maman.' I have no recollection of those events. I can only guess that they had been too painful for me to remember.

If my stepmother had been different the trauma could have been less scarring for it is amazing how resilient children are. The choice to forget my own mother or to dwell upon her elusiveness was made impossible because Mama was for ever referring to the woman.

Should I spend time with the workers - I was like my mother, only happy when being with the lower classes. Should I as much as mention the handsomeness of a human male - I was a whore, like my mother! Should I get my clothes dirty - I thrived in filth, like my mother - and so on and so forth.

I grew up believing my stepmother's views implicitly until I was in my teens. In retrospect I see that her criticisms were designed to make me see myself as being guilty, immoral and useless! In fact, those I used as a deterrent against her views which she judged to be plebeian. But, far from having an adverse effect, they had a protective influence for, under the cover of their umbrella, I excused and absolved myself. How could I help being what I was, I used to think or say, had I not inherited my own mother's depraved atavism?

Short as I was in spiritual needs, I never strove for material things. I had many toys and games and I was able to twist Mama's little finger in order to get all my wants.

To the left of the house, at the edge of the woods, there was a small clearing half surrounded by rhododendrons. I spent many hours there playing on my swing, rope ladder, trapeze and rings. For years I tried touching the tree branches with my toes, only to manage it at times thanks to windy days! I would also gather wood material, stones, foliage and using old blankets, cloths and strings I built rug houses. There, in a world of my own, my dolls and I played and slept, only pretending you understand. Infrequently we found ourselves entangled under our collapsed den.

It was also there I realised the irrevocability of death when, on a summer morning, one of our budgerigars had been found dead on the floor of its cage. I put it in a box and placed it by the swing where I hoped it would revert to its former self. Alas, no matter how often I exhumed the little bird and stroked its feathered head, nothing would revive it. Finally convinced, I returned it to the ground, made a cross with twigs and laid it to rest. There was no sympathy in my bereavement from Mama or from Hubert who, as a rule, discarded with disdain and ridicule anything I, or everyone else, did or said.

Hubert was not only Madame Firmin-Didot's son he was also, to all intents and purposes, my stepbrother, although never once were we addressed or treated as such. I had been told by Mama that he was my godfather and I accepted it. He was fifteen years my senior and I looked upon him as a young man, someone to play with, someone to copy and to share things. Unfortunately that was rarely so.

He had a fine presence and his stern gaze disconcerted me. Long afterwards I understood, yet did not condone, why, smothered by his mother's domination and protectiveness, he was so heartless and arrogant. Only twice do I remember him being away from her. The first was when, in his twenties, he went on a skiing holiday and then, of course, during the war. Mama always said that he was of a delicate disposition, but the only time I saw him bedridden was when he had the mumps!

It was not unusual for me to be frightened of him, yet I wanted to imitate him. Sometimes I wore an old pair of spectacles because Hubert wore glasses and I still feel the discomfort when I walked about with a pencil in my pants because I wanted to be like a boy!

Even so I had some good times with Hubert when we might play table tennis, croquet or a snail-shaped hopscotch together. He also took me with him on his long strolls across woods and farmland and also ferreting rabbits in their warren.

During the dark evenings Hubert and I regularly played cards or did jigsaw puzzles. We had snowball fights in the winter and when the thaw came we went trudging across the flooded meadows. All of these most enjoyable and made me feel very grown up! But sadly, even on those seemingly friendly occasions, there was mockery and contempt in Hubert's attitude to me and tended to my ending up in tears. Hubert in my eyes was "a big boy". As to be expected he was too rough, too strong and was a tease, but that was not why it so often hurt inside. It was because there was never any warmth coming from Hubert to compensate for the bullying which commonly took place between children. His wily laugh showed that he really enjoyed tormenting me and he always held me responsible for it. One such experience took place when I had requested to accompany him on a winter walk. We waded our way through floods, he ahead, I trailing behind and nearly waist high in swirling icy water! One field after another, I thought it would never end! 'Wait for me,' I whined and eventually he did, for short whiles. Otherwise I have the feeling that I might have drowned, but there was no kindness in his help. 'You asked to come, didn't you!' he was saying with a wry smile. 'Come on, get on with it!' I snuffled all the way home. Now, although that anecdote makes me laugh, I have sometimes since wondered whether there had been some resentment on Hubert's part in my salvage? For resentment towards me he definitely had and that worsened to tyrannical proportions as time went on.

As my story stands, I had not yet the ability to analyse situations but I had mastered deviousness to a fine art and I was increasingly becoming a "little pest". I had learnt to calculate the things which made Mama scorn Hubert and tell the domestics off! For example, I used to pass my finger over the copper saucepans which hung in the kitchen so as to leave a small clean line across the barely visible layer of dust and I slyly used to point this out to Mama. I would do, or say, many such things I knew would anger

Mama towards Cook, the domestics and Hubert. This would ingratiate me with her. It was an inwardly glowing pleasure for me seeing my stepmother storming and tongue lashing at the staff and sometimes her fury went as far as to slap their faces. I was not going to be the only one to be chastised, what a relief! Afterwards Mama found something to do or say, according to my mood at the time, which I would take as a reward.

Hubert disapproved of those common scenes. Pointing at me he would shout at Mama and so an argument started, whilst I stood silent and jubilant.

'She can't do anything wrong! She is a cow!' Hubert went on.

'That's not true,' Mama answered, 'be quiet, will you!'

'Oh, yes it is, you are always supporting her!' Hubert continued, pale with temper.

'And you are always getting on at her. I will not allow it, be quiet! I know best!' bellowed Mama, on the point of crying. During those verbal fights I inwardly allied myself with Mama, in triumph, and used to think, 'so there Hubert!'

However Hubert was just as devious as I was. He retaliated with a vengeance. To punish me for whatever misdemeanours he thought I had committed, he used to grab me by the upper arms and shake me to and fro in the air with all his might. Many are the times when bruises or finger marks showed on my arms. The worst of his punishments was when he carried me, struggling under his arm, to a small landing at the top of a disused stairway and locked me there in complete darkness. I remember, with horror, the sound of my screams, the never ending wait and the terrifying doubt in my mind, 'would I be rescued or forgotten?' It was agonising. Mama objected to Hubert's action then and always lectured him for it.

There was an episode which now I find amusing. Hubert was reading the paper and I was making a nuisance of myself for I wanted him to play cards with me. He lost his temper and, jumping out of his seat, he seized me in his usual way and shook me like a garden sieve. On removing my cardigan I saw his thumb print on my arms and made a beeline for Mama.

When she set eyes on me she gasped, 'Whatever is going on?' There was a faint smell of smoke about and, as I looked at the mirror, I could see a pretty ribbon of the same coming out of my hair! 'Your hair is on fire!' choked Mama and so it was! From Hubert's pipe a speck of red cinder had dropped on to my top curls which were smouldering gently! I must give my stepmother her due as, on that occasion, she did not blame me and, kindly and efficiently, restored my hairstyle. Instead Hubert, for once, took all the blame.

That was one of my victories.

Chapter Ten

THE SHATTERING REVELATIONS

There was also the day of the revelations that were divulged in 1938. I was nearly seven years old. It was a beautiful warm spring day. Outside in the corner by the vestibule window Mama and I were knitting, both sitting on our red and white gingham cushions, she on her cane armchair and I on my child's wicker one, there were flowers, flowers everywhere. The caressing of the breeze was full of bird song, I was blissfully happy. We were conversing quietly, I mostly questioning, she answering The topic? The how and why children should address grown-ups. It went thus.

'I can't understand why?'

It's done 'Because.'

'Yes, but, what about?'

'Only plebeians say that and ....'

'Why?'

'Because I am telling you so.'

There was a pause, and then I looked up at my stepmother.

'I call you Mama, don't I?'

'Ye..ee..s,' she answered hesitantly.

'I always do, don't I?' I insisted, dropping my knitting on my lap.

'Yes! Yes! So what of it?' said Mama firmly. The tone of the conversation had changed. I was puzzled; a need to be reassured was called for.

'I could call you mother darling, couldn't I?' I asked.

Mama's voice rose noticeably.

'Certainly not…' she said.

'Why not?' I probed, 'You are my mama, yes?'

'You may call me Mama, but mother? That you never shall!'

'Why not?' I persevered.

The answer came loud, clear and brutal.

'Because I am not your Mother, that's why. You see when …' but I didn't hear anything else. All, including Mama's face, became blurred, I was stunned.

'Listen!' Mama's voice strengthened 'when you were a baby I picked you from the gutter. You were in a box on the floor of your mother's slum. I used to go there and give you your bottle. Sometimes I brought you here for the day and took you back in the evening.'

Aghast, I was doing my best to understand what it all meant.

'But why?' I attempted.

'Do not interrupt! I am explaining to you. Your mother used a hot brick to keep you warm. One day I found you with a severe burn on your hand. To keep you warm, your mother had wrapped a hot old brick in paper. It had become undone and your hand suffered a third degree burn. I brought you here and kept you.'

I looked at my scar.

'How, why?' I asked. 'Who is my real mother? Where do I come from?' I struggled.

'Your mother had a reputation; she was a nasty woman, battered her children with sticks as thick as my arms.' I glanced at Mama's arm and believed her.

'Where is my mother?' I demanded.

'She lives in the forest with her good-for-nothing drunken husband and your sisters.' Was the answer.

Plucking up my courage and bewildered, I asked whether I could see my mother. Mama went wild and said:

'I have done all I could for you. Is this my reward? You are just like your mother. Typical! You want to go back to the muck where you came from?' Regaining her composure she went on, 'You will NOT see your mother. There is no need for such a question. Besides, she has abandoned you. She was filthy and cruel...'

The flowers faded, the birds became silent, above the sun was still shining bright, but no longer on me. The pain of those shattering revelations gradually diminished though dormant this was to extend to nearly half a century. The search for my real mother was to become of paramount importance.

Chapter Eleven

THE SECOND CHANGE OF DESTINY

My father was a heavy smoker. I still remember looking through the contents of his bedside table and amusing myself with his many pipes and menthol imitation cigarettes.

In March 1938 Papa became ill. There was less and less movement coming from his quarters and the shutters were permanently fastened. In the house the atmosphere became increasingly anxious and sombre. I overheard that my father had had an operation on the back of his throat, the uvula. The doctor thought that was the cause of his constant coughing. It was not.

On the morning of the 25th of July 1938, I entered his ante-room ready, as usual, to give him my morning kiss. Mama, who watched him day and night, was standing with her back to the window sobbing. 'It is all over, Papa is dead,' she gasped between her sobs. My beloved Papa had died of lung cancer. He was forty-five, I was just seven. The door of his room was ajar, alone I went to him. The place was very dark and it seemed for a while that the whole world had become dark too. The pain! Oh, the pain inside! My odd reaction was to be brave. I felt a lump in my throat but I did not cry. I managed not to show any sign of sorrow. I ran to the kitchen where I found the servants overcome with grief. Cook wept ….. 'My dear little one, what a tragedy that is in your life, if only you knew, if only you could understand.'

I was shocked and uncomfortable and yet, I wanted to laugh. Cook continued, 'My dear child,' she said adamantly, 'today you have lost the most beautiful feather in your hat (The most beautiful jewel in your crown).' This remark puzzled me at the time and I pondered over it for many years until far, far later, when I fully understood its implication. But how could I, on that day, comprehend the repercussions which my father's death would have on my future? I knew then that I would never see him again. I know now that it meant that I had lost all chances of being given financial, educational, and personal rights owed to me as his one and only child. It was becoming obvious, I can see it now, that the worm had started to gnaw the apple! The anxiety caused in me by the succession of traumatic events was beginning to take its toll. I had never belonged to my own mother's world, having spent my first seven years under the possessive cover of le Petit Château, and the reason for my being there had vanished upon my father's death. Cook was right.

Three days passed and Papa was put into his coffin. My stepmother insisted that I should kiss his ice cold brow before the lid was screwed on, 'After all,' she said, 'he was your Pèr… your papa,' she quickly corrected. So, on my knees, Hubert, Gamekeeper and bailiff watching I did so and ran away. I desperately searched for comfort, I found none.

My stepmother was not unwilling, but certainly unable, to cope with carrying out sensibly her role as a parent. I was left floating in the air with no rope to cling to.

I wanted to give her my love and receive hers but, most of the time, it was more of a "contretemps" than a success. I see now that a crumbling foundation on which to build my uncertain future was all that lay ahead.

The vestibule was rearranged into a Chapel of Rest. Papa's coffin was draped in black crepe and lit by four big church candles. It was covered by masses of flowers and wreaths.

The whole population of the village and many people from the nearby hamlets queued to pay their last respects.

My persistent request to attend Papa's funeral was refused, instead I was sent to the family doctor's home for the day. Yet I had to wear mourning clothes for a whole year.

A few days after the funeral I spent hours in Papa's ante-room with Mama and I watched her emptying out the entire contents of a tall wooden filing cabinet which was always kept locked. There were piles of documents and letters. Mama carried them to Papa's bedroom and, in a wood burning stove, burnt them all. Why?

strictness for three years. The first eighteen months not a single stitch would Mama wear that was not black, then she allowed herself some grey and white (fig 19). She wore the "widow's head-dress", a flat toque trimmed with white from which a black veil dropped down to her waist. She wrote on traditional mourning paper, white sheets edged with black.

I did not wear black, I suppose Mama thought that I was too young.

I was dressed in black and white for three months, then grey replaced the black and pale mauve followed.

After Papa's death Mama often cried. She became morose and used to say, 'If only Papa were here,' or 'Be good! What would Papa say?'

Countless times during the following thirteen years, Mama reminded me that Papa's last words had been, 'Promise me never to abandon Pierrette,' and told me that she had vowed to do so. For years afterwards she never let me forget it. She kept repeating, 'I'll stand by my promise. If it were not for that I would not keep you.'

From my father's last breath, my identity, my status, my freedom, my inheritance were calculatingly and deliberately obliterated.

Fig 19: Mama in mourning July 1938.

Chapter Twelve

MAMA'S UNDERTAKING, RUMOURS AND MADEMOISELLE COLETTE

As Papa was no longer with us I saw Mama as my only support and often worried she, too, might die. Talks of war added to my fears. I had heard several tales about wars, in particular about the First World one, during which Mama used to say she had been a Red Cross nurse. Her family thrived on sexual and, or, gruesome yarns and innuendo, not the least she. Her brothers and nephews were frequent visitors at le Petit Château and a great deal of the time the subject of conversation was in that vein. Over and over I heard how Mama had held the leg of a black soldier whilst it was being amputated without anaesthetiic. And... Yes, the saying about black men was true... they were... "humm... well-built!" "No thank you!!" Snigger snigger everyone. I didn't know whether to laugh or not. There was also the story of the Prussian, who had hacked out people's tongues and, more terrifying for me, had cut off children's hands.

As we listened to the radio I vaguely understood that things of the world were reaching critical proportions. 'Your stepfather would be most worried,' Mama would say to Hubert. 'What shall we do?' To my questions I was told that there was a possibility of war in the near future.

Meanwhile, in that late summer of 1938, my stepmother became somewhat bored with the seclusion which mourning etiquette imposed on her. Le Grand Château was still waiting for the Prince Charming, but no dashing young spark, riding on a white horse, appeared! Instead, brandishing a large feather duster, brooms and furniture polish, the châtelaine, followed by an intrigued little girl, arrived. It was some weeks since my father had died and my stepmother had dwelt upon the daunting task of reviving le Grand Château. I helped her to open both indoor and outdoor squeaky shutters, to sweep away the cobwebs and the spiders which scuttled in all directions. We unlatched the windows, removed the dust sheets and wound up the clocks. We scrubbed, cleaned and polished everywhere. Even the top floor got its share of attention. Many windowsills had built-in cupboards under them, the sills being the wooden lids.

Oh, the frustration those cupboards caused me, for in spite of using my waist as a fulcrum, more often bottom-up and head halfway down, it took all my strength to bring "the finds" to the light of day! There were photographs and postcards, albums, writing boxes, books and games, each window an Aladdin's cave! Every room divulged its guarded treasures. It was a carnival of discovery. For several weeks Mama and I worked hard until the whole château was sparkling, homely and alive again. From the kitchen to the theatre everything was ready. For what, I often asked myself. A reception that never was? Le Grand Château was abandoned once more and left to its wraith-like silent solitude. Mama had completed her undertaking. For me, the dream place had ceased to be the same. Its privacy had been disturbed and although the old building held on to its secrets, the magic spell had been thrown away with the dust. The worst was yet to come …..

Autumn was approaching, Christmas would be the first without Papa. I struggled with my catechism and a new governess was expected soon. I wanted my stepmother's supportive understanding, which was non-existent, and yet I needed some freedom from her possessiveness that constantly impeded my formative years. Mademoiselle Colette gave me both.

That artistic and intelligent woman knew how to educate and entertain at the same time. She was serene, kindly and patient. With her I learnt all my "tables", albeit whilst I lay on the floor under the desk! She taught me to read and write fluently and, for the first time in my life, I received encouragement and appreciation. She gave me much, much more.

Together we made and fully furnished my first and only doll's house. Mademoiselle Colette's dexterity was amazing. Empty matchboxes, velvet remnants and glass beads were transformed, in front of my baffled eyes, into padded sofas, chests of drawers and table lamps. I was thrilled. We played together, looked at things together, learnt together. When Mademoiselle returned to me after her Christmas holiday I knew then that I had a true friend in her. I even asked for a small bed to be put in her room, much to Mama's scoffing and masked hurt. 'I can't understand why? Ungrateful child that you are. Still, if you must, you may,' were her comments.

Whilst Mademoiselle Colette was on holiday Christmas came and went. Children in France do not hang their Christmas stockings. The tradition, when I was little, was a rather charming one and I adhered to it. On Christmas Eve I would select the shoes and carry them around to the fireplaces, putting one of each in front of them. The choice was difficult, the carting even more so, but I had help from Papa and Mama who prompted me as to which chimney Father Christmas might come down! I was then put to bed where I found it impossible to go to sleep for excitement. Eventually tiredness took over, but no sooner was I fast asleep than I was woken up at eleven o'clock, hastened out of bed and, still half asleep, was dressed up to go to midnight mass. But in 1938 as I was taking my first communion I was allowed to stay up for the sitting by the fire, before we set off to church. I did so from then on for at the age of seven, I had reached what the French call "the age of reason". In the olden days, the English called it "the age of discretion".

It was a 1½ km long walk to the church and back, in snow and freezing wind. The ceremony lasted the best part of two hours! I did enjoy the procession that brought the baby Jesus to the crèche on the dot of midnight, and the singing of many carols which I liked so much, "Il est né le Divin Enfant", and so on. I would have enjoyed all that much more had I not had to endure the excruciating pain of my frostbitten feet! Fortunately, the thought that perhaps Father Christmas had called, whilst I was holily engaged, kept me going but of course, he never had! We returned to the traditional Christmas feast which we ate by candlelight. Oysters, white sausages, a delicacy made of white bread, milk and truffles and found in the shops only during the festive season, turkey and Yule log, served by one of the maids who hurried between the downstairs kitchen and the servery.

Christmas morning was always bewildering. Odd as it seems, I often cried when I opened my presents, I could not believe that all the beautiful things were for me. One particular year I was so overwhelmed by a lovely doll that I ran back to bed, without even daring to touch her; I hid under the blankets and sobbed. 'Do not be so stupid!' said my stepmother. Papa was still alive then and fetched the doll for me. Christmas times were very happy in those days.

Back to the last Christmas before the war, Mademoiselle Colette returned and continued to be her lovely self. She gave me an ultimate respite. From her stay with us, there was no trauma, no pain, no sorrow to report. Without her "golden" help I wonder how I could have faced the imminent upheaval that followed. However, winter 1939 was a contented one. Instead of spending it with Mama I was still closely supervised, but in Mademoiselle Colette's room, which was much more fun. Spring took us outdoors, even though we never went beyond the estate's walls.

Alas, increasing rumours of a possible war with Germany were a constant topic of conversation. Phrases like "Mobilisation générale" and "German invasion" were flying above my head. I kept hearing the charwoman telling Mama that more men had been called up. Hubert was turning increasingly pale and trembling in his socks! Quite oblivious of the crisis which endangered the world, and unable to grasp the gravity of the situation, I carried on being happy with Mademoiselle Colette.

I even, at times, showed signs of excitement at the idea that our non-eventful life could be enlivened a little. Long live the innocence of children.

July brought the summer holiday too quickly. The political situation was deteriorating and alarmingly. By then I had understood that war was almost a certainty. Therefore Mademoiselle Colette had to rejoin to her family. Would she ever come back? Probably never? I was torn apart. My newly acquired hopes and security tumbled in front of me like a sand castle caught by the tide. Mademoiselle Colette went. She will never know how much profound gratitude I still owe her. I was eight years old, thanks to all she had given me I was emotionally stronger to cope with her departure.

Chapter Thirteen

BURDENS, FANTASIES AND NOSTALGIA

As I grew older I managed, now and again, to escape from my stepmother's autocracy. I began to roam the estate on my own, exploring hidden corners, generally relishing my newly found freedom.

Some spring and summer mornings I was awoken by the dawn chorus, the call of the cuckoo coming from all directions, the "hoop, hoop, hoop" of the hoopoe and wondered whether or not I would hear the bleating of sheep grazing the sward. I simply could not wait to go outside, there were so many things to see, to hear, to smell, to do. I wanted to do them all at once.

I might go cycling across the park, I might cycle the length of the wooded "grande allée" that skirted the far end boundary wall then freewheel all the way down to le Grand Château steps. To the right a branch of the river housed hundreds of frogs and was lined with magnificent rare trees. Visible from all the buildings and from long distances around, one could see the impressive branches of the solitary Lebanon Cedar facing the front of le Grand Château. It was common knowledge in our family that this handsome tree, together with its "brother sapling", had been brought back to France by the famous Swedish botanist "Linnaeus" (1707-1778). During his return voyage the scientist nursed his "treasures" in his top hat and delivered them thus to their destinations! One baby cedar went to the Paris Botanical Gardens, the other to Chandai. I know that "ours" is still standing but I am ignorant about its "brother".

A short distance away from the cedar, also standing on its own and rare, was a large round building. It was built in a most attractive design of different coloured bricks made in the estate brickyard. It had a gabled roof with a cockerel weather-vane on its apex and dormer windows all around.

The building floor was of well trodden bare earth. In the faraway past the Lush Oasis had been a coach and horses relay, I had heard, and for many years continued to be used for the purpose it was built, "Un Manège". The very top was a pigeon loft. Only a few pigeons lived there, the others had been shot! More recently the ground floor had been partitioned to make a wine cellar and also a cider store. For me it was simply a place to play and ride my bicycle.

Before the last War, 1939-45, the inside domestics comprised a cook and her assistant, the butler and two maids. Rolande, the elder of the two, worked as they all did, from early morning till late at night with a half day off each week and I think, one hour during the day. I will return to Rolande later. I still remember well some of the estate workers, such as the bailiff and two gardeners, which brings to mind a still puzzling anecdote. Why oh why did I, aged again seven, climb up a ladder leading from the vegetable garden to the garage dormer window and, on reaching the top, sit on the door front, pull down my pants and, legs apart, shout for the two gardeners working below to hear "Sausages, sausages!" I shall never understand. The end of the story? I returned home very carefully and uncomfortably. The men having thrown a bucket of muddy water at me. As casually as possible I passed Mama who, with luck, happened to be reading on the bench outside, and I promptly went to change. Mama called "Pierrette! What are you doing?" "Getting a handkerchief" I answered... a lucky escape!

There was also Duval, a deaf and dumb, feeble-minded man who had served with Papa during the great war and to whom Papa had promised help and care for life. Duval was forever hoeing along the drives, paths and around the "chapelle". Wherever one went, weather permitting, Duval was there with his hoe. This is how I became acquainted with him.

Old photographs and hearsay agree that, from the time I was in my pram, I was often where he was, though for short periods only. I imagine that he must have been in his thirties, but I looked upon him as an old man. He had the manners of a grateful subordinate but could, just the same, have frightened a young child who did not know him. I was perfectly accustomed to him being around, however, as my awareness developed, my feelings towards Duval became mixed. He started to hide in the bushes and wait for me to pass by. When I neared his hiding place he used to whisper in his guttural and distorted voice, 'teek-teek', whatever that meant to him and in so doing, he would expose himself. I was curious and apprehensive all at once. Then he began to beckon me to follow him into the cider cellar where, each day, he went to fill up the pitcher. Now and then I answered his advances and in the musty, murky corner, he subjected me to his sexual activities. Those, unacceptable as they were, induced my discovery of the male anatomy. For him, I can now say, the hopeless certainty of his impotency! He never fondled me but guided my hands and once touched my lips to his own use. I was under eight at the time and although those happenings were not physically malicious, psychologically they took their toll. I felt ashamed and confused and the fear of being discovered was unbearable. So why, I now ask myself, did I continue to go to the cellar? I needed advice, I felt such a sinner.

This is where Rolande, the maid comes in, but she was no use. I began to confide in her the burden of my sexual awakening, and a burden it was, but Rolande did not hear me, worse, she blamed me. She kept showing me a small red notebook which she had entitled "The Book of Very Naughty Behaviour". She used to threaten to show it to my stepmother each time she thought I had misbehaved. Instead of helping the situation Rolande worsened it. I could not read what was being written so I was unable to check Rolande's writing, hence I shall never know whether or not she catalogued my confidences. I only know that all this deepened my insecurity. I do not bear Rolande any ill will for I think that she didn't know any better and, in a way, I could say that she had been my outlet. Also she had enormous patience with me in my younger years. One of her responsibilities was the linen room and it was there that we spent time together she sat for hours mending, sewing and darning whilst I stood on the chair behind her playing at "hairdressing"! At the same time Rolande sang for me. In her soft soprano voice I still remember hearing such musical fairy tales as Little Red Riding Hood, Cinderella and "Ma Mignonne Aiguille". I have never seen these songs written anywhere, nor met anyone who knew them. I assume that Rolande, dear Rolande, must have learnt them, as I did, by hearing them over and over when she herself was a little girl. For decades I longed to hear them again, so much so that when, in my forties, I acquired my first cassette recorder, I sang and recorded them all. Now I can re-live those happy moments, although it is not the same as listening to Rolande.

And what of Duval? After a year or so the happenings came to an end as my interest in natural history broadened. By the time World War II was declared far more important things had superseded Duval. All that remains to be said is that when I was about twelve I accompanied Mama to the gardener's house, where only Duval lived. We found him in his dark, squalid room, lying on his filthy bed and making raucous noises. By the bed stood a blue enamelled pail, the contents of which were obviously weeks old. He was by then nearing death. Only years on a most reliable ex-member of staff at that time, said that Duval suffered with his kidney and prostate. Being a simpleton, he, by using a wire hoping to encourage his body functions, used to insert his urinary tract with it! But blood escaping was a plenty, whilst what he expected never did. So much for Mama keeping Papa's promise to help and care for Duval in perpetuity! Duval was taken by motorcar to L'Aigle hospital where, the next day, he died of uremia. Oh! the smell, the neglect, the suffering, the sordidness of it all! I was nauseated, sad and angry, but I kept silent.

By the time Hubert's education had ended there were talks about mine. His tutor was no longer with us; he had left quietly and rather suddenly. I was over five years old and it was time, said Mama, that I learnt to read and write but more important, that I should study the catechism. I was delighted at the thought of going to school, especially at the idea of being with other children. I rarely had contact with people of my own age save during our summer holiday, which was spent at my stepmother's family home, the Château des Dervallières. Occasionally Papa's sister, her husband and sometimes their daughter Aliette visited us. We played happily together, in particular we "practised swimming" on a square low table in the centre of the vestibule. Having removed the heavy plant, we rested on our tummies and agitated our arms and legs in some semblance of a breast-stroke. We were convinced that, come the summer, we would be swimming merrily in the nearby Iton. It was great fun and laughter.

From time to time, a little girl from the village came to play. One of our games consisted of standing on the lowest steps going to the lavoir and there, both poised, we did "wee-wee" into an empty lavatory roll! We never did reach our target, the river. Even when we stood on the lavoir, but there was always a projectile winning distance - shared secrets!

Apart from those short encounters I lived in an adult world and whoever came to our house, I was still the only child. Is there any wonder that when education was mentioned I became a little excited? I soon sobered down when Mama told me there was no question of my going to the village school. Under no circumstances was I to mix with the village children. She made that absolutely clear but I was not told why. What disappointment! Instead I was to have a governess. I was very dismayed and somewhat apprehensive.

From autumn 1936 to July 1939, I had a succession of governesses. In late 1936, Mademoiselle Delabre arrived. A tall, slim young woman whose hair and clothes were "a la mode": the first neatly waved and short, the second mid calf length and straight. As I have said before, my stepmother's eyes were small and blue; Mademoiselle Delabre's were "forget-me-not" blue with a soft touch of silver and were the most beautiful blue eyes I had ever seen. I took immediately to her kindly face, her smiling mouth and her patient nature. She taught me the alphabet and the numerical digits.

Mademoiselle Delabre was much enamoured with the Corsican pop- singer of the time "Tino Rossi" who in a slow velvety voice, used to sing 'Catari, Catari'. I see now Mademoiselle languishing as she listened to him on the radio and the lost, dreamy expression in her "forget-me-not" eyes. With their usual contempt Mama and Hubert never failed to tease the poor woman unmercifully. Mademoiselle Delabre did not stay very long. As a matter of fact none of my governesses did; a few lasted a couple of months, some a week or so, one stayed only two days. She was nicknamed "the hopeless fool"! There were periods without any. It would be true to say that the worm had started to eat the apple and that I could be sly and unwittingly, cruel at times. Probably because, whilst there were governesses in residence, I was surreptitiously encouraged by Mama to tell tales behind their backs. When I did they were questioned in front of me, thus turning any warmth they felt towards me to bitter resentment. I was always blamed for their departure, of course. However, the last one was altogether an exceptional woman. Mademoiselle Colette, darling Mademoiselle Colette, dealt admirably with the bizarre environment of le Petit Château, she stayed nine months with us and would have been with us for longer, but ….. I will give her the credit she deserves at the appropriate place in my story.

Thus began my general education but my stepmother took charge of the religious side, which reminds me of another story. It was on the snow-capped Christmas Eve 1938, I was full of restrained excitement and rising awe.

Since my seventh birthday in June, I had reached the "age of reason". This dictated that in the near future I was to take the Holy Communion for the first time. This was a daunting obligation as well as a great honour. During the last six months I had spent what seemed to me endless hours of learning by heart the Juvenile Catechism. At home I had answered, parrot-fashion, all the questions asked by Monsieur le Curé, who had said, 'Very well done, my child.'

That afternoon, holding my Mama's hand, I walked unflinching the one-and-a-half kilometres to church where I was to make my first confession. Of all my soul's preparation this had been the most difficult. Having faithfully completed my Novaine, nine compulsory consecutive days of devotion to Notre-Père, my sacrifice box in which I put little pieces of paper for each mental offering to God was almost full.

I had tried so hard to inflict sacrifices on myself such as not answering back, not putting any jam on my bread and butter and especially not crying when being smacked on the face for just being there or when being chastised unfairly. Now, kneeling on my prayer stool, facing the altar beside the Confessional, head bowed and rosary in hands, I was at a loss to think of anything to confess.

'Help me, mon Dieu!' I pleaded under my breath.

Too late. Head still bowed, looking from the corner of my eye, I saw two black shoes moving in my direction. As I looked up, the black silhouette of Monsieur le Curé disappeared into the Confessional.

'You must go now,' prompted Mama. Choked with apprehension, I moved slowly towards my goal; in doing so I dropped my rosary.

'Oh sorry, God,' I whispered as I picked it up. In darkness behind the green curtain, on my knees and forehead pressing against the wooden partition, waiting, I heard a small door sliding. This was it! I looked up, just able to see Monsieur le Curé's face through the lattice.

'What are your sins, child?' breathed the priest.

'I... I... I can't think of any, Father.'

'Child, child,' the priest said gravely. 'Such an admission is a deadly sin. Pride, you understand.' He paused. 'Anything else?' he asked.

'I don't want to tell a lie,' I mumbled.

'Very well,' continued the priest, 'as a penance you will say one "Ave Maria" and your penitence prayer.' When I looked questioningly through the lattice, Monsieur le Curé was signing the cross. 'God be with you. Go in peace,' I heard.

At last I had gained sanctification. I was now pure enough to receive God in my heart. I did take Communion that Christmas at the Midnight Mass.

Contrary to what I had been led to believe, I was not born a sinner - no one is.

I had been much maligned from birth until these days. Yet in spite of - or perhaps because of - frequent soul-destroying influences and many shattering sequences of events, I am still the person that I was born to be.

On looking back I can see now that I was more and more emotionally unbalanced. How could it be otherwise? When I was with the staff they used to suggest, after a while, that I went upstairs where I should be but, with the family and their frequent guests, I was told that I had no right to speak! 'What do you know about that? You can be quiet!' I didn't belong anywhere.

But I had plenty of ruses up my sleeve to amuse myself. Here are a few samples. There was the day when, in a flash, I jumped onto the large ironing table and danced all over the beautiful white sheets in my muddy boots, much to the despair of the three women who were ironing them. They slapped my legs which turned as red as their angry faces! The sheets, "Hah!" the wretched sheets, had to go back to the boiler.

There was also the afternoon when my stepmother was expecting the vacuum cleaner saleswoman. When the woman arrived I followed her into the sitting room. Mama sat, urging the shy visitor to do the same. The saleswoman put her Electrolux and briefcase on the floor and, as she timidly sat on the edge of her armchair, a small "prrrt" escaped from the cushion! The poor woman didn't know what to do. Blushing and excusing herself, she readjusted her posture and, in so doing, sat perfectly on the top of my hidden "Whoopee Cushion" which let off the most noisy and realistic succession of "farts".

'Truly sorry, Madam,' choked the unfortunate "de lux" woman.

'Not at all, not at all,' my stepmother managed to say through her muffled laughter. I swiftly skipped out of the room.

I still laugh about that episode and the following one too.

Again in the sitting room the family lawyer was sitting opposite Mama. He was a hairless, chubby little man with a ruddy face. This was a business meeting from which I was excluded and I did not like it. I had recently acquired two small aeroplanes, one red, one blue. Those clever little toys were propelled by an elastic band which one twisted before launching them and they flew very well indeed. I chose the blue and twisted the elastic as far as it would go. I opened the sitting room door and, hidden by the fireplace, aimed at the round face and let go! "Pfffrrt", away it went, a little blue arrow across the room and, "oops", landed neatly on the top of the lawyer's head! His complexion changed from pink to purple. My stepmother flinched slightly and, as she called out my name, I detected her embarrassed but controlled rage. 'Pierrette!' There was no answer, I had shut the door behind me and vanished.

Some of my secrets had a sexual twist to them. For example, I used to lock myself in the lavatory with a pencil and an encyclopaedia. In great anticipation there I sat looking in the book for coloured works of art which represented nude women and, when I found them I would press the well sharpened pencil on each nipple, navel and pubic area that I saw. Also I used to find pleasure in capturing into a small pipette the many gnats that lived in abundance on the window panes. Later, I let them free again.

Such pursuits gave me sexual pleasure. The excitement was certainly sexual but confused. There was pleasure in doing "naughty" things in the lavatory which I did enjoy but did not comprehend.

But secrets were not in the foreground of my growing up. When I was young in Normandy, the four seasons were well defined. Each brought to me its own elation, pursuits and a kind of certainty. There was the harvest and the cider making, the snow drifts and the rainbows, the holidays and the church festivals. Their memories still arouse conflicting responses in me. It all happened seventy-odd years ago but now seems more like over a century. That is because nothing changed fast in our village apart from some households who owned a car and a very few who had their own electricity, most other families lived on their inherited knowledge and superstitions. I too, adhered to some, such as when spring came I made sure I carried my talisman, any small coin would do, as the saying went that good fortune came and lasted all throughout the year to those who held money in their hand when first hearing the cuckoo!

At Christmas Mama and I put up the crèche together. As late as sixteen, each May Day, I used to erect a blue and white altar dedicated to the Virgin Mary, a statuette of whom, surrounded with flowers, stood in evidence for the whole month. When I was an adolescent I no longer erected the altar, instead, each May morning before breakfast I used to dampen my face in the dewy grass. A guarantee for life of a beautiful complexion!

Each April and October I rejoiced at the turning over of our wardrobe. From the box room Mama fetched the heavy suitcases and would exchange our clothes for those suited to the oncoming season. I also found exhilarating the vegetable and fruit preserve-making days; I particularly liked the "petit pois" days, which started immediately after breakfast. All the domestics took part in the outdoor exercise. My stepmother always joined in the shelling and, naturally I did too. The gardener arrived with wheelbarrow loads, then we all sat around one of them, a bowl on each lap, and the shelling began in earnest. Dozens of jars were filled with peas, a few baby carrots and some young lettuce leaves. Within four hours of being gathered the vegetables were in the tall metal sterilizers and cook was keeping a vigilant eye on their thermometers! Marvellous memories of fun and duty equally shared.

In 1937 Mama and I were not involved in such a day for poor Mama was convalescing from a long, and ghastly illness.

In spring of that year she became unwell. Intermittent, but increasingly large, swellings developed on the sides of her neck, together with crises of violent vomiting. This was finally diagnosed as "Actinomycosis", a fungal infection usually affecting cattle and extremely rare in humans. It was thought she contracted the disease by sucking an infected blade of grass, presumably whilst walking through the cow meadows.

My stepmother was dangerously ill until some injections of "Propidon" were tried and, witnessing the tears rolling down her cheeks, I can vouch that it must have been the most painful cure to endure, but a cure it was. During Mama's agonising five months I seldom left her. Everyone tried to persuade me away from her bedside but to no avail. I took my meals at a small, low table by her bed and the rest of the time I played quietly in her room. My anxiety at the thought of her death, which seemed so imminent, was constant.

Mama fully recovered and in July, Papa, myself and she went on our holidays to the "Dervallières". These were happy holidays, two weeks of play, joy and affection for Papa was with us and it was good to see Mama alive.

It is just as well that those holidays are remembered as a ray of sunshine for they were to be the last of my early childhood.

Chapter Fourteen

FRANCE IS AT WAR –
THE NEW HOUSEHOLD

1939 - A year remembered the world over, by mid-August the news bulletins were everyone's main concern. The paralysing shock on the household when we heard on the 1st September that the Germans had invaded Poland. The order of mobilisation in France was passed at the first issue of that news, it did not get underway until the following day. Oh - the consternation which descended all around me and the fear that I might have my hands cut off!

When I woke up next morning Mama reminded me that we were at war with Germany. From that day until the end of the war, all windows without shutters or curtains remained painted dark blue. The general atmosphere was one of fearful expectation. This did not last long, for after the initial stupefaction, nothing then disturbed the peace of the Lush Oasis. I was back in Mama's room and still went rabbit shooting with Hubert.

I cannot say how long it was since the mobilisation but one ill-fated morning, the maid brought the mail with breakfast to our bedroom. My stepmother examined the post, her jaw dropped, she called Hubert saying in a quivering voice 'Oh! Mon Dieu, non!'

Hubert, I see him now as if it were yesterday, still in his pyjamas, took a letter from his mother. Hesitantly he opened it, glanced at it and, shaking his head, he uttered with a wry smile:

'That's it.'

My stepmother did much crying and gesticulating but to no avail. Hubert had been called up. He had to go. When or where he went I knew not. For a while he was no longer at home, then from time to time he reappeared. I heard later that he had been invalided out on health grounds, but that is all very vague in my mind.

Some of my stepmother's relatives lived in Paris, others at Nantes. At the beginning of the war things were extraordinarily quiet and uneventful. I heard people say how surprised they were that Paris had not yet been bombarded, but eventually there was news of air raids here and there. Some women and children began to move from the towns to rural areas.

It was arranged that one of Mama's nieces, her two children and an older aunt were to come and live at le Petit Château.

Hélène, the young mother, was a woman of class, tall and elegant. I didn't have much to do with her. She spent her time looking after her youngsters and writing to her husband. There were two things about Tante Hélène that I particularly liked. It was her jewellery, not the valuable pieces, but two sets of necklaces and matching earrings, one blue, the other pink. Why those have stuck in my mind to this day I have no idea. It could be that they were the first novelty jewels I ever saw. Or was it their colour? The other focus of my admiration was how the numerous shades of pinks and reds of her lipsticks and nail varnish blended so perfectly.

The older Aunt Zabeth, whose name was Elizabeth, was not a true aunt but the younger generation called her so. I think she had acquired the title through being a very long standing friend of my stepmother's family. She was rather short and often walked with a stick. Her round face and slightly trembling double chin were always pale and powdery. Her grey-blue eyes were animated, so was her small, versatile mouth with which she added her say at the slightest opportunity! Her facial expressions were incredibly similar to those of "Becassine", the main character in a well known children's book of the time. Aunt Zabeth, this overwhelmingly pious spinster, kept encouraging me, in the "name of Our Lord" to make sacrifices of all sorts. Those, she used to assure me, would save my soul if, or when, the last judgement was passed.

The new household settled quickly. Tante Hélène nursed and wrote, Aunt Zabeth prayed and Mama knitted. Alain, the four year old boy, and I tried to play together but without much success. Mostly it resulted in screams and tears from Alain and interference and jeremiads from Mama. That was predictable. The consecutive strain of my dichotomic upbringing was, at that time, very much in evidence. For eight years it had been the norm that one minute I was pampered, the next I was scarified. I had been the youngest child and when Hubert grew up, I became "only" child. Overnight I found myself the eldest of three children under the same roof. It was the first opportunity I had to assess and assert myself. Although it was subconscious, I did it with method and satisfaction. Alain, the spoilt brat, suffered the consequences of my vindictiveness. I was no longer the only one to be castigated, it was my turn to dominate, to make someone cry and I let it be known!

Chapter Fifteen

WAR DEBATES, THE EXODUS

In early May 1940, shortly before my ninth birthday, the words Hitler, prisoners, bombardment, Maginot Line and evacuation were constantly mentioned. This started to worry me terribly. I began to think that war was not going to be such "fun" after all. On local roads a mild panic had started. People looking lost and carrying a few possessions were travelling in a dispirited and aimless fashion. There were already some refugees in the village houses and farms. Our household was having animated discussions as to what to do.

'What about the children?' questioned Tante Hélène.

'I shall face the enemy,' blustered Mama, holding herself firmly upright. 'If I am to die it shall be in my own house.' Then she added, 'I AM NOT BUDGING!'

'I don't want to die,' whined the little boy, Alain.

'I don't want my hand cut off' I whinged.

'Let us pray' whispered Aunt Zabeth comfortingly! And so, day in day out, the arguments went on.

What I was able to grasp of the situation bore little resemblance to the atrocious reality. At the time I understood that the Germans were approaching and that they were thought to be invincible. The western allies maintained unjustified hopes that they could win the war by forcing economic pressure upon Germany. Whilst the debate at the Petit Château continued, Aunt Zabeth was flicking over the pages of her prayer book.

The debate in the House of Commons was particularly stormy. On May 7th, Leopold Amery, using Oliver Cromwell's words, was saying to Chamberlain, who resigned the next day: 'You have sat here too long for any good you have been doing. Depart, I say, and let us have done with you. In the name of God, go!'. In the name of the same God, the following day

Aunt Zabeth was mumbling over her rosary, when simultaneously over the air came the news that Churchill had become Prime Minister of England.

These names meant very little to me. I was pleased to have my dolls to play with, the Lush Oasis to roam about and Alain to tease. It helped to brighten the gloom.

As I was doing the inventory of my possessions and deciding which toys to take with me, if or when we left, the men of war were also stocktaking.

In early May 1940 the two conflicting parties seemed to be fairly equal, certainly in their physical strength.

The Germans had 132 army divisions, 114 infantry, 10 Panzer, 6 light, one cavalry and one airborne. The Dutch, Belgian, British and French combined had roughly 153 similar divisions. There were about 2,700 tanks on both sides. The significant difference was that the German Panzer were grouped together whereas the French tanks were scattered here and there attached to infantry formations. The worst discrepancy between the Allies' total and the Germans was in air weapons, for there were about 3,000 front-line German aircraft, against 1,800 Allied ones. However the German superiority was found in their warfare skills. Their organisation, training and leadership surpassed by far those of the Allied armies.

My assets were five dolls, a bicycle, a large toy chest and much more. I thought myself superior in rank and position as I was the eldest and on my own territory. I was winning all the battles against the poor disadvantaged Alain. How cruel can children be at times!

By mid-May we were sitting In the Salon before lunch when a long, fiery discussion developed. The news was bad. The Germans were crossing the Meuse and it seemed inevitable that they would soon reach Normandy. Mama felt responsible for the children and was finally persuaded to flee. It was decided that "Les Dervallières", her family home, would be the place to go. Only the date remained to be fixed. Normally I would have been overjoyed for this was where we used to spend our summer holidays; but not this time. When, on May the 27th, the capitulation of Belgium was broadcast we began to prepare ourselves. I knew little about the words capitulation, debacle, exodus which fell on my ears all the time, but I had become aware that this was no laughing matter.

Trunks, suitcases and food baskets were organised. Tante Hélène and my stepmother were to drive their respective motorcars. On the morning of our departure both vehicles were loaded to bursting point. The two children and their mother sat in their car, Mama, Aunt Zabeth and her rosary sat in the front of ours. I was more than willing to struggle into the back seat, cramped between the dog and the food basket, having heard a day or two earlier that the Germans were at Rouen's doors. Mama led the way. Red-eyed we waved at the servants and drove slowly towards the main road. We had joined the Exodus.

The first day was terrible. It was frightening, hot, endless. I was in great pain with a septic thumb and Aunt Zabeth's reassurance that the braver I was the more saintly I would become didn't do much to lessen the agony! Along the road, people who, like us, were hoping to escape the invaders looked harassed and tired. Women, children and a few men travelled the best they could, on foot, on drays or on bicycles. Some in small groups, others alone. At times we overtook short lines of refugees, at other times deserted roads stretched ahead of us. During the journey I saw two "dog fights" in the sky overhead; those frightened me for a while. They were noisy and the blue sky was full of little grey and white puffs of smoke. With the sun shining on them they were very pretty. We plodded on till shortly after dark when we arrived at Sablé, a small town about sixty kilometres southwest of Le Mans.

No sooner had we parked in the town square, which was already packed with refugees in transit, the sirens sounded. The town went dark and all the traffic stopped. This was a new experience for me. I had never heard such a strident clamour before, nor had I been so alarmed. I was shivering all over with fear, pain and hunger. When silence returned it was a deadly one. In their vehicles the flock of petrified humanity sat breathless, speechless and motionless. Within seconds, that seemed like hours, a throbbing was heard as if all the hearts of the people in the square were beating in unison with mine. I looked up through the car window and, against the starry sky, I saw another kind of flock of "steel birds", the metal hearts of which droned above us.

Shaking like a leaf I curled up and waited. No bombs dropped on Sablé. The sirens heralded our luck and relief! Mama's permission for the dog and I to get out of the car and "be excused" was indeed a great relief too. Then, in the calmer night, people shuffled in and out of their motorised shelters. Here and there I could see the light from their torches moving cautiously; with the help of ours, Mama gave us some refreshment after which, without knowing it, I fell fast asleep.

The early morning sun woke me up, my thumb had improved and soon we were on our way again. Little do I remember of the last leg of our journey to Nantes, via Angers, until we arrived safely at "Les Dervallières" (fig 20). Less than two weeks later, the Germans were there too!

Fig 20: Mama's family home.

Chapter Sixteen

LES DERVALLIÈRES

GRAND CHÂTEAU'S PILLAGE, DEVASTATION

La Contrie, where the Dervallières estate had been situated, was one of the rural areas of Nantes. The large Renaissance-style château and its surroundings were spacious. It was the family home of the "de La Brosse". In spite of having central heating and running water, it lacked the comfort and intimacy of our home; it did not have the cosiness and character of Chandai's Petit Château. Even though I spent many happy days there with adults and other children, for reasons best known to my stepmother, I was never treated like any of the latter, and often I felt lonely and isolated.

Before the war, several families with children of all ages lived at the Dervallières. Some children had their nursery on the top floor, where Nanny, in grey uniform and white bonnet, looked after them. The older ones had an English governess, Miss Chadwick, called by all "michaduique"! The youths played tennis, canoed on the lake, cycled around the park or went for rides in the donkey (Friquette)-drawn cart. I never had anything to do with the nursery or with the governess. On occasions I was included in the outdoor pursuits, but wherever I went I was treated as an outsider and, whatever I joined in, the other participants always made me feel as if I were there on sufferance. I spent most of the time with Mama, but when I was very young I played with one of the little girls who was four years older than I and, in a small way, was my friend. But she died of septicaemia when she was eleven.

The Dervallières entrance hall was floored with black and white marble tiles. It had a grand, imposing staircase sweeping up to a very large landing overlooking the hall with its long marble balcony, alongside which breakfast, on a massive oak table, was taken. I was the only young child who took lunch in the dining room. Almost invisible and ghost-like, I sat on my cushion on top of a leather chair next to Mama, facing the intimidating master of the house, Grand-père de la Brosse.

I spent my sixth birthday at the Dervallières and never forgot it. As two maids served dessert, a third came down the servery steps carrying a cake with six lighted candles. She came around the table and set it in front of me. All conversation stopped and it seemed as if millions of eyes were suddenly focused upon me. I blew out the flames and everyone offered me good wishes. I was overwhelmed; a little cake just for me! But, oh horror! I didn't like it. Nonetheless, Mama insisted that I finish the portion she had given me. One by one the others stood up and went to take their coffee in the hall. I was left alone and eventually, in tears, I forced the wretched treat down my throat. What a shame that this rare kind thought, instead of being remembered as a treat, should have ended in tears.

When we arrived as refugees at the Dervallières in 1940, it was crowded. One of my stepmother's sisters, who normally lived in Paris with her two children, Jacques and Jacqueline, had already taken up residence in what had been Grandfather's quarters before his death. We were to share it with them. So instead of the bearded face, which I used to see in the double bed during my previous visits, now I was to wake up every morning to the sight of Mama and her sister's faces.

At the foot of the double bed, and almost touching each other, were two single beds and a cot. There I slept between Jacques and a younger child called Tangui. Although I was at least four years older than he, I had to go to bed at the same time because he didn't like being alone. I resented the fact that, not only was it earlier than my usual bedtime, it was also I, and not Jacques, who had to suffer the little boy's exasperating behaviour. To send himself to sleep he used to toss his head from side to side. Worst of it, he muttered rhythmically, and almost without stopping for breath, the word "locomotive, locomotive, locomotive", which usually lasted about half an hour and was hardly conducive to sleep! Looking back, I wonder why that didn't make me murderous, probably because I had never heard of murder! Not once did the thought of killing him enter my mind, but instead, I kept telling him to 'shut up' which, of course, made no difference at all!

A week or so passed, I heard new words being spoken, Dunkirk, swastika, Nazi, Reynaud, Marshall Pétain, surrender - none of which meant much to me. To my young mind, we had gone through the exodus to be safe from the enemy and that was how things stood. I was aware that the war was still on but I was not unduly concerned. What I did not know was that on June the 16th Rommel had crossed the river Seine with the 15th Panzer corps; and the 4th Army's 38 corps, led by Monstein, had reached La Ferte-Vidame, forty miles south of the bridgehead and only thirteen miles from Chandai. When Mama told me the news, I realised how lucky we had been - and how wise to have left le Petit Château just in time. It was comforting to be at Nantes and out of the reach of the conquerors. But I began to wonder, were we really safe? The answer came soon enough.

It was three days later, when luncheon had just ended at the Dervallières. Some people were drinking coffee in the hall and a few had carried their cups outdoors. I was skipping on the edge of the terrace (fig 21) and trying not to step on the lines between the flagstones. The day was sunny,

calm and very hot. In the hush of the midday heat all was still and peaceful. It was almost too quiet; not a ripple on the lake, nor a rustling of leaves, nor a bird song. On the front lawn, under a tree, Friquette, the donkey, was flicking her tail now and again and occasionally twitching her ears. I

Fig 21: Just as quiet in 1936.

was debating happily whether or not to dunk a lump of sugar in Mama's coffee. I did so, then went inside. There, I found a mood of awe stricken but resigned expectation; a general atmosphere of disquiet which unnerved me.

It was June 19th, 1940. The German 11th Motorised Brigade had taken Nantes and St. Nazaire. As I ate a second sugar lump, I heard an unfamiliar rumbling in the distance. I ran outside. As far as the eye could see, grey-blue motorbikes with sidecars, followed by military vehicles, were driving through clouds of dust along the drive towards us. The Germans had arrived. The first motorbike stopped abruptly at the foot of the stone steps. I didn't wait to see any more, but flew up the sweeping double staircase, ran along the corridors and climbed, two by two, the spiral steps leading to the very top of the building. There, hidden in a dark corner, hiding my hands under my arms, I waited, terrified.

To my amazement I heard no screams or gunfire so, after a while, when I felt braver, I retraced my steps, albeit on tiptoe. Leaning over the banister, I looked down. Two German officers, caps in hand, stood by the coffee table talking quietly in their own language with Mama and her eldest sister. Encouraged by such unexpected civility, but still shaking at the knees, I took the risk of joining them. A little while later, the SS officers replaced their caps, clicked their heels, saluted Nazi-fashion, then, saying 'Danke schön,' marched out of the front door.

They had requisitioned the east wing of the ground floor. Immediately, the billiard room and the sitting room were vacated, by whom I did not know or where they went. By the evening, the Germans had settled in and were organised downstairs. Sitting on a corner of the front door steps I watched the comings and goings. The Germans had given me smiles and chocolate. Far better still they had not cut off my hands!

The Germans had arrived at Nantes two days after Marshall Pétain had asked Germany for an armistice and General de Gaulle had fled to England in a British aircraft. The date of the French capitulation was June the 17th 1940.

Now that my stepmother had come face to face with the occupying army and had discovered that life at the Dervallières had changed very little since their arrival, she decided that we might just as well live in occupied Chandai as in occupied Nantes.

Arriving back home I was happier than when I left, but apprehensive. We did not know what was awaiting us. Our two faithful staff and the dogs greeted us warmly. No Germans were present, they had been and gone - for the time being.

For a brief interval it was wonderful to be home again. Tante Hélène and her children returned to Paris but Aunt Zabeth was still with us. She settled into Hubert's quarters, while Mama and I went back to our own. Mama first noticed the sign of pillaging by the Germans when her eiderdown was missing. My first shock was the loss of my doll's house. But, before I had time to be sad, Rolande told us that le Grand Château had been the target of the worst assault. Mama and I went there immediately. The door was intact and closed, but it was unlocked. We wondered why. Maybe Rolande had been ordered to hand out the keys? I do not know.

The heartrending sight which hit us as we walked from room to room has scarred my heart. Whichever way we went, Mama and I were bereft with disbelief as we witnessed the evidence of abominable destruction, vandalism and hatred. Some things had been looted, the majority remained, although many were damaged. Furniture had been hacked, scratched and scorched, linen and curtains shredded or slashed, glasses and china broken. The museum was ravaged and looked like a battlefield. And the books! Oh, those beautiful and irreplaceable riches! Nothing but insanity could have led to their having been destroyed in that way. The ashes of some lay cold in the hearths, the pages of others were torn, half burnt and littered the floor, their leather bindings used as fireguards. Gone was the intimacy of the "blue salon", gone the memories of the reception room, gone the "marvels of the sea" collection, gone the stuffed pine marten, the squirrel, the owls and the hummingbirds, gone all my motionless and silent friends! Where had the secrets of le Grand Château gone? They had disappeared forever. Everything, everywhere, was nothing but destruction and devastation.

Chapter Seventeen

THE REQUISITION OF
LE GRAND CHÂTEAU

AN ALARMING SITUATION

Besides Mama's eiderdown and my doll's house nothing was missing, or had been damaged, at le Petit Château. Home was still home, the only change being the photograph in the frame above the sitting room fireplace. Before the exodus an arrogant looking Général de Gaulle, in uniform and seeming about to orate, was now a Marshall Pétain who, with crossed arms resting on his desk, cast his "fatherly" eyes upon us!

Despite the mere fact that France was occupied, life for me at the Lush Oasis continued unchanged. So far my summer days were as heavenly as those in spring had been. I went back to my loving interests. I could just about curb my eagerness towards the familiar wholesome pleasures awaiting and, of course, was not the war now over? I thought!

Suddenly, intoxicated with happiness, bursting with love and almost levitating with joy, I was in total harmony with the elements.

My search for treasures continued to take me around the park and I also went to the village shop with Mama. Alas! there the tranquillity of the past no longer prevailed. German soldiers went hither and thither about their business and convoys of tanks and armoured vehicles drove along the main road.

The calm of the Lush Oasis did not last long! The conversations between Aunt Zabeth and my stepmother about the war intensified once more. I understood that the world situation was not so peaceful as that of "my little world".

Between the 3rd and the 8th of July 1940, the French and the British were going through serious differences. Hitler was planning the invasion of Britain. At Vichy the new French government, now under the Germans' supervision, offered no help to the British. Instead it broke off diplomatic relations with London. To retaliate against the British behaviour, which took place during that first week of July, the French dropped their bombs on Gibraltar. It was touch and go whether France declared war on Britain. She did not!

In the course of those few days my stepmother sold some of le Grand Château's furniture to an antique dealer. I see the woman now, holding the artefacts upside down and looking for the "maker's" signature. Whilst I was rambling in the woods I found my doll's house and its roof and furniture on the rubbish tip. Those were moments of deep sadness.

Less than two weeks had elapsed since our return home and one day a chauffeur driven German car pulled up in front of le Petit Château. A high ranking German officer stepped down, his decorations, including an Iron Cross, glittered on his immaculate uniform as he paced forwards. The front door was opened. Side by side Mama and I were waiting. The officer marched in, clicked his heels, extended his arm Nazi fashion and said 'Heil Hitler!' My stepmother sustained her unshaken authority, we both held our breath and remained mute. In poor French the German asked whether my stepmother was the head of the household, to which she answered, in perfect German, 'Ich bin es!' 'Ah, you speak German?' the man enquired in his own tongue. 'Eine wenig', a little, replied my stepmother. And so a conversation developed between them. Already I was able to pick up a few words of German, although, over the next five years, I was to reach fluency.

Between the onset of the War and the evacuation, le Petit Château's staff had been reduced to two, Cook and Rolande. After the German emissary's nerve wracking visit the depleted household gathered in the sitting room, where Mama passed on the news of the requisition. The German troops were to arrive the next day. Le Grand Château was to become a barracks, the top floor of the wash house was to serve as offices. Losing no time, that same rainy afternoon my stepmother arranged for the furniture to be removed. Drays made several trips from le Grand Château to one of the farms' lofts and straw barns. Many books and other belongings were stored in "La Chapelle" and in the gardener's house. Heartbreakingly at the end of the day le Grand Château was by no means empty, only a small amount of heritage had been saved. Even so, masses of antiques and artefacts had to be left.

My confused mind was telling me no more visits to le Grand Château, with or without Mama. Already I was grieving for the loss of my secret sanctum.

Next morning the weather was clear, my mind lucid. The despair brought by yesterday's events was replaced by exciting curiosity of today's expected ones. The morning dragged on. After lunch I began to wonder whether or not "they" would come. Inwardly I felt slightly disappointed for, although I was still a little wary of the Germans, I did not fear them anymore. I thought that their coming would bring some "divertisement" in what I felt at the time, our grouchy life.

It was early afternoon when we heard the revving of motorbikes. They arrived by the lower drive. From the upstairs windows I watched the convoy making its way to le Grand Château. Motorcycles with sidecars drove ahead of personnel carriers, followed by vehicles packed with stores. With hindsight I believe those troops were the Panzer Grenadiers which, in accordance with the Germans' war tactics, used to precede the tanks.

Of that very first day of the Lush Oasis's occupation I have no unpleasant memories. I found the whole performance rather entertaining. From various view points I spent the best part of the day beguiled, yet amused, observing the unloading of men and materials. It was a noisy affair, with raised voices. The shouting of orders, the continuous hammering indoors, the to-ing and fro-ing outdoors was abrupt. Long pieces of wood, shorter ones and planks (I discovered later had been the troops' bunk beds). Bedrolls, kit bags and gas masks were all carried hastily inside. Considerable clatter was heard from the razzle-dazzle of the kitchens. It lasted long after my interest had dwindled, then, as if by magic, there was a void silence. Men, vehicles and materials had vanished! The plot was thickening!

In the morning I woke to a German voice shouting the reveille. Within no time at all the troops were out and about. I had no intention to stay in or near le Petit Château whilst so many things were happening. And all those handsome, young men with white SS on their collars! No sooner was breakfast over I went to "reconnoitre" the estate. I found the "vanished" vehicles. They were well camouflaged along the alleys of the park. There was no magic about it! I made my way back down the far end drive which ran along the garden walls and ended at Cedar Lane. From there I saw troops lining up in front of le Grand Château. I walked up to the terrace. Sitting on the upper lawn, I watched the first parade down the slope below. The first of many.

The wash house was situated behind La Chapellle, a short distance from le Grand Château but a little nearer to le Petit Château. On the top, the bright and only room had five windows, and wide shelves the length of two walls. There was also a round cast iron stove waisted with spaces to accommodate the warming flat irons. The vast ironing table took up almost the whole room. It was to be a very long time before I understood why the Germans had chosen that spot for their secret communications centre. The building stood amongst high trees, making it invisible from the air, hence it was perfectly suited to their needs and a reasonable distance between Paris and the coast. I only went there once during the occupation, a quick peep, but long enough to see the road maps, papers, telephone, and wires all over the place. An officer told me to keep away so I never went again. The Germans used it throughout the occupation.

The first batch at le Grand Château stayed about a week. From then on and right up to June 1944 companies of Wehrmacht and SS came and went at irregular intervals. At each changeover, one or two officers came to inform my step-mother of their arrival. When, on some occasions, a high ranking officer would sit in "Papa's" chair conversing with Mama, I sat attentively and understood more and more German!

The presence of the occupants did not impede my free rambling, if anything it made it more interesting, for there were always new activities going on. Groups of soldiers, with or without firearms, marched up and down, sometimes singing, sometimes shouting. Unperturbed, my prime interest was still leaning towards nature appreciation. I collected butterflies, their life cycle fascinated me. I took my hobby very seriously. Into an airtight jam jar I used to put a fluff of cotton-wool, already imbibed with ether. With my small green net in one hand and the jar in the other, hopeful and happy, I gambolled in search of the flying gems. I also gathered caterpillars, cocoons and chrysalises. I pried into nooks and crannies of the outbuildings and inspected the gardens and undergrowth. Le Grand Château's exterior shutters were a particularly productive ground of harvest.

My "experiments" took place in one of the greenhouses. I fed the caterpillars and, when they had metamorphosed, I kept vigil over the cocoons. The excitement began when the emerging butterfly showed its head, then its front legs as it struggled out of the dried protective sheath. My patience was unlimited. I watched its proboscis curling up for the first time like a miniature spring. Finally the whole insect, wings crumpled and moist, stood trembling precariously on the empty shell. Ecstatic! I held my breath. It was then that the miracle came to its climax. Within a few minutes the small appendages dangling pitifully each side of the butterfly's body like two pieces of screwed up tissue paper, stretched and opened giving shape, colour and life to the fragile, powdery wings. For a while, I held out my hand to the newborn and, as it wobbled along my fingers, I carried it outside. Then gently, oh! Ever so gently, urged it to fly. The butterfly took to its wings. I watched it flitting, unsteadily at first, then just a tiny speck against the bright blue sky. A symbol of freedom!

I collected bird's eggs and flowers with the same dedication. I asked to have my own garden, and was allocated a small piece of ground between the two greenhouses and given a spade, a rake and a watering can as well as a specially made dark green wheelbarrow with removable sides, scaled to my size. I worked hard on my little allotment, growing carrots, lettuces and flowers. It was magic! At a later date I kept rabbits in a disused kennel. I looked after them all by myself. In my fourteenth year I was very strong and healthy, I carted full, heavy wheelbarrows, mucked out the runs and washed them, and harvested baskets of rabbit food each day, dandelions, plantains etc. I had started with only a few bunnies but as everyone knows rabbits are quite proliferous and mine were no exception… My favourite was "Willy", a medium size creature, jet-black fluff with the brightest blue eyes. I have never seen a rabbit with blue eyes since. He was named after a German officer who also had beautiful blue eyes.

At the house anxious talks were receding. My stepmother was involved with the storage, distribution and dispatch of goods allocated to the French prisoners of war. On parcel days women from the village would arrive at le Petit Château carrying their holdalls, bursting at the seams with treats for their loved ones. The exercise took place in the dining room. Mama distributed the provisions from large cardboard boxes and the helpers busily packed individual parcels. There was much tongue-wagging, a few tears and some laughter during the process. The result of the afternoon was a pile of neatly wrapped and labelled boxes bound for Germany.

Summer was now over. Whilst Chandai had been sinking into its new routine and I had been "admiring" the Germans' manoeuvres and drills, the Battle of Britain was taking place. The first mention of it came to my ears ten years later! Oh! the irony of it all. To think that when I was nine years old my life was enlivened by German troops preparing for the invasion of Britain, the very country which, one day, was to give me my own freedom!

On the 16th July, 1940, Hitler planned to invade England, Operation "Sea Lion", and made preparations for six weeks ahead. His prior assault was by air, but by early September the Battle of Britain had been won, the Luftwaffe losing. Invasion was thwarted and Hitler turned his attention to the Russian front. One night, at dusk and without warning, we heard a thunderous noise immediately followed by a tank. Amazed, we stood at our bedroom window and watched a military convoy, having used the upper drive, skirting our home and making its way to the woods. The Germans had never used the upper drive before and this unnerved us a little. We grew more worried when, after the tanks, came the ammunition carriers and the sight of the many petrol bowsers. Inquisitiveness grabbed me by the arm! I promptly disappeared. I went to nose around and found La Grande Allée chock-a-block, so was Pine Lane. There were vehicles everywhere. I meandered about that arsenal, touching this and that and exchanging a few words with the soldiers. 'Guten Abend!' I'd say. 'Guten Abend,' they said. 'Was ist das?' I was asking here and there. 'You speak German?' they asked, in their own tongue. 'A little,' I boasted, in theirs. The cheek of it! After a few exchanges I returned home to find that the verbal exchanges between Mama and Aunt Zabeth differed distinctly from those between the Germans and I!

'Where have you been?' Mama asked.

'To the park,' I answered.

'Whatever for? You are always going where the men are,' Mama pursued discontentedly.

'It was interesting,' I continued, explaining what I had seen. Mama and Aunt Zabeth were quite agitated.

'Do you realise that we are in grave danger?' Mama asked.

'I didn't think, why?'

'No, you never think, do you?' Mama went on. 'What if a bomb were to be dropped on the woods? I am most fearful.' Only then did I become aware of the danger which hung above our heads, puzzled too, for Mama had neverbefore mentioned the possibility of Chandai being bombed. Indeed, I do not remember it having been mentioned again.

'We had better pray that this does not happen,' prescribed Aunt Zabeth.

'Should we be bombarded the whole village, including us, would be an inferno,' Mama went on. Those words were the last I heard as I fell asleep.

Next morning Mama and Aunt Zabeth were all smiles, the convoy had gone. It was one of the most alarming situations we had yet faced.

Chapter Eighteen

MÉMÉ AND PÉPÉ WEISS
ASSAULT ON BOTH CHÂTEAUX

Under aunt Zabeth's influence I was, in a fashion, becoming more pious, but my growing up line of thoughts did not altogether agree with the ecclesiastic ideal! My academic education had come to a halt when Mademoiselle Colette left and, at this moment in time I did not go to school, had no governess, no friends. My horizon was the estate's boundaries.

In the course of 1941, the lodge, which had stood empty for some time, was inhabited again. This was a small single-storey stone building with a tiled roof. A few steps and the little balcony laden with geraniums led to the only door. The door of the kitchen, dining room, sitting room combined. A large book case occupied the facing wall. Each side of it were the doors of the bedroom and the study. On the right behind the front door was an old sink with a cold water tap, on the left there was just enough room for the small range. Between the range corner and the bedroom was the spare bedroom door. Three sides of the cottage were completely surrounded by large trees, which made the rooms dark and damp. However the kitchen-cum-living room was always warm and cosy.

My stepmother let it; not as a gatekeeper dwelling, but as a refugees' abode. For my good fortune, the new tenants, a retired Jewish couple Monsieur and Madame Weiss from Paris, soon befriended me.

Madame Weiss was adorable. She had a kind, loving and stable personality, with a sharp sense of humour. Like most women of her generation she was devoted to her husband; nay! Subservient! Although being the dominant he too was committed to her though for different reasons. Had she not given him and brought up their four children and entirely dedicated her life to their family? Now in the winter of their life,

they were "lovers" again as they had been when courting.

They were inseparable (fig 22). Arm in arm they went to the village, hand in hand they strolled to their vegetable garden and many times I arrived at their nest to find her sitting on his lap and cuddling in a big armchair by the stove. Monsieur Weiss was a retired accountant, and this is why I met them soon after their arrival; an agreement was made with my stepmother for him to give me some tuition in mathematics.

A deep affection quickly grew between them and I. The lessons took second place while my calls increased in frequency and length. Before long our mutual endearment warranted my calling them "Mémé" and "Pépé", which in English would be "Nana" and "Granddad".

Fig 22: Still lovers.

According to my stepmother's impotent criticism, this was too familiar a way to address them… and "common" at that! But familiar and common though it might be, it bore no relevance to the sentiment which I felt for Mémé and Pépé, and I continued to call them so. At last I had found people who treated me as a child of ten needed to be cared for. They gave me love, help and altruistic attention at times of uncertainty. I received from both, the much wanted understanding and comfort lacking in my upbringing and much more besides. Madame and Monsieur Weiss were avid readers and later they lent me books. When we were not talking about the facts of life, we played cards and mahjong.

This unexpected turn of events was to be the key to unlock the security door that my stepmother had so meticulously fastened. I spent less and less time at home.

"I am going to the lodge", I used to tell Mama.

"'What? Again? You are never here, wait a minute....' Mama intercepted... but I was gone and sometimes I didn't even return for my meals. Naturally I was not always going to the lodge straight away, for I still gadded about on the estate and went to le Grand Château when it was free from Germans. I am sure that Mémé and Pépé laid the foundation stones of the wall of strength I still have; onto which I relied for protection throughout my life, but I am still sad that they died before I was old enough to express my eternal gratitude to them. It seemed in my young mind an imprint of decency and pride.

Another wonderful thing sprang out from knowing Madame and Monsieur Weiss. During the summer holidays their twelve-year-old grandson, Jacques, stayed at the lodge and better still, their youngest granddaughter Françoise. When she first appeared on the scene, she was under school age and used to stay for long spells at the time, later she only came for holidays. There is no means by which I can express the joy, the soothing feeling and the elation that being with other children brought me. Although there were five years between Françoise and I, and now and again I did tease her, we played very happily together. Either at le Petit Château or around the estate, at the lodge and even beyond the gates as far as the lower farm. Françoise was a sweet and delightful little girl. One of her thumbs was all flattened for she was sucking it at any opportunity. She thought the world of my stepmother who, in return for this incited and blind admiration gave Françoise kind but queenly attention... Mama's very attitude I despised so much once I had ceased to be a child, that to the eyes of a very young girl gave her brilliance and respectability. To this day, Françoise still melts with admiration at the mention of Madame Firmin-Didot! Françoise is still sweet and delightful... but the tale must go on. And indeed bar from one "war" day, summer 1941 was a wonderful one.

But what of the war? Had it not been for the occasional reference to the Germans, by some villagers as "Les sales Boches", I was near to forgetting it. On reflection I remember that, to me, the ambience in the lush oasis and the village, was more of a holiday than one of war!

Reality returned one terrible day and took me by surprise. The occupants might have been celebrating the first success of Operation Barbarossa? Their invasion of Russia was not only a quick victory, it also had a jocular tinge.

In spite of all the evidence and many warnings from well informed quarters, in London, Paris and even Tokyo to name but a few, Stalin blindly disbelieved the imminent German threat. The supply of raw materials and grain which he diligently used to send to Germany continued to be delivered right up to invasion day. On June 22, 1941 at 2am, the last Germany bound train carrying the Soviet goods rolled through the main front line of German soldiers who were ready for the assault. An hour and a half later the ever confident and highly amused troops launched their attack! Tausend Dank, Herr Stalin! It is possible that the festive mood at le Grand Château was prompted by the destruction of thirty-three Russian divisions, in less than three weeks, or by the achievement of Hoth's Panzer Group 3, to cut the highway between Smolensk and Moscow on July 15 and 16. In 23 days the Germans had captured 300,000 men, albeit at the cost of many lives.

To whom or what the frolics at the "barracks" were dedicated, I still cannot tell and knew even less then. But evidently there was jubilation. The SS company of the time cheered and sang in open excitement. In mid-afternoon we heard repeated clamours coming from le Grand Château. Somewhat concerned aunt Zabeth, Mama and I went to the front door. Transfixed with outrage, as if glued to the threshold, we saw all sorts of things flying out of le Grand Château's windows. Books, chandeliers, furniture catapulted in the ground as we gazed, stupefied, stunned and powerless. In a quivering voice Mama was saying, "Oh! A wardrobe!" And a few minutes later – "Oh! No! The marble fountain! Please stop!" Then, out flew one of my "treasure troves"... 'Please, no! Not my mahogany dressing table!' Mama pleaded, alas to no avail... It too was launched into space and from the spot where it landed its wreckage was thrown onto a huge bonfire, where its ashes joined the cinders of ruination.

All the while I kept close to Mama, my reaction, as it always was in times of tumult, was wanting to laugh… especially when my stepmother was pleading for mercy!

Meanwhile, the sporadic havoc never seemed to end. Nothing could be gained by staying to watch Lucifer hard at work, so heavy hearted we went back to the sitting room. I could see that Mama and aunt Zabeth were ill at ease, every so often they checked the situation. I felt unwell and the need to laugh had left me, fear had taken its place. What if our home was next on the list for destruction? Outside the fire grew bigger, the flames fiercer, the shouting louder.

As daylight came to an end, so the light-headed troops stopped their satanic marathon. The last thing I saw, when I leaned out of the window before going to bed, was a ribbon of smoke escaping furtively from the pile of demonic embers. The ordeal was over! Thus thinking, relieved and exhausted I went to sleep… But I was wrong. There was more to come. In the depth of the night we were awakened by the singing and hailing of inebriated officers. Mama got dressed immediately. Aunt Zabeth and I used our dressing gowns. I can still see Mama opening, with the greatest of care, one of the windows. Through the shutter's slats we saw a group of six or eight men swaying and staggering on the terrace just under our windows, and looking up. We locked all our doors, listened and waited. I shall never forget Mama's perplexity and aunt Zabeth kissing her rosary's crucifix in the harsh light of the bedside lamp, their faces screwed up with fear. Near them I sat on Mama's bed, for I was shaking so much that my legs would not support me.

Outside the singing deteriorated into bawling and we heard stones crashing against the shutters. It was atrocious! The roars went on, the noise of handfuls of stones cracked at the protected windows like bullets of miniature machine guns. What could we do? We feared that at any moment the men might smash their entry into the ground floor and that it could be the end of us. In the grip of this potentially fatal situation, Mama kept expressing her concern over the family silver, hidden under her bed!

Was it not peculiar of her, I now ask myself, to show such stubborn preoccupation about material things, albeit valuable, while our very lives were possibly at stake?

A good hour must have passed I suppose, when eventually there was silence. We peeped out of the window… the terrace was free and so were we! Aunt Zabeth kissing her rosary crucifix, again returned to her bed, I stayed in Mama's. I was very cold, still shaking and turning my back to her for warmth and protection – none came. Of the happenings of war time, this was the most frightening of them all.

In the morning le Grand Château was deserted, the silence heavy. I went to poke through the ashes of the bonfire. It was an impulsive but hurtful and melancholy gesture. Perhaps I needed the conformation that. the ignominious episode had not been an awful dream but the cruel facts. I found many twisted and scorched remnants and straight away went to show them to Mémé and Pépé, who lovingly pacified my mental turmoil.

Chapter Nineteen

THE REQUISITION OF
LE PETIT CHÂTEAU

RAM PATH

Autumn brought its misty days, winter its snowfall. Neither carried much recreation to rejoice in nor odiousness to weep about. I shared my time between the lodge and home. Often I left in the morning to return well after dark. I never used a torch, usually I jogged all the way home looking straight up above, for my only guide was the line of treetops against the sky.

I welcomed Spring 1942 with glee. My freedom was further increased by having another bicycle. It had been a while since I had outgrown my first one. Cycling became one of my favourite pastimes.

Early in the season, when my outdoor freedom extended, my stepmother found hers indoors suddenly restricted. A strikingly handsome German officer rang our doorbell one morning. He was a Colonel with SS Standarten Fuhrer badges on his collar and the edelweiss flower badge on his sleeve which would indicate that he belonged to the SS.Abschmitte, 26th SS-sub district. He also wore other decorations, including two Iron Crosses and even higher, the Knight Cross. This impressed Mama and I.

The German's attitude matched the implacable severity of his uniform. Although he was civil enough he spoke in a commanding tone and certainly did not sit in Papa's chair to converse with Mama like some others had done before. No! that one had come on a mission and meant it! My stepmother was a trifle taken aback, nevertheless she kept her arms crossed and chin up even when she heard the "Colonel's" orders. It was the requisition of our home! At that point my stepmother's knowledge of German helped the situation considerably. She and the officer discussed at length, although not in the most amiable manner which I took for granted during such meetings. That was a verbal fight! Mama wished to stay put, the German wanted us out. At the end of the battle a compromise had been reached. We were allowed to keep our four en suite rooms but were to share the rest of the house. Heil Hitler! said the Colonel before his departure, nearly touching my stepmother's nose as he saluted! So it was that le Petit Château became a German officer's quarters.

Rolande left at that time. Did she still, in her enfeebled voice, sing fairy tales to little children, I wonder? Cook continued to work for us. I now suspect that from her first working day she probably had been in service at the Estate, but this is only a guess. She was skilled in all aspects of her job and watching her, I learnt much about that art. Cook's mother, just about retiring age, was the washer woman and came each Monday. I had grown fond of the old woman known as "La Petite Mère Suard".

She lived alone in her cottage where I often went to see her. It stood on its own on the top of a long but gentle hill in a small country lane. From the Lush Oasis the path going to the cottage started from a narrow gate at the end of a hump bridge across the river. "Ram" path was so called because indeed, three quarters of the way up, there was a ram. That particular ram did not bleat however; it was lodged in a small brick building and its never ending "sprishsh, sproshsh" indicated that it was working. That hydraulic pump, the Ram, supplied Le Petit Château with water. The pipe and tube went from there right across the width of the Lush Oasis and up and down again to the reservoir at its very top. There were only two water points in our house, but many around the estate.

I simply loved using Ram path and did so for many years. Going up towards "La Petite Mère Suard's" cottage, on the left was a flower meadow and on the right a marshy tangle of thriving aquatic vegetation. In spring and summer I picked armfuls of wild flowers, in autumn coloured leaves, and in winter I walked from one iced puddle to another to hear the cracking! I never ventured too near the tempting, but awesome, place opposite "Ram Lodge"! There was a large pond and a wealth of things to observe and admire each season.

As I knocked at Mother Suard's door I used to see a lace bonnet rising, then slowly disappearing from the window, and I heard the shuffling clack, clonk of the black sabots on the brick floor. The white bonnet reappeared on top of its usual head and smiling Mother Suard was on her doorstep. When I brought her flowers she put them in a vase on the round table by her window.

The cottage was two-roomed, with only one being habitable. This contained an old range, a kitchen cabinet and in a recess, the bed. Mother Suard was shrunken with age and I, still growing, was of the same height. She was the dearest of nonagenarians, minute and frail in her long black clothes and crocheted white shawl. She always sat between her table and the range. I sat facing her and, as we babbled on, goodness knows what about, I watched her arthritic fingers working at full speed like spider's legs weaving its web. To and fro, up and around went the thin thread, whilst dangling from her thinner than matchsticks knitting needles, the intricate and delicate work of art took shape.

We generally had a drink together which we drank out of an ex-mustard glass container. This was, and still is, a most popular drinking vessel used by French country people. According to the weather we either took cider or coffee. My visits were never very long but they lasted over many years.

When the toll rang for little Mother Suard I heard that she had lived just short of her century. As soon as the news came I went on my bicycle to the cottage of my long-dated friend. All the shutters were fastened and Cook was away. Another page had turned, another life had ended, another friend had gone.

Chapter Twenty

OUR HOME SHARED WITH GERMAN OFFICERS

MY ROMAN CATHOLIC CONFIRMATION

Whilst far away from the lush oasis, the relentless WWII was still raging. There was fierce fighting in North Africa. Because of his determination to keep hold of Libya, Churchill had reinforced its position by making its Western Desert Force the Eighth Army, while Rommel was then in command of Afrika Korps in Tripolitania.

On November 18 1941, the British Commander-in-Chief Middle East, General Sir Claude Auchinleck, attacked to free Tobruck. At the same time the Soviets were fighting tooth and nail against the Nazi. By November 26, the Germans had lost 743,112 men, excluding the sick and frostbitten ones. The closest the German Army came to Moscow was within sight only of the Kremlin golden spires, which like the donkey's carrot was never reached.

By the beginning of March 1942, a matter of weeks before the requisition of le Petit Château, the Russian front had accounted for the loss of 1,005,636 German lives! Even though the insignificant dot on the map marked Chandai was a long distance from the USSR, my stepmother remarked on the Germans' overall change of mood. They were becoming more aggressive, she said.

During these dramatic times of worldwide unrest, I, being a few months into my first decade, remained unperturbed. In early 1942 my concern, if any at all, was nearer to home. For now I was not only watching the troops at a distance and at close range too, I was also living with them, so to speak. It is strange to relate that I remember very little about the shared occupation of le Petit Château. Now and again I was passing the officers along the corridor and on occasions I saw an orderly cooking for his superiors while our cook was preparing our meals that we took in our own rooms.

How Aunt Zabeth and Mama spent their time I have no idea. I should think that between church services and the odd social visitings, there must have also been some socialising with the Germans in the sitting room. How else would I have acquired so quickly the ability to understand some German?

Inside our home all was very quiet, not so outside. The trampling of boots and the drillmaster's calls were frequently heard on the terrace. I much enjoyed watching from the windows the squads being trained. The instructions were rigorous, stringent and noisy. Strictly no vacancy for dilettantes there!

On reflection, I think that I was surprised, seduced even, by the glamour of the Germans' attire. Without knowing it, I was drawing a parallel between the troops' authoritarian life and my own life under my stepmother's autocracy.

Between spring and autumn 1942, I saw many military parades and drills. Sometimes when I routed across the woods on my own, I used to ape the soldiers. I goose-stepped a few yards, saluted "à la Nazi" and lashed out a juvenile "Heil Hitler" to the trees! There was an occasion when I did this in front of Mama whose reaction was not, to say the least, favourable!

Although I spent hours at the Lodge with Mémé and Pépé and gallivanted all over the place, I did now and again stay at home. Aunt Zabeth showed me how to play a two-people patience, there was no winner or loser, it was called "Sympathy". Mama and I played it too. Given the opportunity, I still do.

From March to September of that year everything was uneventful apart from the following episodes. The first was when, at a distance, I saw two armed Germans forcing forwards a Polish prisoner of war who had been working on the land; the Pole was carrying a spade and the Germans had their guns against his back. In a walled corner of the Lush

Oasis he was made to dig a large trench, then he was shot. For many years afterwards little bunches of flowers kept appearing on the lone grave, from whom? One will never know. After the war his remains were exhumed and properly buried in Chandai's cemetery. Anger swept though the village when the news about the Polish prisoner was heard.

The window near my bed was a convenient "observatory". From there I once witnessed a German soldier fulfilling his punishment. It was a painful thing to witness. There was no leniency or remittance in the SS's rules and regulations. When a man had faulted he was punished; and severely at that. On that particular occasion, the chastening took place on the tableland. I watched it from beginning to end. On the ground rested a preserving pan, it was full of water. The object of the exercise was for the accused to pick it up by both handles and to carry it as he ran the length of the tableland and half the way back. The pitiless part of the punishment followed. Never letting go of his burden the man had to kneel and stretch face down on the ground, stand up again and start from the very beginning. This performance was relentlessly repeated until finally the soldier collapsed with exhaustion. All that time my heart went out to the man; mentally I struggled with him, and I felt aggrieved when he succumbed. I was puzzled too! What crime had he committed to deserve such a harrowing sentence, I wondered? Later we were told by our "co-habitants" that the accused had stolen a gold watch. I now suspect he did not step out of line again in a hurry!

Although I didn't go to school, I was never idle. My interests and curiosity kept me constantly on the go. Wild life, cycling, playing at the Lodge and now I took up a new hobby. It was fishing. My tools were primitive but it was amusing to prepare them myself. These were of two kinds, the rods and the traps. The latter were made out of empty wine bottles. With a stone and a stick I hammered a hole in the funnelled bottom of the bottle, then I replaced the loose glass with some bread, corked the bottle and tied up a long string to its neck. Et voilá! For the rod, any old twig, with a length of kitchen string, a bottle cork and a fishing hook worked admirably! I used bits of earth worms or bread for bait. It was as simple as that. To the river

I marched, I can see myself now, carrying my accoutrement, three traps, a rod, bait and bucket… A "fishergirl" if ever there was one! My fishing ground was behind the washhouse. I set the traps a few yards apart along the accessible stretch of river and while they were being filled up I fished with the rod. Minnows were the subject of my attention. My patience was always rewarded. I never came back empty-handed. Sometimes I returned my captives to the water, sometimes I took them back to the kitchen where I prepared them, fried them and ate them there and then. Later I pestered Mama to distraction for her to give me Papa's beautiful wooden tackle box, to have peace she did so. It contained everything that an angler could wish for... what a treat! I launched myself into the art of fishing, but I remained faithful to the unfortunate minnows!

Now the lucky owner of long and flexible rods, now and again I also went frog fishing. To the left of le Grand Château there was an overflow area of the river Iton. Its two-hundred-yard length which ended at the back of a small house was part of the estate boundaries. At ground level the south bank followed the cow meadow. On the old building side there was a high bank, lined with splendid trees. We called this stretch of water "the dead river", but even though it was almost stagnant, for the locks at both ends were never in use, "dead" it certainly was not. The vegetation which covered the steep bank was rich in species, quality and quantity. Damselflies of many colours, scarabs with iridescent wings, bugs of all shapes lived there in harmony while birds and vole families kept the balance of nature. The aquatic flora and fauna were equally luxuriant and frogs were in plenty… These lovely creatures were easily caught. No worms, no flies, no bread was necessary. A square inch of bright red thin material attached to an open safety pin at the end of the rod was all that was needed. The poor frogs couldn't resist; they bit and snapped at it with all their might.

1942 was indeed a busy and eventful year. Françoise spent the summer at Mémé and Pépé and we saw each other every day. She growing more ecstatic towards my stepmother. I increasingly attached to her grandparents. In June I was to go through the ceremony of my religious vows, the "Communion Solanelle" (this could translate into English as "High

Communion"). I was not allowed to participate in Chandai's church "High Day", the grand ceremony attended by all children of that age together to unite in the celebration of their Roman Catholic solemn vows. The little girls are dresses as a bride, all in white, long dresses and veils, the boys wore black or grey suits with a long white armband. Before and after high mass they enter and leave the church forming a procession. Each carrying a church candle which they disposed of during the officiation. After mass the communicants go home where presents and a feast are awaiting. In mid-afternoon they attend Vespers (evensong). When the religious ceremonies are over, there was usually a home celebration, when guests, family and children alike lose their inhibitions. Much frolicking, singing, story telling and dancing went on until the early hours of the morning as the company got more inebriated. The poorer the family the more flamboyant, lengthy and merry the "do"! Of course not all families celebrate that day with such an exuberance! Some have more moderate and sanctimonious views on the meaning of it; and there are considerable variations according to regions, social rank, and sanctitude of the people involved.

After many months of catechism learning, I successfully passed my written examination, and the priest examiner gave me carte-blanche for my oral test. Thus initiated, I left home one sunny morning and with Mama I travelled to Paris where we spent ten days at her sister's flat. Arrangements had been made between my stepmother and the Mother Superior of a convent for me to join in its "High Day". In order to bring my eleven-year-old soul to the required state of purity, I had to follow a novena (nine consecutive days of prayer and devotions).

Fortunately I didn't have to be a boarder. Altogether these were not happy days. At the flat the atmosphere was contrived. I secretly envied Aunt Manette's children who were doing their homework in the evening. How vividly I wished I could have been like Jacqueline working at her desk and working on her translation and English comprehension. Especially when Mama pointed out how much she would have liked me to be clever enough! If only I would work... she used to say! This made no sense to me, as I had no one to educate me at home and, so far, the village school had been prohibited!

On the Monday Mama took me to the convent. It was only three Metro stops away. I returned to the flat for lunch each day. My commuting alone in Paris unnerved me at first but it was the highlight of my stay, for it made me feel very grown-up and responsible. During the week I went to be fitted with my "bride" outfit; all went well. Sunday was approaching, I could almost sense the halo above my head! On the Friday night there was an air raid. The furniture and windows shook as the bombs dropped on Paris and we roamed about the flat to the glimmer of Mama's torch. Poor aunt was petrified, she spent the time in and out of the lavatory. I understood that this was her usual reaction to fear. During the raid I had mixed feelings. I was mildly amused and slightly fearful, but mostly I found the situation uncanny. So often I had heard about bombardment but never experienced being the target and on looking back, I think the sounding of the siren was the thing which I disliked the most.

My communion day was a serious and dull affair. For some reason I kept thinking about my real mother. Between mass and vespers I expressed the wish of her being there which naturally darkened the situation even more, displeasing Mama enormously. 'After all that I have done for you, is this my reward?' she said for the umpteenth time. We had goose for lunch but no dancing, merriment or rejoicing took place that day. I went to bed early to rest for the morrow which was to be my conformation day. This went according to plan. I kissed the Bishop's ring when he gave me communion, but when following the ritual His Grace gave me a gentle tap on the cheek, I shunned away… May the Lord forgive me! I now realise that this was the protective reflex I was conditioned to use to avoid my stepmother's hand.

We left the next day and what a relief it was to be back at the Lush Oasis!

A few weeks on I was about to make my way to Mémé and Pépé when I happened to look out of the window. I had become blasé about yet another military drill but something unusual caught my attention. I looked twice and became glued to the spot. I could not believe my eyes. Was

I imagining things? Day dreaming perhaps? But no, my observation was correct. In the front row, marching with the soldiers, stood a little boy! I was flabbergasted! The child, looking not a day older than I, was in full SS uniform and goose-stepped perfectly. His clicking of heels and salute were faultless. "Heil Hitler!" the "little" man shouted at the top of his voice when the drill ended.

I was perplexed but nevertheless most impressed! My wish was to meet that contemporary of mine, but I never did. I did not see him again. Who was he? Where had he come from? Where had he vanished to?

Chapter Twenty-One

THE FINAL EVICTION
FROM CHILD TO WOMANHOOD
THE INJUSTICE OF LOUISETTE

It was still summer 1942 when, one morning, there was a knock at our door. It was a German messenger who handed a piece of paper to my stepmother, saluted and was gone. The châtelaine had been summoned to the salon where a Captain was waiting for her. When Mama returned she was in a portentous state. Then, standing, distraught and in a quivering voice, she told Aunt Zabeth that she had been given the requisition order to vacate the Lush Oasis, including our concessionary rooms. So, after nearly two years of holding the fort, poor Mama finally lost her own "war battle". She had been given three days or else!

It was on removal day, whilst our belongings were being carted away, that my physiological clock chose to upgrade me from being a child to a possible child-bearing adult. I had found it necessary to rush to the lavatory. At the sight of blood I became alarmed and rushed to seek Cook's help. I knew nothing about the facts of life but she reassured me. I returned to Mama who, with no further ado and in full view of everybody, showed me what to do. It was a few weeks before my eleventh birthday and a very humiliating experience indeed.

Within the allocated time Aunt Zabeth, prayer book and rosary went back to her Perigueux home in the Dordogne, Cook left, Mama and I, plus dogs, together with the help of a newly employed "daily-cum-cook" called Marie Louise, took possession of "the Little House", situated just outside the Estate's walls, where we were to remain until beyond the end of the war. The Germans issued us with a Pass to the Lush Oasis and there were a few other people who, for different reasons, also qualified. From then on, whether on foot or cycling, I used the narrow gate on the side of Pépé and Mémé's cottage. It was lovely to have them so near.

Living outside the Lush Oasis extended the range of my discoveries considerably. I cycled kilometres of roads, country lanes and wooded areas. I met new people, visited others but, most of all, I learnt anything I could about the world of nature. It was no longer possible for Mama to keep tabs on me! In more ways than one the German occupation was to be my own liberation.

Summer was over, September days were noticeably shorter. Françoise and I were making the most of our remaining play days before she rejoined her parents in Paris.

One day, all of a sudden, my stepmother said that I was to go to school. Somewhat shyly I agreed. She had been giving it some thought, she continued; I was to go to the village school! I was tongue-tied! Not knowing whether to show joy, apprehension or astonishment, the latter muted me. After eleven years of exclusion, followed only eight weeks earlier by my "exiled" communion ceremony, I was to be mixing with the village girls! For a few days I was not sure whether to believe Mama or not. My doubts dissolved when she took me to see the teachers. Two grey-haired, unmarried sisters, Mesdemoiselles Froger. I was delighted with the school. It was an old grey building with two classrooms attached to the teachers' house. Inside the school the air was stale, a melange of ink, paper and carbolic acid, but I liked it. I liked, too, the wooden desks and seats all in one. I was particularly attracted by the two holes in the desks into which the white stoneware inkwells fitted so well. I was excited. I couldn't wait to start and sit facing the huge blackboard on the wall. Mama and I went to the village's draper to buy material for my school pinafores. School at last! I was extremely happy and shared my happiness with Mémé and Pépé. For a while the SS, the drills, the comings and goings of the troops and all my hobbies took second place. I began to daydream about lessons, exercise books and the playground, but my euphoria was lessened when I learnt that one year at that school would be all I could attend, for then I would be of "secondary education" age.

When my stepmother took me under her tutelage she, by some means or other, had expressed her wish to the villagers for them not to speak to me and I not to mix with them unless in her presence. As a child I thought that Mama's rule was for me only. Later, when I probed the charwoman about that puzzling regulation, she whispered, 'Oh! my dear child, it is not easy. If only I could speak!'

I knew that one of my sisters still lived in the village, she was called "La Petite Louisette". My stepmother forbad any contact between us. So strict a rule so frightened the villagers that it brought several cruel episodes, such as, for example, when I went to the village shop with her every so often and Louisette happened to be there; the sweet child, shuffling her few cents in her hand, bowed to my stepmother and stumbled over her 'Good afternoon, Madame Didot.' To which, from her height, the latter replied, 'And how are you getting on at school, dear child?' This made me feel ill at ease and miserable. Timidly Louisette would say to me, 'Alright, Pierrette?' The situation was heartbreaking. I wanted to answer her smile whilst, at the same time, I was trying to avoid her eyes. I was also thinking, "I" don't go to school.

My stepmother's attitude soon drove Louisette close to tears and made me even more overwrought. When I went to the shop on my own sometimes "La Petite Louisette" was there too. As Madame Didot was not around our emotions would get the better of us and we used to exchange a sentence or two. I was so pleased we had done so that I could not keep it to myself and thought that, when I returned home, Mama would understand and share my confidence. How wrong and naïve I was! Heartlessly I was condemned for my action and, by the same token, I was slapped across the shoulders. From that day on I kept my brief encounters with Louisette carefully to myself. Yet that was not enough. There was another time when I thought the secret of our little chat was safe and secure, but alas! the next day I was summoned to Mama's room. 'Pierrette,' she began solemnly. 'Yes?' 'I have been told by the charwoman that you were seen speaking to Louisette yesterday, is it true?'

'No…, well…, yes…, it was not.' And so yet again, in no uncertain terms, I received my reprimand. The last time I saw "La Petite Louisette" was on an Easter Day. Outside the church's side door a few faithful, waiting to shake Monsieur le Curé's hand, were chatting with my stepmother. Meanwhile Louisette, who had left the church by the "commoner's door", was walking towards me. The weather was splendid. I, proud and light hearted in my new Easter outfit, and, by the look on Louisette's face, she too in her brand new hat. Suddenly she was near me. Before I had time to blink she had embraced and kissed me affectionately. Mama saw us, in a flash flew towards us and, with all her anger, slapped Louisette across the face. It was outrageous!

For a moment Louisette was thrown off balance by the blow and her hat, her precious hat, flew off her head to land a few feet away on the grass. I was grabbed by the arm to join the company and later when I defended myself from my stepmother's reproaches, I felt that I was betraying Louisette. In reality I was not, for the episode had been entirely caused by Louisette's impulsion. Like me on other occasions, she should have known better, but she was only twelve years old and I was eleven. I shall take the memory of this ignoble incident to my grave.

I never saw her again. In the far, far distant future I was to hear that she had had a baby girl, Dominique, and then a short time after she, Louisette, had died in poverty.

THREE CHANGES OF DESTINY

Chapter Twenty-Two

AT "THE LITTLE HOUSE"

The Little House, "La Petite Maison", was now home and I loved it. The garden surrounded by chicken wire was made dog-proof. At the rear, a small path alongside the river with a tiny "lavoir".

Mama, who had been forcibly relegated to only two rooms in her own house, became extremely busy in one way or another. She took to her Miss Brodie bicycle. The front wheel had a hand brake, the back one she worked by using the pedals in reverse, she let me use it sometimes. Of course it was far too high, but such enjoyable hard work. I had to climb astride the frame, and pedalling as if pressing grapes, I pressed hence up and down and naturally if I pressed backward the bike and I hit the dust road, all good fun. Some Tuesdays Mama and I would go to L'Aigle market together. If alone I covered most of the way holding onto the back of transport lorries… It was quicker, tut tut!

There was no running water in the Little House, simply a pump attached to the wall by the sink. The kitchen was homely with a large wood-burning stove, floor to ceiling cupboards and two wooden tables, a round dining one with four chairs, and under the window a deal table with drawers. To the left there was a small dining room and on the right almost clandestine, a narrow door in the darkest corner of the room was hardly noticeable, it opened onto equally narrow and askew steps that ended on a landing. This had two doors. The one on the left opened onto the main room, its end divided into two adjacent bedrooms, one for Mama and one for Hubert or guests. I had a bed and bedside table in the main room, later I did my school work there.

Funnily enough we associated much more with the Germans since we had left the Lush Oasis. We had good times. There were short and long visits. Willy, Hans, Franz and Fritz are the best remembered as happy ones.

They were all young and good looking officers. Except for a few Wehrmacht, of the troops occupying the Lush Oasis throughout the war I believe were mostly SS. There were days when our favourite habitués joined Mama and I on the garden bench in shelling peas and tailing green beans for bottling. We also played games on the kitchen table, we particularly enjoyed a game called "Alma". I still have the board....

Mama did not participate with us, it was too obvious that she preferred spending time upstairs with her high-ranking officer. He was the highest in command and the longest to live at le Petit Château. I disliked him a lot. He came too often and stayed too long upstairs with Mama for my liking. But I could not fail to be impressed by his manly attractiveness and his immaculate uniform. His name was "Strönewald". There were instances when Mama was alone upstairs and, on hearing the gramophone playing, she came down and danced with us to the tunes of the old "78" German records; "Tango Marina", "Die Blau Danube" and others. All very jolly and would end by our saying schön! And sehr gut! Then danke schön! all round, we might also eat together. But in spite of laughter and frolics, was not the war still on?

All these encounters were short lived, for soon the men would leave for the front, fewer returning.

I remember two of them, they were only eighteen, one of them was not at all frightened of anything, the other was so afraid that any time he heard an aircraft he shook like a leaf. On the morning he left for the front he cried like a little boy. He could have been any mother's son. He never returned. He was shot on the first day of the battle. The other one returned wounded in his left arm but alive. War is a sad thing...

The first summer in the Little House passed quickly. The living quarters of the mill were occupied by a woman and her fourteen year old son. During the long holidays a cousin of his stayed there too and she, like me, was eleven years of age. Also Françoise played with us but, being five years our junior, did find it difficult to keep up! Whimpering and moodiness flared up! She and I were to share many future memories over seven decades to come.

Going to school for the first time in my life was marvellous. Nothing remotely resembling my governesses' teaching, especially that of Mademoiselle Colette.

On the top of the eight foot walls of the school were spikes of glass. Mesdemoiselles Froger, of a certain age, shared their life. Both always wore black or grey ankle-length dresses and sensible black stockings and shoes. The slim one taught "les enfants", the other, better endowed, took care of the big girls.

We sat, four in a row, on wooden benches attached to our lift-up desks, with a ceramic inkwell plugged into a hole in the flat top of the desk. I loved school. I walked there and back on my own twice a day, following a little path between pastures and meadows.

I soon made friends, one in particular whom I was allowed to visit in her home. Two families of the same name lived in the village. One at the top of the slope, the other at the bottom, and consequently known as "les Viviens d'en haut" and "les Viviens d'en bas". Those at the top lived in poverty, the others had adequate means. Socially they did not mix. It would not have done to "mix the tea cloths with the table napkins", as the French would say, and still do today!

My friendship with the two children from the bottom went on for a few years, the one with Monique from the top, and one of nine children, lasted but a few weeks. It was curtailed by Mama after Monique's first visit to the Little House. Poor Monique, she was still nervous after her gauche curtsey to Mama who, after all, was still the châtelaine, albeit living at the Little House. Monique arrived wearing a navy woollen cloak and a beret and put the latter upside down on my writing table then, with her head slightly down and shifting her feet from one to the other, she answered humbly the kind enough questions put to her by Mama. 'Yes, Madame Didot. Don't know, Madame Didot. Thank you Madame Didot.' Then Monique and I sat down next to each other, whispering, talking, simply being two happy schoolgirls. It did not seem long before Mama came to us and said that it was time for Monique to go home. We got up and I noticed that Mama's gaze was glued to Monique's beret. I then realised it was crawling with lice! Mama was obviously shocked and later proclaimed that Monique was never to visit again. Even so, I kept friendly with her but only at school.

Once at the Little House, cook, Marie-Louise, worked part-time, or full-time. A short, rather square-built woman with a flat, round face. Her forehead was narrow and her eyes and mouth small. For reasons only known to themselves, Marie-Louise and my stepmother became, one might say, confidantes. Their alliance was to shape my future. Meanwhile, Marie-Louise was merely part of the Little House's life.

She was easily frightened. When during the battle of L'Aigle, our nearest town, eleven kilometres away, was bombed, she was petrified. Bombs exploded, some quite near, and shells flew above the Little House. Thinking that she would be protected, she sat, head down, under the kitchen table where the cutlery was kept. For each bomb that dropped and for each shell that whistled past the house, she jerked up her head and shouted, 'Help, Mon Dieu!' or 'Hoooo!' In so doing she knocked her head against the cutlery drawers and the rattle of wood against metal unnerved her so much that she knocked her head even more! It was so funny to watch!

After a while I begged Mama to let me install myself in the barn (adjacent building). All that space! my bed facing the light of a small window, albeit somewhat reduced by a fourfold standing screen, behind which I had made a cosy space where I had books, paper, all manner of items of all descriptions to occupy my brain and hands. It was exciting and all the more when the wind howled around and against the naked tiles!

At the top of the barn large stoneware jars were used for preserving eggs and salted meat. Once, when up there, I heard a movement. Slowly and apprehensively I moved towards its direction that seemed to be hosting something live. My first thought was a bird or mice, so, bravely but timidly, I put my arm deep into it. My whole body froze in horror and my hand came out ten times quicker than it had gone in! There were maggots stuck to it. The jug contained nothing but maggots! I had used them many times before as fishing bites, but never did again! Even the thought, let alone the sight of maggots still makes me cringe with repulsion.

The barn had a small window overlooking fields and river. It also had a very old wooden door facing the Little House's garden at about 2 metres above ground level, once the way to the hay loft. To get out, climbing down the vegetation was far more diverting than using the stairs, I thought.

During our stay in the Little House, numerous were the nights when Mama woke me up in the middle of the night. "Just in case", she would say. You see, night after night (so it seemed) we would hear the planes, heavy with bombs, passing above us, a continuous low key rumbling. If I looked up at the sky I could see what appeared to be thousands of red specks dotting the darkness.

During the day the bombers were not so noisy as they were lighter by then having dropped their load.

They were a magnificent sight especially in groups of 15–30 in a V formation. I would, many a time, count up to 100 to 200 in one day. Vibrating, throbbing, glittering mechanical migrating Geese.

We remained at the Little House until 1945 or there about – we were still there when the enemy started to retreat and these weeks were indeed most precarious ones. The Germans, realising they had no chance of winning, felt vulnerable and edgy. Meanwhile the Resistance was most active, and putting many villagers' lives very much in jeopardy.

My stepmother's fluent German proved to be very useful in settling disputes and fierce arguments between villagers and Germans. She was called upon to help on numerous occasions when, by foot, by bicycle or in the back of a military car, she would go immediately. Usually she managed to appease the situation satisfactorily; unfortunately, as we shall see later, in the aftermath of the liberation, her own situation did not reach such a satisfactory conclusion.

The Resistance may well have done heroic deeds, no doubt helping French patriotism and honour, yet its indiscriminate actions also caused unnecessary atrocities and suffering. The following story illustrates clearly my comments.

On the evening preceding the final departure of the German troops, the village which stood in the shallow valley was surrounded by guns. The danger lay in the fact that at the top of the South slope lines were English and on the opposite North the Germans were poised to attack at dawn. During the night a 19-year-old young woman went to warn the enemy about the Allies being fully prepared for battle. There were, so the rumour echoed the next day, only a handful of occupiers, few tanks and little ammunitions. On hearing their predicament they retreated, hence the destruction of Chandai including its inhabitants was avoided. The brave informer was acknowledged and most congratulated her action, she should have been given a medal, she saved us etc etc…

Not so in the thinking and actions of some "resistance" braggarts, as we will see in chapter 24: The Liberation.

Chapter Twenty-Three

THE DUST ROAD
ITS WAR AND MINE

As a whole, except at the time of my father's death, the Dust Road had been rather dormant, now all of a sudden gained major importance. All through the war it gave the occupants access to the Lush Oasis and naturally, after the Liberation, it did so to the English. After the war its quietude was never restored as the flour mill was modernised into a pork factory and the wooden wheel stopped turning. In the course of 1943 the Dust Road was mined. It started from half its length to the building attached to the Little House. It made our home the end of the road, as it were. Most comforting I must say!

There were three occasions when the Dust Road and I shared the ugliness of war, one of them being the day Françoise (not yet seven) and I heard but did not see an aircraft in trouble, on looking up we saw both parachute and man in flames. In a split second he was a human torch and, before we knew it, crashed at our feet. On impact his skull cracked open expelling his brain, which splattered the side of a disused military vehicle nearby. Françoise did not see that, I put my hand over her eyes and immediately took her to Pépé and Mémé's house. On returning outside, and astounded, I looked at the body. His clothes were charred, his face and hands blackened and on his finger a dark red stone ring stood out like the last ember of a dying fire.

A few people hurried to the scene, someone covered him with foliage, others kicked him.

The Dust Road was also the site of worse happenings when I too was there. This occurred after the Liberation in 1944 when the Dust Road was to be de-mined. One hot and sunny morning a zealous and patriotic self-important man carrying a machine gun appeared near the Little House.

The man was marching a group of German p.o.w.'s and, having reached the road and pointing his gun at them, insultingly ordered them to detect the mines. 'Sales Boches! Allez, allez!' Less than an hour later the inevitable happened, the mines exploded. It was carnage and, I am not ashamed to say, the one in charge paid for his arrogance by losing a leg. From a hole in a surrounding hedge there was an ashen head dangling on its own. Two dead were on the ground, one survivor stood and the open wound of another one stretched from his chest to his abdomen, yet he still found the strength repeatedly to call, 'Mutter, mutter, mein mutter!' As usual I was the only witness.

It was about that time, on returning home one afternoon, I noticed the abandoned German tank, which for weeks had been parked half way up the slope facing the Little House, was ever so gently making its way downwards. Gathering speed it shot across the Dust Road and bulldozed over the Little House's garden, demolishing the front of our home. It was stopped by the large wood burning stove in the kitchen.

Shortly before the Liberation of Chandai, in the spring of 1944, I was walking on the Dust Road when a car bearing a swastika flag slowed down on its way to the Lush Oasis. The German officer sitting in front acknowledged me with a smile and I did the same. Many years later I learnt it was Field Marshal Rommel, the only military V.I.P. to travel next to his chauffeur.

Fig 23: A museum tableau of Hitler planning at L'Aigle in Normandy.

Unbeknown to me the "Battle of Normandy" was nearing.

Chapter Twenty-Four

THE LIBERATION
MY STEPMOTHER'S ARREST

The increasing anxiety shown by the "visiting" Germans at the Little House became more pronounced, soon there were to be no more calls, convoys had not been so obvious of late, and no more groups of soldiers carrying bayonets, singing, marched along the dust road past our home. Everywhere the occupants were keeping a low profile. They appeared to be in a state of expectation.

On the 6th of June 1944 there was great agitation all around. Mama and Marie-Louise had heard that the English had landed at Aromanche. The rumours were that the Germans would put up a fight. Mama was most alarmed. On that day, and for a few weeks to come, we were still here and there surrounded by small clusters of the enemy.

Several convoys of lorries and tanks drove through Chandai towards the front, I thought that they would meet the English on the way and that there would be some fighting but the Germans were defeated and surrounded.

On the 9th of June the English liberated us. In late morning I heard that the English would arrive by the "route de Crulai" at the top of the village. I went to position myself on the wall at the far end of the park and waited.

There I was, all on my own, perched astride as if riding a fixed stone horse. My stomach in my mouth, half excited, half afraid, from my observatory I watched the everlasting convoy of lorries full of armed soldiers, tanks with cannon at the ready, vehicles and men all camouflaged with leaves, branches, nets and army jackets etc. I was not surprised because I had seen many such convoys passing my gaze, the only difference being that they were khaki colour instead of the usual field grey.

After a while, I went back to the house, then went to the main road. There were people standing, screaming, cheering, dancing on the pavement whilst the Liberators were greeting us back, throwing cigarettes, chocolate, smiles and kisses.

I, myself, apart from picking up the goodies, was looking at all that as through the eyes of the "romantic teenager" that I was. Comparing the good-looking men in dissimilar style and colour uniform was 'interesting'. The route de Crulais's convoys were going north to south, the ones on the N.24 were driving toward Paris, west to east. I could not tell of their way ahead after passing Chandai…

Suddenly, becoming aware of the serious situation it could have been, I felt a retrospective fear, especially on hearing the following account.

It concerned the nineteen-year- old girl who had saved the village. On the evening of the 8th she had been informed of the Germen positions ready for attack at dawn. She also knew that at the opposite end of the village the English too were preparing their attack. A hollow between the two hills the village itself would be the battlefield. The brave young woman went to tell the Germans of the situation; fortunately for all of us inhabitants the enemy troops capitulated. The next morning they were gone!

What had happened to her? Well! She had been picked up by the Resistance people who by then had taken the law into their own hands; she was tied up, shaved and sent to prison! So much for saving Chandai and most of its inhabitants!

People were arrested, shaved and sent to war camps for having or not, as the case might be, collaborated with the occupiers. Some French men came out of their hides, some German prisoners were walking at gunpoint. In the distance, anti-aircraft guns could still be heard.

1944's summer weather was glorious. My usual friends including Françoise arrived here for their holidays. It was splendid. I had received no education since July 1943. We had complete freedom including the entire Lush Oasis. We roller-skated through the empty Grand Château, we swam in the river and much, much more. At last, to me, it seemed to be a normal young person's life.

Hubert returned suddenly, from where? one wonders? – he was rarely at home. He was a great walker and used to visit "Cook Marie-Louise" in the village (as quoted afore).

Close by the village church a country house had been, during the war, a safe haven for children's holidays. One of their female workers, Madelaine Gashtoft, struck up a friendship with my stepmother and, I assumed, with Hubert as well for I once saw her sitting on the dining room floor with both her arms around his legs! After the Liberation Madelaine was seen jumping onto a passing vehiclefull of English soldiers bound for Paris where her parents lived. She and Mama had, beforehand, broached the subject of my education and Madelaine was soon to supervise it, Mama informed me!

The last week of September, or thereabouts, on a beautiful morning there arrived, without warning, some Frenchmen unknown to me. Mama, I and Marie-Louise were in the Little House's front garden. The two men had come to arrest my stepmother and I. Mama protected me and asserted that I was under aged to be labelled as a collaboratrice but the men would not take no for an answer and Marie-Louise had to fetch my ration book whilst we all waited. The officials then forgot all about me and with only her suitcase and half the contents of her handbag Mama, Madame Firmin-Didot, was driven away. Two estate workers, the gamekeeper and one of the gardeners, had denounced her to the Resistance.

I took Mama's bedroom and remained at the Little House with Hubert. Marie-Louise cooked and cleaned.

At the beginning of October Hubert drove me to Paris where he left me at St Joseph du Parchamps convent. There I was to be a weekly boarder being looked after at weekends by Madelaine Gashtoft who lived in her parents' house.

No more Mama, no more Little House, no more Chandai or friends… The anticipated pride to be learning and wearing a uniform did not alleviate my abandonment. I wept non-stop even in my sleep, for the whole week, the longest I had ever done so in my first fifteen years. The weekends were no better, although I did not cry. Madelaine did not look after me, she was mentally unbalanced. Oh! To think that she had been responsible for looking after children!

Even though I was entirely free, yet she abused my gullibility by forcing me to obey her. The bribe was for me to kneel across a broom handle until I couldn't stand the pain anymore. She made me repeat the exercise several time, telling me that if it did not hurt enough, I would never see Mama again; at the same time she would also assure me that she, Mama, would be home by Easter.

Most weekends, either I roamed alone the streets of Paris or went to the cinema – up to three performances a day – I was drowning, searching to be rescued.

There were only two enjoyable happenings to relate from my living at the Gashtofts.

Madelaine's parents who wore the coarse yellow star were both musicians. On a Sunday afternoon I did not go to the cinema, instead Madelaine and I sat in their sitting room listening to her father playing the grand piano while her mother sang, it was indeed "ear" opening!

The only lighting was from the Menorah candles.

I was transported!

The other event worth a mention was to be present amongst the crowd of millions of frantic celebrants. The whole length of the Champs Elysées heaved with patriotism. Slowly the parade went past, Général de Gaulle (Charles!) standing halfway on the top of a tank, waving both his arms in the air, shouted " La France c'est moi!!" There was dancing and from all directions La Marseillaise sounded.

The first Christmas without Mama I returned home. As a result of my disturbing behaviour at the convent, the Mother Superior asked Hubert not to bring me back after the holiday.

The oncoming spring was to be joyless and lonesome. Them, at last, it was Easter. Madelaine had been right. After two months in prison followed by three in camp Mama was back! Her waist long hair had not been cut so now we were both free.

VIVE LA LIBERTY!!

Chapter Twenty-Five

BACK TO THE LUSH OASIS

MARIE-LOUISE

Her incarceration over, Mama took in hand the domestic tasks for a while, one assumes that cook Marie-Louise had taken a 'sabbatical.' Hubert continued his 'doing nothing' but on occasions mentioned going or having been to see Marie-Louise!

She lived in the middle of a row of cottages at the north end of the village, and was known as 'the village whore' (not openly you realise)! A substantially voluminous ginger-haired native of Brittany, her appearance was somewhat disorderly. She had a flat moonlike face with crafty blue eyes and her numerous wrinkles were badly concealed under layers of make up, whilst her thin straight lips were clumsily covered by abundant red lipstick. She had a husky voice and her cynical laugh frequently issued from between her smiling false teeth. How Mama ever did discover her I know not. She started her employment as a washer woman but I cannot really recall; however I do remember that all the time we stayed at the little house (including the time when Mama was in prison and then concentration camp) most days Marie-Louise looked after the little house, and I would almost swear though I cannot prove it, that it was she, Marie-Louise, who initiated Hubert to the pleasures of the flesh . . . It was a common occurrence to hear him say;

'I am off to see Marie-Louise now' or 'I went to see Marie-Louise today!'

I too went to see her sometimes. We might call on people, or perhaps go walking.

During one of these gallivanting expeditions after the liberation, we were walking home along the main road, and in those days there were plenty of convoys going either way through our village; Marie-Louise decided that she had enough of walking and that it would be much better to try for a lift …

So with out further ado she waved at an army lorry lifting her skirt! Well! I was so embarrassed, and not a bit brave, and I was thinking of Mama's reaction when she heard about the lift. Anyway, in climbed Marie-Louise and I followed; we sat among the soldiers and to be sure there were an awful lot of giggling and shuffling, I looked at my feet and prayed to God that I should be dropped at the village; There were about three kilometres between our embarkation point and the lane going to the house and I am glad that it did not take too long before we reached it, with immense relief I jumped out of the lorry and left Marie-Louise to her own devices … She went off with the soldiers …

Her cottage was sordid. I remember her bedroom most vividly, it was where she seemed to spend the best part of her time! There was a double size iron bed - never made … Next to the window adorned with torn and filthy net curtains, stood a marble washing table with a washing bowl and matching water jug.

From my numerous visits to the place, one particular instance jumps to mind: I had arrived late in the morning to find Marie-Louise lazing as usual amongst the pillows and eiderdown, she claimed to be suffering from rheumatism. No sooner had I entered the room she promptly threw off all the blankets and uncovered her breasts. She asked me if I could see any hair …? Embarrassed, I replied 'yes', so, rolling onto her side, she reached out for a pair of tweezers conveniently lying on the bedside table, and handing them to me she then requested that I should pluck her nipples! This I did with innocent care … Whilst she wriggled and giggled commenting that 'it tickled …' I was fourteen, such naivety seems, now, unbelievable; to end up the 'session' Marie-Louise got out of bed, went to the washing bowl, put it on the floor and standing astride she relieved herself splashing and spraying all around.

This was to her a matter-of-fact occurrence, and I was not unduly surprised to witness the event, it simply brought to my mind the vision of cows urinating in the fields! I left and bicycled away.

In my (den/attic) I wrote poetry and short stories, but now my already much used bicycle took precedence.

We went back to the Lush Oasis in 1945. Hubert returned to his own upstairs 'en-suite,' Mama and I together took the ground floor one immediately under it. By then le Petit Château had lost its cosiness and old fashioned charm. The delightful Louis XVI period sitting room together with the Empire dining room had been converted into one large salon. Once monthly the Empire dining room had been a "parcelling" room. On parcel days women of all ages came to le Petit Château carrying overflowing bags full of goodies and government rations, such as tobacco, cigarettes, soap and little treats.

Gossip, stories, tears and laughter were rife but friendly and enjoyable. Everyone handling with care brown paper and string. Addresses were written by the best hand-writers. All the parcels were piled up waiting to be collected on the morrow by a special war postal lorry.

The salon had replaced the billiard room and sadly the country house type kitchen had been abandoned for a dismal affair on the floor above it next to the new dining room. A new laundry and a charwoman were employed, Mama took charge of the cooking whilst Hubert and I continued our lives of leisure.

I remained faithful to my bicycle and my unwavering passion for all things of nature, in particular botany and ornithology took flight, calling me to the best places where the wild flowers grew and the birds nested.

I seriously collected eggs, mosses, graminées and tree leaves.

Reading and writing were also some of my interests, naturally Hubert disapproved of course!

'Reading again?' He would say. 'Why don't you make yourself useful instead?

'It's interesting.' I'd defended myself.

'What is it, anyway?' He'd scoff.

'The History of The Solar System' I boasted.

'Oh yes? You can't possibly understand that, your intelligence wouldn't stretch that far!'

'I do understand it!' I put in.

'Besides why don't you go to school?'

Impudent of him who had never attended one!!

There was another attraction to my country life, la grande ferme near by mentioned in chapter one. I often went there and took part in milking and butter making. To a young girl it was challenging and most interesting. I had learnt and was learning new things. In the winter, milking was done in the cowshed, otherwise it took place in the fields.

I sat in the back of the horse and cart with the pails, three legged thirty five centimetre high stools, a large funnel and of course the milk churns. Once a week I participated in butter making. Both of these I only did when I felt like it, you understand! I had other 'important' things to attend and Mémé and Pépé waiting for me.

Although I was not going to school, the heart of summer was still holiday time as I had other youngsters to play with.

In all there were three consecutive idyllic summers 1944-1946. Except for Françoise, all of us were in our early teens. We swam the river, roller skated the now skeletal Grand Château's ground floor and spent our time doing and talking all day about nothing in particular, as indeed the youngsters do today. We were four boys and two girls plus 'grasshopper'-high Françoise who, when we used the troops bunk beds to snog and kiss each others lips only, was left by herself. Never for long though, the 'one rose between two thorns syndrome'.

Fed up with Huberts chronic jeremiads about my being at home all the time, Mama gave way. I was to attend L'Aigle religious secondary school run by nuns, in 1946.

I was to use the village postal car which also took passengers. My stepmother's request for me to travel exclusively in the front, was obeyed. Her reason, explained to everyone including myself that, 'le pére Bureau,' my real mother's ex-husband and allegedly, my blood father sat at the back each morning. I was strictly forbidden to look or speak to anyone. This made me very unpopular all round, already I was being much maligned by villagers, so that additional restriction made it worse. Mama's insistence had been difficult to understand and for a short time my mind was in turmoil. How could the man travelling behind me be my father? Was not my Papa whom I had kissed, in his coffin? And why, if le Pére Bureau was my father did he not acknowledge me? I never made head or tail of the situation and no one spoke!

Even so, credit must be given to my stepmother who, each school day got up at six to light the wood burner stove and had my toasted bread and café au lait ready on the table. It was quite a distance to walk both the length of the lower drive and the whole of the dust road to be picked up passed the la grande ferme but I always enjoyed it. The drive took a good hour, the route going from village to village and through forests, all enchanting to me whatever the season.

Soon after beginning of term I dropped Latin and religious education. I thought that talking and amorous flirting with the nineteen years old driver was far more to my liking! I would leave school early to join him on his afternoon round.

One golden autumn afternoon, he insisted 'you love me, don't you, yes? Well prove it!' were his words. So on a bed of dead leaves, looking at the blue sky and listening to a robin's song I yielded to his wish. I was still aged fifteen but no longer chaste!

Following the only two more such occasions, he broadcast, without my knowing, that I was 'une fille de joie!' I left L'Aigle school at the end of that year.

At home there were still to be many hours of amusements between the three of us. Sometimes with Hubert's few contemporaries. We danced the Lambeth Walk and the Horsey-Horsey in our vestibule. He and I also played 'ping pong', now called table tennis, l'escargot, a snail shaped hopscotch and croquet of course. Card games, jigsaw puzzles, were also on the menu as were snowball fights. Mama and I indulged in diabolo, a skill that she excelled (fig 24).

On returning home Marie-Louise had called on Mama fairly frequently, they had had terrible arguments, really Mama would have liked to discard

Fig 24.

her, but for some reason only known to themselves which I shall never know, Mama did not dare upset Marie-Louise too much, in case the wretch should open her mouth and reveal wartime secrets. Very likely it would have been quite detrimental to Mama's reputation and safety.

So eventually Marie-Louise was re-employed but only in the kitchen. Owing to ill health there was a lapse of time without Marie-Louise. She did return for a very short time and then disappeared ...

Chapter Twenty-Six

UPSTAIRS OR DOWNSTAIRS?

We were "cookless"!

I returned downstairs, enjoying every culinary experiment, luckily it was all successful. I severed the carotids and plucked the poultry, removed an eye from the rabbits to bleed them, starved the snails, scaled the fish and suffocated the guinea fowls by twisting their necks.

Then to the table waiting and washing up.

But what I did not like each morning was that, when I took the breakfast trays, one of our most frequent guests would, without fail, verbally and physically exhibit sexual obscenities. The same man included his dog in forced behaviour edging towards bestiality. How I detested these frequent and warped exchanges.

Trays collected and washing up done, I would start organising luncheon and planning dinner – both these completely home-made meals. Pâtés, terrines, delicatessen were to join: cheese soufflés, escalopes and chocolate mousse. Saturday, the pot-au-feu whilst Fridays, naturally, was fish. I enjoyed doing it all as well as eating it.

Fig: 25: Myself when downstairs.

I was always praised for my efforts, especially by the visitors, and if the truth be told, some of them came all the way from Paris primarily to sample or retaste their favourite dish.

The tradesmen such as butcher, baker, our gardener delivered my orders, in other words I had full responsibility for "downstairs", including menus. So, having finished the duties until the early evening's ones.... I was free, it was wonderful... FREEDOM! I galloped rather than walked down the tradesman stairs, jumped on my newly acquired bicycle, and was away. It was called "Mirkye" after an admirer of mine himself named Mircky The target of my haste was "Ping-Pong" (table tennis nowadays). I thrived on it as well as my opponent-friend Gérard. We played it for hours at a time, sometimes up to five hours. Chaise-Dieu-du-Teil, a small village a few kilometres from Chandai, had an outdoor swimming pool (where Gérard and I had met). It also had a sort of embellished wooden building where many events took place. In England one would say "the village hall" – one end a stage, at the opposite end, close to the roof, there was a small platform accessible by narrow, wobbly wooden stairs: the "room at the top", one might say! It was used to store things but more especially as a projection cabin from where, once a week, films were shown.

In the fifties this was a wonderful novelty. A long white screen was unrolled from the ceiling above the theatre stage ready to receive the projected black and white images. It was a well attended affair, somewhat noisy, chairs were knocked against each other, people shuffling, installing themselves they moved next to a newcomer disturbing the entire row. Some hailed each other, changed places, shouting, laughing, smoking.

All of a sudden a cockerel, shaking himself and cock-a-doodle-do-ing, appeared on the screen – a messenger heralding the actualités (news). In an instant silence reigned, only to give way to the crrrr-crrrr of the projector and of course the news reader. Then, all lights came on again, together with more commotion, the hubbub resumed, the interval had begun.

Gérard and I were "friends only" for several years. Mama knew about him. He was gentle, kind-hearted, and via a nearby châtelaine (one of Mama's many acquaintances). He was an avid reader of good literature – but oh! Dear me, his grandfather, during the eighteenth century, had been Mama's great-uncles's coachman. Well, would you believe it! Tut-tut. Furthermore he, Gérard, was a gamekeeper, worst of all you know he was a factory worker... What did I think I was doing? Was not uttered but thought by Mama's indirect comments. Hubert in his usual way scoffed and smiled wryly. Thirty years on while on holiday in France, Gérard and I met in Paris, but while I had moved on he was still static. However a short and pleasant walk down memory lane.

" It is going to be most difficult to find you a husband."

No comment from me.

"You are going to be difficult to marry."

Silence.

"I cannot see what can be done."

This was Mama's harking on and on.

I was now sixteen going on seventeen, I would soon be of marrying age and whom? PRAY? would want me!

I had but a few admirers in my life. Amongst them, seventy years on, one still figures in my memory's notebook.

It was in the middle of an "upstairs" period. I was enjoying the midsummer weather, the birds were still nesting and hence singing, but the lilacs and violets were over.

The l'Aigle pharmacist's wife, a friend of Mama's, called to present Henri, her nephew. He and I took to each other straight away. His surname – are you ready? De Chanack de Lonzac de mon Logis! (talk about name-dropping!). Anyway, to all of us including me he was Henri.

We found that we had a lot in common, particularly a love and respect for all things of nature. He was, as I was, on holiday, being at the time a boarder at a finishing school run by nuns.

To return to Henri, he asked to see me again and I looked forward to reading his letters, before our next encounter.

It so happened that later that year I went to L'Aigle's market where, it also happened, I met Gérard. We chatted briefly: How was I? What was

I doing these days? And, of course, what about the table tennis? That was it…. But somehow, someone had seen me speaking to Gérard and had promptly reported the fact, either to Mama or to Henri's aunt… Disgrace of disgrace, you know! And so I never again saw nor heard anything from Henri, from my "veterinary surgeon to be".

His family had a vineyard (in the Dordogne I believe) where the well-known Tavel rosé is still being made.

At home, the alternate stages of upstairs, downstairs were less frequent. I spent longer times upstairs and less at the domestic work. Nevertheless when attached to the kitchen the laundry had several changes of washerwoman. Thinking of a particular one and our shared time together always warms my heart. To all, she was known as La Mére Cherruel.

The warren's entrances were two-fold. There was a medium-height wrought iron double gate (already mentioned in chapter ????) and a narrow high wooden door attached to a wall. The latter was part of the one-up-one-down cottage occupied by the clog-maker, where I have spent many hours, many times, many years ago.

My timid knock at the door, a muffled "Come in", a gauche turning of the door handle and I would be facing the man seemingly emerging from an ocean of wood shavings. He was sitting on a low stool in the centre of the place, the smell of wood together with that of the gently burning open fire was even better than Mama's Guerlain perfume!

Between the warren and the gamekeeper's cottage, together with the disused brickworks, there was a pasture, the south side running along the river, whilst its north skirted an A-road called la route de Crulai, the very road where I had first set eyes of the "liberator" English troops four years since. I used to go that way quite often, looking for mushrooms, looking for birds' nests, fossils or wood butterflies. There were many narrow lanes criss-crossing the warren, but there was a larger and straighter one at the bottom of the slopey entrance. An eight-foot-high chicken wire fence kept rabbits and uninvited humans at bay.

Leaving behind the warren, I would wind my way across the field amongst segmented hedgerows and apple trees of all shapes and sizes, and there on the right, a few steps from the lane, was another one-up-one-own isolated cottage… Mother Cherruel's dwelling, the threshold of which I never did cross! But it was there that its only and lonely inhabitant took her last breath.

On a very cold morning, one of the rare passers-by noticed her door open. On further inspection, he found her still, wearing her nightdress. She was no more…

Mother Cherruel was a true and true Normande. She always wore the traditional long black skirt and black apron. She trotted in black clogs or clog-like footwear, thick black stockings, not forgetting her black shawl and bag.

At irregular intervals one had seen a black articulated shapeless heap plodding along the Lush Oasis lower drive… a stick and cloth bag in hand. Mother Cherruel was going a-shopping. When we were short of a washerwoman, it was she, with her sanguine face and padded lips, who came to assume this weekly task.

It was during these apparitions that, during her meal breaks at the kitchen table, she sang for me… She taught me many old songs… melancholy melodies of her younger days, now well over a hundred years old.

I sat spellbound facing her (sometimes) moistening eyes; her pensive look seemed to be searching ahead the abyss of her faraway memories. She remembered the Crimean War and of course the three after that!

I still have the exercise books intact (perish the thought of homework!): words, date, place where we shared precious moments, some jolly, some sad. Dear Mère Cherruel, over sixty years have passed but I shall never forget you.

To justify the title of this chapter, I hope to seal any doubt about my dichotamous Lush Oasis life.

One particular evening in early 1949, guests had been invited to dine at le Petit Château. Amongst them was one of my late father's nephews, Pierre Firmin-Didot, a good-looking man in his twenties. When, being smartly dressed, I arrived in the salon, the only available seat was beside him, occupying a small two-seater. Shrinking with embarrassment I stared straight ahead. His embarrassment was as obvious as mine. Trying to sound casual he said:

"Do you live nearby?"

"No, I live here. I am Pierrette" I almost whispered.

"Aaah?" he breathed.

I was about to endeavour to explain when the door opened.

"Dinner is served" was announced. This brought silence to all, but mostly relief to me! I dare say to Pierre as well!

Fig 26: Myself when upstairs.

At the oval table, conventionally he sat to Mama's right. I sat at Hubert's left, hence we were facing each other. There were a few glances and smiles between Pierre and I, but no communication… Not a word from anyone came my way. I did not follow people to take digestifs and coffee in the salon, instead, feeling somewhat nonplussed, I made my way via the staff stairs to my room. Shame about Pierre, I should have been used to being a non-entity.

And what of Pierre? He was never seen nor heard again at le Petit Château.

There was also Bernard de Pont Alba, my father's only first nephew, who rarely called on us. He was distant and a trifle too haughty for my liking. To my mid-teen eyes, he was tall-dark-and-handsome. Mama and I were conversing one day and, simply in passing, I happened to mention Bernard's handsomeness and with a dreamy look the word marriage came out! Oh! dear! what a mistake! Mama went berserk!

"If you think that a man of such breeding would as much as waste a glance on someone like you, you are indeed too silly" she bellowed.

"Why? I thought that…" I was interrupted.

"Bernard is a man of the world, why should he even speak to you? It is inconceivable! Have you taken leave of your senses?" … etc, etc…

So that was that. Bernard and I were never to set eyes on each other again!

Being useful, servile and smiling was what I was expected to be at all times, especially towards the frequent visitors who were almost exclusively male and all Mama's relatives. This attitude of the household, combined with a strong Roman Catholic influence, distorted and damaged my consciousness, almost obliterating my self-esteem.

Having been told for as far back as I could remember that I came from the muck, the offspring of a whore and that in spite of my stepmother's efforts (her words) I was just like my real mother, guilt set in. Conflicts in my mind caused fearful battles. Life was a constant conflict which I was subconsciously trying to disentangle.

From the age of six, I had to learn by heart endless pages of the catechism, which preaches tolerance and kindness. Yet I was told to "Be quiet!" and smacked without warning. In my early teens I began to rebel verbally as well as actively. But religion had a fierce hold on me, until I realised the damage it had done to me. It took me a long time and caused me a lot of suffering to free myself of the Roman Catholic claws.

One would be forgiven to understand the mental and psychological conflict "upstairs or downstairs" brought. Deep confusion if ever there was one! From belonging nowherem, now I had to be part of both upstairs and downstairs! Already as a little girl (one may recall) I had to adapt to the frequent changes of governesses. In this new phase I had to adjust being in turn cook/washerwoman yet legitimately the daughter of the house, or simply cook according to staff's comings or goings.

If downstairs on summer days, I got up quietly at 5am and went to the wash-house. The washing was done using a plank resting at an angle across a large wooden vat. I scrubbed away, then in a wheelbarrow transferred the "whites" to the previously heated copper boiler. A fierce wood and coal fire (my first job) supplied the heat as long as one kept it well aflame.

Next came the full-up vat of the "colours". They were the first to be rinsed from the "lavoir" at the bottom of the steps along the river.

By 7:30am household and personal laundry were swaying in the morning breeze.. most satisfying!

It was now time to prepare and serve breakfast. This had become more up than down of late. It was late 1948 and Marie-Louise had re-emerged! First visiting Mama as mentioned before but her apparitions led to her having a longer stay.

My enjoying freedom was sheer bliss.

I was at home only a little and when I was Sabine understood me.

Chapter Twenty-Seven

SABINE'S MARTYRDOM

In 1947, Mama and I had one of our arguments and, in the heat of the moment, I voiced the words "Finishing School". My stepmother consulted the telephone directory, found a convent number, rang and six weeks later she deposited "both my trunk and I" at St Paul de Chartres. The next day I ran away and called at the hotel where I knew she had spent the night with a certain Monsieur Badaire! "You asked for a Finishing School", were her parting words after she had escorted me back! It was an extremely good school where I learnt a lot and made a forty-year lasting friendship. The time at Chartres was to be remembered as wonderful, and tearless.

On one of my six-weekly holiday weekends I had as usual carried two large suitcases. Hubert had fetched me at L'Aigle station. I was wearing my navy pin-striped suit and felt very grown up. On arriving home, I saw two new faces in the salon. I kissed Mama and shook hands with (I was informed) Simone and Sabine. The latter smiled kindly, the former uttered bonjour. I promptly vanished to my room.

There were to be several such visits by Sabine, even one where her mother came to stay bringing her personal maid Margot with her.

Halfway through the long summer holiday of that year, one of my schoolfriends also came to le Petit Château. Mama and Monsieur le Curé, plus some of the neighborhood people organised a "Kermesse" (fête); it was to take place all along the Grand Château ground floor.

It was a resounding success, including the evening ball.

There were two young students lodging at the vicarage – the two had the same first name, Michel Aimé and Michel Magne – the first escorted my friend, the second was my companion. We kept in touch for many years; the first was a violinist, the second became known later on – even wrote the music for "Bonjour Tristesse" "Le Journal d'Anne Frank" played by François Sagan. His self-destruction was a big loss to the musical world.

In the course of Noël 1946 and New Year holidays at home the news was official! Hubert and Sabine were engaged to be married.

Evidently the visit of Sabine's mother and Margot had been to sum up the suitability of her daughter's future. If only the poor "lady" had known she could have prevented dearest Sabine from being subjected to an unremitting life of hell!

She, Sabine, was a gentle, genuine and religious (non-bigoted) woman of the world.

In the corridors of gossip I had heard that "Monsieur Hubert's intended had fallen head-over-heels for him". I liked her enormously. She talked to me with understanding kindness and appreciation.

A good while before the wedding and being into one of "my upstairs" stretches Mama and I were sitting in her bedroom, she by her desk knitting of course! I, by the woodburning stove mending nylon stockings. Dinner was over, darkness had come early, it was warm and comfortable, the dog stretched on the floor and soft classical music enveloped the tableau.

"It will be a long journey", Mama suddenly muttered to herself.

"Where to?" I asked.

"To Cheverny, Sologne is far from here" (talking wedding).

"Will I be going with you, in your car?" I asked in a matter-of-fact way.

"I am not sure, you must ask the permission to Hubert…"

I was dumbfounded!

"It is his wedding, it is for him to say" Mama's assertive voice riposted.

Silence from me… I was thinking.

Whereby, unexpectedly, Hubert, no less, entered the room.

"Ah" said Mama, unsure. "Hubert, Pierrette has to pose you a question". Mama stood up next to him. I left my work and, facing them both, my head down rather than up, fearful of the answer, I enquired my attending his holy matrimony, then I held my head high and waited. Hubert looked down at me, wearing his usual obsequious rictus, finally nodded saying "I s'pose so."

Once the decision had been made, Mama had my outfit ordered, and later on the lookout for a matching colour large-brimmed hat proved to be an ordeal! I was one of a few wearing a short dress (fig 27).

There followed a grand reception, a copious buffet and an abundance of wine.

Predictably, not having been introduced to anyone, I stood alone by the main door. Some of Sabine's friends said, in passing, "…beautiful day… what a delicious wine… delicious dish…" and they were away! Sabine told me to go and get myself a cup of coffee… What a BIG deal! I would have been better staying at home with my hobbies!

The first weekend off from my second year of the finishing school in November 1948, Hubert stormed into my bedroom.

"Wake up. Wake up!" He choked out of breath.

"Yes, yes, what?" I grunted.

Fig 27: Sabine and Hubert's wedding.

"Quickly! Sabine had a baby boy."

Before I had reached Sabine's quarters at the end of the corridor I had declared that I would not return to school… I did not. The date was 28/11/1948.

Apparently the whole affair had been expedited, the midwife had already left. Mama facing the "fait accompli" seemed slightly ambivalent. Hubert did not know whether or not to sit down or to stand up. I was admiring Sabine's incredulous expression holding the wee thing. Both amidst ruffles and lace (fig 28). The newborn's name was Gonzague soon to be baptised so.

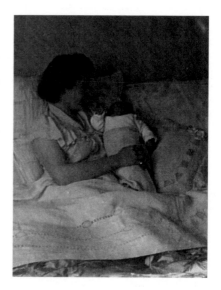

Fig 28.

Alas too soon after the sunshine came the rain. Less than a year on Sabine heard of her mother's fatal illness. Love and duty called, she had to go. Hubert approved about leaving Mama in charge of the infant.

So, for a good number of months Sabine had to travel until her mother's death. Poor Sabine, not only had she lost her mother, she also had lost her son! Not in the flesh naturally! But her own maternal right. Hubert and Mama categorically insisted that the boy stay and be looked after by Mama. He saw his mother, they played and talked together but Mama WAS in charge! It went as far as brainwashing, telling the child, as I witnessed, "Do not go with your maman, I'll give you some strawberries" and "If you want something do not call your mother but always your Papa" – enough said on this so, so sad a story.

For my part, I had left behind my childhood foibles, for example, sniffing the seats after people just left them, neither did I find amusing, when Mama's brother returned from his walk holding his underpants dangling on the top of a long upright stick! There were also indoor amusements (?). It used to be a recognised practice at some French courts, and I am told at the English one, to "Brûler les pets" – ignite one's flatulence!

At home, conversations, anecdotes, gossip, even newspaper articles, anything possible was expressed in double entendre, always attached to sex or sexual connotations. There was once in the local paper news that a Madame Courtois Suffi had given birth to a dog litter – five of them – all having hands!

Perhaps I should try to justify my dislike of dogs. It is hard to define whether or not this is an innate feeling (sentiment) or whether it has been brought about by my childhood experiences.

We always had dogs at home and I was constantly reprimanded because of them. Amongst the various breeds we owned over the years, one of them, named "Doc" because he had been bought from the family doctor, was a big black animal, the size of an Alsatian. I used to play with him ever since I took my first steps; in fact we were exactly the same age. He had been the guardian of my pram and in a way I was quite fond of him. He died when we were thirteen and I thought that perhaps I would die too. But when I was little he used to frighten me for he used to practise his mating behaviour on me, he would catch hold of my waist and would not let go; I used to call for help and my stepmother untangled us, always shouting at me and telling me: "There is no need to shout like that". And often she smacked me, only occasionally did she smack the dog.

I recall one instance when I was on all fours playing on the dining-room floor. I must have been around five, the dog jumped on me and I could not get free. My stepmother than laughingly called the maid to witness the event: "Rolande… Come and see, it is so funny!" Oh the pain and humiliation.

When Sabine had arrived on the scene, I had found in her a comforter. She and I did not think that genre of divertissement remotely funny, this constant uncouthness brought us closer to each other.

Sweet "gentile" Sabine, she had to endure so much, Hubert and Mama were tyrannical, even when we played bridge. On one of these seldom occasions, Sabine was looking lovely, wearing her brown suit. We were talking, the four of us, and Hubert called her quote "a stick of shit"! Sabine and I both felt the injurious remark the game(s) went on.

Sabine had always disagreed with my working downstairs, she used to say that I was not the "servant".

She gave birth to her second son, he was born nearly, oh so very nearly in the lavatory pan, when the midwife arrived, mother and baby were breathing happily! Mama was somewhat grumpy. One may recall that Hubert's quarters were immediately above Mama's, she used to monitor the happenings at night.

"You demand too much of Hubert" she would say. "Again last night, Hubert is too tired" she commented… "You must not call on Hubert so often!" and so on, and so forth!!

This time Sabine managed to keep her baby, Antoine, born in early 1950. In 1952 her third and last child was given my papa's first name of François, though they were not related. I had left the Lush Oasis by this time.

When still at home, there was to be a longish stint downstairs. The butler/wife and baby mentioned earlier had moved on and no replacement had knocked at the Petit Château's door. I took hold of my apron once more and enjoyed more experimenting cookery and all.

After her mother's death Sabine had brought Margot to Le Petit château. Small Margot who had worked for Sabine's mother all her life was now Sabine's personal maid. Like Mother Cheruelle, she dressed all in black and wore a black ribbon choker. Minute were her short pointed fingers, minute was her thin pointed nose wearing thin metal spectacles, in short two "Little and Large" singers as Margot too sang for me across the kitchen table. She had a pair of collared doves, in a cage, but they had some free time and pecked food out of her mouth.

Sabine and I had developed an affectionate and understanding acquaintanceship; secretly we shared our heart and mental ill treatment from Mama and especially from Hubert.

When, years later, I called at the Lush Oasis to see Mama I was a qualified psychiatric nurse and an RN officer's wife plus, my little Erica aged under 10, Hubert had to put up with our visit. Mama as usual taking her handkerchief from her skirt waist, wept on my face, Sabine kissed me warmly – and this is Erica? Abominable as it was, ten years on, when Mama was dying and I called to see her Hubert marched to my friend's vehicle telling us to depart immediately or else he would phone the police! Sad, despondent and furious we drove away and I never saw Mama again. But during Hubert's threatening of calling the police Sabine was looking down helplessly from her bedroom balcony. I knew she wanted to speak, her wisdom and wifely duty told her not to try… All she could do was to shrug her shoulders.

For years to come we sparingly wrote and phoned each other. When, in a faraway future, I was able to fetch many of my own belongings, left in store at the Lush Oasis, Hubert not only refused my wish to see dying Mama, he categorically forbade my entering the estate… Sabine collected all the things she thought would be mine and had to deliver them from her car to me (fig 29). Unfortunately some were left behind never to be rescued. It was so difficult not to cry but in spite of Hubert's nastiness, Erica, Sabine and I went to a nearby restaurant for lunch (fig 30). We

Fig 29: Sharing emotions.   Fig: 30: Clandestine meal with Sabine.

reminisced and amongst the stories that made us laugh was the following.

There were thousands of field crickets' holes in the grass everywhere. From the first spring days when the air had lost its morning nip one would hear, from sunrise till late in the night, the insects' din all around.

I would crawl in the grass and cued by the calls of my little friends I would discover their homes well concealed under the mass of thin blades. As soon as the crickets saw my shadow they would perform a head to toe jump and dive full speed into their burrows. For their own sake, not for long, because I would pull out a single blade of grass and introduce it into the hole, rotating it for a while, hence tickling the animal, which did not like its privacy being intruded upon and who, quite angrily, would reverse back to the surface. It was then that I would capture the innocent creature and put it in a jar with some grass and sometimes with ,many others of its species. These little things were very attractive, they had extremely delicate wings with the most beautiful patterns on them. Very often I carried my prisoners with me and rested the jar on the dining room window sill, on the terrace bench, or on my bed as the case might be.

The adults were not too keen and always made awful faces when they saw me and my treasures, for there had been some unfortunate incidents when the captives escaped in the house, much to the dismay of the inhabitants. Another time a far worse thing happened, I left the precious jar on the table outside and very sadly forgot about it; when I returned the sun had been shining all day on the unlucky beasts and, I am ashamed to say, they were all flat on their backs with their legs ion the air... Dead!

Eventually, life went on... Our letters dwindled and we lost touch. In the eighties in the course of my holidaying in Normandy, I heard about Sabine being in hospital. When I visited her, it was evident that she was too ill for lengthy talk. She was not allowed visitors' physical contact for fear of catching any infection. The sad end of the gold-hearted Sabine, I was not told, it certainly was not long after my visit.

I have permitted my pen to go ahead. This was necessary in order to give 'saintly" Sabine a mention she well deserves.

Chapter Twenty-Eight

SHORT FAIRYTALE, BLOODY NIGHTMARE

During my late teens, the already mentioned Marie-Louise resurfaced at our home, sometimes as cook, other times as Mama's visitor. The frequent visits always intrigued Sabine. She failed to understand what such a woman should have in common with the châtelaine. But in spite of all her efforts she never did work it out.

It was in 1949 when Marie-Louise was working as cook for a short spell that one day, I happened to walk across the kitchen when out of the blue she said:

'I know of a "gentleman" who would like to meet you."

'Oh?'

"I told him about you", she pursued. 'He wants to meet you, he has a car and he is very handsome.'

I could hardly believe my ears! Some man with a car interested in me? I, who had been going out with a factory worker? Tut-tut! I thought.

'Really?" I enquired further. 'How can I see him?'

"Well,' said Marie-Louise, 'I can arrange a secret meeting.'

'Yes, yes!' I choked, beaming – already in love!

At the time I was reading a lot, mostly romantic works – Musset, Montpassant, Thomas Hardy and many others. In addition, much to the disdain of Hubert, Mama and I were "hooked" by a "weekly" in the vein of "Woman's Own", avidly following a love story called "The Green-Eyed Soledad"!

The possibility of a secret rendez-vous threw me off balance. I could not wait. Where would it be, when would it be? Mama must not know. I lost my appetite – and my sleep.

Strongly influenced by my romantic/sentimental reading, my

erroneous imagination took over my thoughts and drowned "a la" Barbara Cartland style.

The meeting went according to plan. Three days later, I felt thus…

Two-thirty p.m., a magnificent June day, I met HIM. The man of my dreams. The man of my life. My hero!

With trembling knees, I went down the servants' stairs, whereupon emerging at the back of the house I saw, facing away, a maroon 4CV Renault, parked a few metres from the house.

Plucking up courage, I stepped forth.

Seeing me coming the man got out of his car and came towards me. As we shook hands my blue eyes must have turned into sapphires! Dazzled by two rows of snow-white teeth hatted by the most voluminous black curled-up moustaches and no less voluminous eyebrows.

Now, looking back, I realise that Charles was merely a dark-haired man with blue eyes! Nevertheless the fact remained that I followed him to the car whence he literally swept me off my feet!

To an isolated clearing he took me, and there under the semi-shade he said:

'I could do so many beautiful things because of you.'

Charles was an artist; I blushed, wondering how an ARTIST could find any value in someone like me! From then on, most evenings after dinner I walked the east drive to meet him at the main top gate and away we drove towards the sunset. Sabine kindly teased me, Hubert couldn't care less, Mama was slightly ambivalent. A few weeks on we left for our yearly holiday to Les Dervallières to join the usual family gathering.

Charles had said that he would write and he did. That was it! I had fallen in love.

The three weeks holiday were spent mostly lounging about re-reading Charles' letters. They were literate, poetic, flattering. They massaged my ego and imagination beyond the realms of reason! On returning to the Lush Oasis Charles and I continued our summer evening escapades and it was not very long before I succumbed to his persuasive amorous demands.

Came autumn, Charles dined at our table each evening. Mama as she used to continue, now and again, to pat Charles' face.

'I trust you, mon petit Charles,' she would say. 'Look after her and take care of her, she is in your hands.' Charles certainly answered Mama's words and amply made use of his hands!

When we had returned from Les Dervallières, cook Marie-Louise left and I took over her job. Away from and in front of the household Charles and I became more intimate. Alas, I was only a short way up to my apotheosis when I struck hell.

It began with morning sickness, guilt and fear. If it came to Mama and Hubert's ears I dreaded to be scorned, despised and, very possibly, evicted from my home. At all costs it had to remain untold. Therefore, when threatened by Charles to abandon me, I complied with all his wishes, amongst which were to kneel in front of him, to kiss his shoe and, in spite of the pain it caused me, to comply with his violent sexual demands.

There was one short meeting between our respective families and the wedding date was agreed and a very "triste" and dismal affair it was to be. No one knew that I was already pregnant. Neither my stepmother nor Sabine attended because Charles was a "divorcé" which prohibited a church wedding. There were six people in all, Charles' parents and a witness and, on my side, Hubert, tall, stern and distant in his navy-blue winter coat, came as my witness.

My husband and I were to set up home in a two-bedroom flat already prepared with our furniture. It was there that the wedding sextet went to eat a couple of sandwiches, share a small chocolate cake and drink a cup of coffee before leaving.

It was a cold mid-January night. Charles declined to cuddle to keep me warm. 'I have to drive a long way tomorrow, let me sleep,' he said.

The next morning we went on our honeymoon, a long, cold journey. Half way between Verneuill and Annecy we hit the snow across the Haute Savoie, endless kilometres of no drink, no food, no heating. It did not help my abdominal pain, for which I was ordered to be silent. Having driven the whole next day up and down the Hautes Alpes it was late and no sooner were we escorted to the hotel room than it was time for dinner. My discomfort was worsening but I had to smile. I was picking up my handbag when Charles became angry. What had I done with his wallet? By then, exhausted and ill, thinking proved impossible. My husband flew into a rage, gesturing menacingly. All for nothing, no wallet was found. So regaining his amiable composure, not to me but to the world, Charles and I went to dine. Nevertheless, the rage was only temporarily controlled, to explode with a vengeance on returning upstairs. I was showered with verbal abuse and ordered to get out of bed. 'You are a bitch, the bedside rug is all you need.' I did not shed any tears, I think that I was too ill, there were signs of my losing the baby. I was confused and resigned. With reluctance I obeyed. Charles' command to go back to bed, 'You are too silly, what do you think you were doing on the floor?' I feared having to abide with my conjugal duty but, instead, my husband turned his back on me and went to sleep. What a relief! As for the wallet? I found it at the foot of the bed between the bedstead and the mattress.

At the end of the next day, after yet another long journey I had no choice but to satiate Charles' sexual appetite. In the morning he was infuriated by the result, a considerably bloodstained bed! Regardless, we went on a coach trip that day where I sat immediately above the wheels. That did not help my discomfort. I was naïve and ill, unaware in those days to the point of stupidity.

When I felt better I enjoyed the romantic qualities of Milano, my mother-in-law's native city; the dinner with the violinist playing, just for us, at La Scala restaurant.

Back home an emergency hospital admission was necessary. Moodily my husband took me there and, after an operation, I was told that my baby boy had been dead for quite a while.

We lived two turnings away from my parents-in-law, his mother lived with them. Every Sunday, including Easter and Christmas, the meals were lovely, very traditional and which we all shared. We also went for meals to the Lush Oasis. Hubert was reasonable, Mama affectionate, Sabine her usual friendly self. I was a housewife with plenty of spare time, the most wonderful of which being to study natural history, in particular "birds". This sanity-saving occupation could only be intermittent because I did expect four more babies and lost them all. The most traumatic was the last. When severe pain woke me up one night I sought my husband's attention. 'Let me sleep,' was his reaction. At bedtime that evening I had endured "rape" in marriage. His response to my plaintive requests, prompted by excruciating suffering, was, 'You are my slave, shut it!' When the alarm clock woke him up I was still miscarrying. Having taken I know not which or how many tablets during the night had made me numb and stuporous.

Without a word or acknowledgement my husband got dressed ready for work. Before he locked the flat door behind him he said, 'I will 'phone the doctor from my parents.' I was rushed to hospital. When I was home again Sabine came to see me and she gave me a set of cake knives and forks. Dear Sabine, such a kindly woman. I still have a few left.

Although I had spent three years with a well educated man, the opposite to my first twenty years, I learnt very little. Charles was a qualified architect and engineer, erudite in the arts and a known artist, particularly in oils. He had his ankles badly scarred from the treatment he suffered whilst in Dachau concentration camp. I never did know about his wartime life except that, because of his intellectual capabilities, he was released.

My husband was eleven years my senior, our lives had been poles apart and so were our outlooks and expectations – our marriage was bound to be disastrous in various shapes and forms. He had lived, I had not!.

I had left him and Normandy for good.

Chapter Twenty-Nine

FAREWELL NORMANDIE

Not long before my leaving the marital home, a new visitor joined our habitués. Mama's elder brother (the one who had once sexually abused me) brought his mistress to the Lush Oasis. She was a pleasant, womanly and very handsome woman. A modest bonhomie exuded from all her being. The couple were deeply enamoured with each other. Both fitted perfectly the indirect, yet constant references to sex. Conversations, interjections, news or speculations always ended in a sexually related conclusion. They purchased a cottage nearby where later Charles and I visited them.

Conveniently, it was when my marriage was at breaking point that Uncle Paul, who had chain-smoked, had been given a few months to live. His concubine was beside herself. She asked me to help in the matter.

Fig 31: The very windows.

Already I had looked after Charles's grandmother , now I was willing to stay at their cottage for a while. Charles agreed. Clara and I shared a room. She guessed my unhappiness and became my confidant. She was horrified by my confessions, 'No-oo, no-ooo'ing and saying, 'This is outrageous! You must leave.' So now that I had found a refuge, I did.

From the window of the third landing (fig 31) I broke the nearest one of my flat, and at roof level I passed from one window to the other, collected a few belongings and never returned.

Clara and I stayed at the cottage after the funeral, and the divorce affairs were organised. Clara and my stepmother remained close friends. It was decided, with my consent, that I went to Paris under the guidance of Clara with whom I would stay to keep her company.

Fig 32: Gossiping friends.

I did not mind keeping Clara company but I was not that keen on sharing not the same bedroom, let alone the same bed! It was she then who confided in me about Uncle Paul and her amorous effusions.

Within weeks of arrival in Paris I applied for the job of dental assistant, bought a white overall and started on time that Monday. I was asked to clean the white washbasin and please prepare the dental instruments. When I went for lunch I had no wish to return, my guess is that the dentist shared my decision!

Chapter Thirty

PARIS FIFTIES

Undeterred by this miserable first attempt at securing a job, Clara and I scoured an appropriate newspaper's "announces". Instead I found a room to let and moved within a week.

When at last freedom came I had no insight on how to cope with it. Fortunately my first landlady, Madame Hirrigary, the widow of an opera singer, was a kindly and caring soul.

On a golden and crimson autumn afternoon I took possession of my new abode. I much enjoyed making it "my home"! On the evening of my arrival, Madame Hirrigary knocked at my door, "would I like this cooked meal?" I needed it! I wanted it! I ate it!

I could not thank her enough. This was going to be the first of such occasions.

Indeed my landlady's kindness did not stop at food; there is also the heart-warming memory of being invited to her sitting room.

Her old gramophone and a pile of precious 78's records were pulled out from under a book case. Both of us sitting on the carpet and between listening, changing metal needles and windings, Madame Hirrigary reminisced about her late singer husband.

It was marvellous, my fondness of music had always been there. I knew by heart scores of songs from the very old to the latest, political to satirical, and many more songs still unpublished, I virtually new them all by heart.

To Madame Hirrigary I owe my, overdue, initiation to classical music and its world. Thankfully there were going to be some more musical times ahead.

As months went by, I had made two friends, Jaques Penot (ex head administrator of the Camargue), now a private secretary to a government minister and a fervent ornithologist. The other friend René Bonnet being a working civil servant who dabbled in ornithology.

Under the safety of Madame Hirrigary all was well. On the other hand there were evenings when, like the feminine version of 'The Midnight Cowboy,' I 'boldly pranced' into Paris's magnetic, yet shadowy lights.

Alone in the unknown semi darkness, intoxicated by the taste of FREEDOM, I walked non-stop barefoot till the early hours. Many a time during my Paris years, I repeated this escapade.

I kept going forth in search of what? I knew not. At twenty-three my worldly awareness was just as adultly naive as ever.

For example, as a fourteen going on fifteen year old, I had been invited for a fortnight at my stepmother's friend family home. She and Mama had been political prisoners together, but she, a woman in her late twenties had been released earlier. The family had two daughters, the later and Anne aged seventeen; far more my age group, far more my cup of tea, far more fun! We became immediately an accomplice in mischief. Furtively each night Anne and I escaped by the ground floor window and went to the funfair, by courtesy of her father's safe! She new the combination number! We returned at two-thirty each morning. One day we noticed that the window, that was always pulled down, was open. We became somewhat apprehensive . . . What if there was someone in there? Dry mouthed we peered into the room but saw nothing.

'You go first,' whispered Anne.

'Why? You go,' I uttered.

'Don't be silly ' insisted Anne.

So I went in and I pressed the switch but no light came on. The street light helped a little and I noticed the wardrobe door was ajar, I went to open it and put my hand on somebody else's. As casually as I could I pulled it towards me. A tall man wearing a trilby hat and coat emerged.

'You are lucky,' he began. 'I have just disturbed a burglar who was about to go up stairs,' the man went on. 'I chased him out of the window,' the man blabbered. 'Oh, thank you,' I said. 'Look,' he continued, bending towards the outside lights to show his wounded nose, 'we had a fight.'

'Thank you,' I said again. 'You must be more careful,' he went on. 'Think what would have happened if I had not been passing at the time.' Melting with gratitude I thanked him profusely saying, 'I am very sorry I cannot pay you a reward for your kindness. I've spent all my money but I have two cigarettes left. I don't know how to thank you enough.' The man took the offering and left via the window. During the conversation Anne kept well on the pavement! That was the degree of awareness with which I started my Parisian life. I was an easily detectable prey for the unscrupulous of both genders.

But now unforeseen predicaments were inevitable. Trying the door-to-door insurance sales to the underprivileged and being paid only on commission did not even suffice for adequate food. The low value note sent me weekly by my stepmother paid for the rent, a few tins of sardines, bread and rice.

A number of us had been given a half week of training, heavy brief cases and maps and thus equipped we were sent to the most unprosperous and unsavoury areas of Paris. My partner in poverty was a most beautiful 18 year old blond, she spent her time practising smiling in the way she was coached to become a model.

We worked late in the day so as to catch people during the evening meals, these in France are between seven and nine thirty p.m.

My companion used to bring her sandwiches, I, had a yoghurt or two. Having nothing else all day but a toast; a small plate of pasta with black pudding the all around whiffs of cooking were difficult to put up with. Also once I was refused a "petit pain" by a baker because I was short of a half centime. Occasionally I was fed at Clara's table. Since my independence from her we were still in affectionate contact.

Before we started work my sales woman colleague and I met at a near by bistro. One evening we went back there to rejoin two men that we had met earlier. As soon as our drinks were finished we agreed to go to their home. We walked along a musty dark street and followed them across the back yard of an unkempt building. All the while they giggled together especially when we kept being told that they always did share everything between them! At the top of an uneven, repugnantly smelly stairs we reached the last landing with a single door. One by one we entered a grisly room. It was just large enough to accommodate two single divans and a chair.

Before the door was shut completely my friend was asked how old she was 'Eighteen' she replied, both men in unison said; "you can go then" I tried to follow her but it was too late one of them had locked the door and removed the key. I still had the idea that my favourite would give me love and attention and I refused the other one's approaches. (The only thing my landlady had requested from me was that in the event of my not coming back home one night I would telephone to let her know, she often did worry when I was very late returning. It was agreed for security reasons that she would alert the police if there were no sight of me there in the morning). Eventually under duress and fear I obeyed then I was let free. I reached my room at the crack of dawn. What a hard lesson it had been!

My thirst for knowledge never waned. By now I was cosily settled and Madame Hirrigary was still a caring landlady who respected me. Never was she judgmental, yet supportive in my hardship.

I started evening courses but the cost was prohibiting. Somehow on Sunday mornings I was allowed to use a typewriter for free. I was the only one in the ground floor room. On a particular sunny summer morning I heard, at short intervals, some interpolations . . . 'Psst! . . . Psst!' A man standing on the pavement was pointing down to the window ledge where upon was rested, in all its glory his manhood!

Quite a few adventures and misadventures took place whilst at first in Paris. I was violated twice and bodily used several times. I very nearly lost an arm to lymphositis and in spite of agonising pain from rheumatic fever, I struggled not to miss work.

Paris of the "Fifties" was the one of existentialism, when all night discussions on literature and the arts took place, especially in the "Quartier Latin" café's on the left bank. Drinking cups of coffee and smoking, I listened and learnt about names such as Jean-Paul Sartre, Francoise Sagan, Sacha

Guitrie, Picasso, Colette, Baudelaire, Charlie Chaplin and Edith Piaf which were on every ones lips. Not on mine, as yet!

Still the world of nature was never far from my mind and I frequently went to the Natural History Museum. Ornithology, Sociology, museum visits, cinema, Aahh! La Vie Parisienne at its best! The doors of music and literature, together with those of recognition, self awareness and yet unknown unremitting affection were flung open. A remarkable woman called Hélène Piton held the keys. Many forthcoming pages will be dedicated to her.

Meanwhile, although I was living a full life and far from being lonely, I was still very much alone. Subconsciously I was, as always looking for acknowledgement of the individual and fulfilment. Alas! promiscuity did not provide for my desperate needs! Rarely was I to see my stepmother and her daughter-in-law Sabine at the Lush Oasis.

My elevated social status was inebriating and difficult to realize. I met the eminent Ornithologist Professor Etchecopard. He took me to his workplace it was spellbinding! Birds, birds and more birds everywhere. Books, showcases and draws full of eggs. He spoke to me as another human being, answering my avalanche of questions and shared my enthusiasm. He then suggested that I join the "Paris Group of Young Ornithologists" and, if I so wished, that I call on him again. I did both and, in so doing, I met kindred spirits such as Jacques Penot with whom my bird watching trips each Sunday morning shared many interests. Together we went to the 1954 Ornithology Exhibition where Prince Murat and I also shared our detailed interest in birds, but Jacques efforts to "propose" marriage remained unappreciated.

My bird watching trips however, in "Le Bois de Boulogne" and René Bonnet's "Sunday Outings" and lunches, without strings attached, I enjoyed. Jacques was our guide on those occasions, he was a much admired water-colour artist of birds and animals and he and I became life long friends together with René Bonnet who, sadly, died in the sixties.

It is said that the fifties were the Rock-n-Roll years but I, for one, never rocked let alone rolled! Instead I kept to my calling on Clara and familial meals there with her living in son. He was always good humoured and worked for a weaving manufacturer. It was on such a visit that he offered me a job. I was to promote knitted elasticised cuffs and waistbands together with tubular knitting by the metre. I became 'une demoiselle de magasin' at le grand magasin du Printemps. What a welcome respite it was to be self-supporting. I continued to see Clara and less and less frequently spent the weekend at the confining Lush Oasis.

Another of Clara's three sons told me of a vacant bed-sit to let, took me over to see it and I immediately accepted it.

Shortly before I left Madame Hirrigary I received a telephone call telling me of my divorce settlement and that a small amount (very small) of money would soon come my way.

Madame Hirrigary's and I farewell was warm and genuine but of different nature. I saw our parting as a self governed independence. I was still totally unaware to be unaware! My emotions ruled my head . . . More the pity . . . On the other hand Madame Hirrigary wished me happiness, success and good luck (you will need it)! In retrospect, I now remember a slight element of sad uncertainty in her eyes and voice. She had wisdom I had none. My gratitude to her shall never ebb.

A small bed-sit, my new home! Situated so it overlooked one of many back yards belonging to the renowned Place des Vosges, famous the world over for its architectural beauty, originated by Henry IV (of France of course). It was to be a wonderful area in which to live, close by most ancient Paris quarters: and with easy access to my work.

Tiny as it was it would be complete freedom and I relished the idea. It contained a two foot divan, a two-drawer chest card table and a chair. A diminutive sink, a solitary tap and a single gas ring. At the top of the dark, dirty and odorous stairs, leading to my "palatial" abode, the landing included a no less odorous "one hole in the floor" lavatory. Devoid of rationalisation my imagination carried me forward. Clara's sons whose help in finding me job and abode, also helped with the fetching of some belongings which were in storage at the Lush Oasis.

To complete the overture of what I imagined was to be a so called independent free and normal life, I had a Post Office book holding the few Francs from my divorce settlement.

As had been arranged between my stepmother and Clara, the latter was still monitoring me at a distance. She kept a stealthy eye on my activities and reported her judgement back to Mama. Once she invited me to dine out. She had spent some time in Egypt and a Pasha friend of hers wanted to meet me. He invited us to dine in a restaurant where everything appeared dark red in a most subdued pinkish light. Sitting between Clara and himself I was ill at ease. I remember only that I did not like answering the questions he was asking in an ingratiating tone. Towards the end of the meal Clara left us alone. At that point he put his hand on mine and said that he would very much like me to come to Egypt with him. If I did so I would have everything I ever wanted and never, never want for anything. He also put in my hand a gold cigarette lighter to keep and would see me again soon. At that memorable evening Clara displayed surprised amusement, an Egyptian nobleman almost proposing to insignificant me was, indeed, laughable! On looking back I see now that, for the first time ever, the survival instinct came to the fore. I refused to see him again but I kept the lighter!

It never occurred to me at the time how close I had been to becoming a concubine! The deed had failed! Both Clara and my stepmother would have to put up with the knowledge that I was still around!

Chapter Thirty-One

BETTER TO HAVE LOVED

In October, 1955, I was entitled to a holiday. I booked with Le Club Méditerranée. It took nearly twenty-four hours by train between Paris and the south of Italy. The carriage was packed with young adults only. To facilitate sleep each traveller was provided with a small wooden board just big enough to accommodate one's folded arms and which was pulled from the rack above before using it as a pillow.

The campsite at Camerota and the climate were lovely. Everyone appeared to know each other but I was never included in any activities. Two days before the last I met Marcel who was a teacher at Colwyn Bay in Wales. We corresponded and later spent a weekend in Paris together. The letter he was going to send me afterwards never came.

Soon after my return, I was in a café drinking and smoking alone at a table facing the stairs when three men arrived. I did not take any notice of the first two but once I set eyes on André his eyes never left mine. It was love at first sight. When I left the café I did not look behind me, I knew he was there. On the pavement he took out a pocket chess set. 'Do you play chess?' were his first words. 'Yes.' It was the most instantaneous and profound togetherness. Nothing else in the world existed for each other than each other. Within a week we shared my minute place. André had studied Art, Poetry and Mime and continued to paint, read and earned very small amounts as a replacement extra at "La Comédie Française". I worked full time during the day as well as living an artist life during the nights and weekends. André eyed and judged all things through the eye of an artist, I had always done so but had never realized it.

Together we ate little, smoked a lot. We shopped little, socialized a lot. I slept a little, worked a lot. Comparatively, André worked little, spent a lot. We cared little, made love a lot!

Sometimes in the depth of night we would work on Paris's old features such as the favourite one, "Le Pont des Arts"; material, canvas, easel and all, we felt as if alone with the "Seine".

Usually I brought candles, a lit-up one in an empty jam jar would do, its flame enhancing the tones of the tout ensemble admirably. What precious involvement these short times were!

In the middle of 1956 a work colleague, answering to the name of Hélène Piton, already mentioned in chapter 30, had befriended me and the more we saw each other the deeper our affection grew. An older woman who knew much about young people, she soon became a greatly needed confidant and, throughout this tale, I have called her "My-Ellen".

At the end of that year, leaving me in Paris alone, André spent the festive season looking after a group of skiers in the Alps and, in January 1956, he went to see his parents in Nice. Whilst on holiday he had written every day beautiful love letters, full of drawings and poems. Those stopped. Missing him too much I packed my bag and, unannounced, arrived on his family's doorstep! I was made most welcome and was privileged to attend the Sabbath and a circumcision. All were kind towards me. Not so my employer who terminated my contract there and then!

Upon my return to Paris My-Ellen had also left her work owing to ill health. I often went to see her at her home in Marly-le-Roi. I used to go alone and also with André a few times. By the end of the summer I was expecting his baby whom we nicknamed "Gad". André and his friends appeared happy about the news. My-Ellen was somewhat concerned.

One dark, autumn evening as I returned home from hers, the discovering of André's infidelity stunned me. Wearing my pyjamas there was a blonde woman in our bed. 'Good evening,' I said calmly. 'Good evening,' she answered. 'Where's André?' said I. 'Gone to buy cigarettes,' then, 'do you know a woman called "l'oiseau"?' the woman put in. Silence. 'He talks about her all the time and always in complimentary terms.' She went on to describe the marvellous sex they had just had. I was "l'oiseau" and my wings were broken.

Totally in a daze I went, by train, straight back to My-Ellen's. On the journey there a rivulet of tears began, no sobs and I remained frozen on my seat to my destination. The tears lasted for three full days. At home each evening I listened and waited hopefully for the last train but, fifteen minutes later, no one called at the door. Was my unborn baby crying too, I wondered? Love at first sight had ended.

Our endearing names had been, literally, "Oiseau and Minet". The law of nature had taken its toll. The pussy cat had killed the bird.

Such an intense, all embracing experience can neither be mistaken nor duplicated. Its consequences were grievous, scarring and hard to endure. Yet I still think that it is "better to have loved".

HAVE YOU EVER?

Have you ever heard
The silence of loneliness?
When cacophonous birds
With no vocal chords
And demented crowds
Whistling soundlessly
Ring the dinning toll
Of memories dead?

Have you ever seen
The darkness of loneliness?
When all sunrises
Without light, not even a sky,
And shapeless silhouettes
In stagnant inertia
Dance the black ritual
Of the blinded mind?

…Have you ever…..ever….?

Chapter Thirty-Two

MY-ELLEN

My-Ellen was the only child of a musical and artistic couple. She had been brought up surrounded by books, brushes, palettes and musical instruments. During "La Belle Époque" they mixed with the Paris bohemians. My-Ellen had followed in their footsteps but, alas, in spirit only for a catastrophic end to her father's attempt in business had left the Piton's virtually "sans un sou".

An expert in musical notations, literature and knitting, as well as being attuned to the esoteric and folklore, that remarkable woman was all of those. Tall and slender, her mannerism inspired respect.

I had been working at the Printemps for a short while when my working patch was relocated. I was now occupying one side of a rectangular counter and working individually, back to back with another "mademoiselle de magasin" answering to the name of Hélène Piton (fig 34).

My-Ellen, as she was soon to become, proposed our having lunch

Fig 33: My-Ellen in 1906, aged 6.

together at the staff canteen. By the end of the meal our equal need for each other had been spontaneously evident. I became the daughter she never had, she the mother I never knew. That is why when, late one evening, with child and broken hearted, I arrived on her doorstep she gave me shelter

Fig. 34: My-Ellen in the fifties.

and unreserved compassion. There and then began an indestructible communion of heart and spirit which, forty years after her death, lives on.

We shared three years of mother and child life together. Her old ancestral home had eight rooms all split-level with nooks and crannies. The building had been divided into two living areas, there were two front entrances and a door overlooking the back garden. My-Ellen and I valued and respected each other's individuality yet shared all of our daily activities. These included guitar playing and singing by the log fire, endless literary discussions as well as the arts and esotericism. Country drives on our motor-assisted pedal cycles, long walks and bird watching were often on the card. We ate upstairs at her kitchen table the frugal meals she somehow managed to prepare. It was all so wonderful, I was at last respected, understood and loved with a secure roof above my head, plus being surrounded by generations of dusty books and artefacts of all shapes and forms. In other words a "dream" place.

Be that as it may, both our incomes were below the poverty line; they had been so on the evening of my rescue too and continued.

One day over breakfast we deliberated about my having a baby. Our feelings swung from desirous excitement to resigned panic. There were only two options. Either to have the baby and, in spite of our fondest love, condemn him or her to a life of deprivation, or risk imprisonment should an illegal abortion be discovered.

A private doctor I knew of in Paris reluctantly agreed to see me briefly and only once. Stuporous and alone, I went to Paris, took the Metro and made my way to his sumptuous consulting rooms. Without preamble and within minutes I was told, for the first time in my life, to place myself in a most undignified posture onto a table. He then, tools in hand, bent towards me and said, 'This looks delicious, one could eat it!' The whole visit lasted about half an hour. When he escorted me to the door he took his exorbitant fee, shook my hand, saying 'Au revoir,' and shut the door

Shocked and forlorn I returned to My-Ellen's all embracing comfort where, after a sombre and apprehensive evening, we retired. It was not long before the syncopic twinges were felt. From nine-thirty that evening to three in the morning I muffled my screams in my pillow. The time came when, astride a large chamber pot, I suddenly saw my baby boy lying there beneath me. My-Ellen answered my call in an instant. 'Oh!' she exclaimed. 'He has André's hands.' All was unreal, Gad already had fingernails and seemed to be smiling in his sleep. The sleep of the dead.

Wretchedness, depletion, bewilderment took their turn in my thoughts. Then, fatigued in mind and body, I drifted into oblivion.

In the morning My-Ellen and I went to the fairy-like part of the back garden where she showed me Gad's tiny spot of newly turned earth (fig 35).

It took the best part of a week for us to recover our equilibrium. For health reasons she, My-Ellen, was no longer working and I would shortly be looking for a new situation. Our days were filled with wood-burning and peaceful harmony. I

Fig 35: My-Ellen's house and garden.

was most surprised, one day when reminiscing, that on our first encounter I had said to her, with great importance, that I was about to write a book on birds! I knew everything about everything, so it seemed! However, she, Mademoiselle Piton, being thirty years wiser than I, had known better. She had understood immediately that, under the layer of my self-praise, there was plenty of potential crying out to be untangled. 'Therefore', she explained, 'I saw you as a very fertile, uncultivated field, the stones of which had to be removed one by one.'

We were both "ill-au fait" with the midwifery world. It is now difficult to believe that neither of us had given any thought to a thing called "afterbirth". My-Ellen had a passion for cats and many had had kittens; I had no experience in the matter but, now that I have learnt, I am sure I would not have been willing to ape the feline!

I became unwell and forty-eight hours later was unable to stand or think rationally. My-Ellen was beside herself and contacted the Paris doctor. He did not want to know. She gave him an ultimatum. He was to come and fetch me NOW or else he would be reported. There was no beating about the bush. He fetched me by car, dropped me in hospital and quickly vanished. I was saved just in time! An extra bed had been added to the other four, it was squashed between the wash basin and the door which was kept permanently closed. All the patients were prostitutes. In the corner, by the window, one of them kept rummaging in her holdall. She dragged it from under the bed, sat comfortably, rested the bag on her lap and appeared to be looking for something. Then the rummaging would start again a few minutes later. Eventually the bag was returned to its resting place. No one took any notice of that strange behaviour but I was intrigued. Noting my interest she enticed me over. With my back facing the others I stood near her whilst, once more, she repeated the almost hourly ritual. After a minute, and on her whispered request, I looked inside the bag and there, right at the bottom, resting in her cupped hands, was a black-skinned foetus. A heart-breaking sight of regretful necessity. I didn't realise how lucky I had been to have had My-Ellen's help. Within thirty-six hours I was back with her.

On our request André came to see me. He gave me no comfort but seemed upset at the loss of "our" son. Before leaving he took me in his arms yet, regardless, was able to sketch the reflection of our embrace in the mirror behind me.

He never communicated again.

My-Ellen and I were unaware of the wonderful years to come, and she, with her unflinching enthusiasm, taught me and shared many of the realities of life, albeit a bohemian one. The good, the bad, the ugly and the beautiful, we shared them all. After the rain came the sunshine for both of us.

Chapter Thirty-Three

ADIEU LA FRANCE

Eventually that traumatic episode joined the memory file. We took up again our common interests, it was all play and no work! Unfortunately it had to lessen considerably when, at last, I found work again, a two month's contract to sell toys for Christmas, afterwards followed by full-time as a delivery girl for a "Sports Gear" wholesaler. The Underground and my legs were my means of transporting heavy parcels five days a week and up to nine hours a day, eating on the hoof, as it were, and very poorly paid. I was there from November 1957 to September 1958. In spite of My-Ellen's help of having my soothing foot bath ready each evening and our meals on the table, I had reached exhaustion.

In the spring of 1959 I met a young Holiday Tour guide. A short man with frizzled hair, his hands were small, so were his feet. In other words he was small all over, a male "petite" one could say. He was about to take care of a holiday coach bound for the International Exhibition in Brussels. This revived my spirit of adventure and, when I went to say goodbye, he suggested my going with him. In haste I telephoned My-Ellen not to worry saying, 'I'll be back in two days!' Her answer to my announcement stayed in the telecommunication's wires. I put the receiver down and was on my way to Belgium. A weekend to remember, packed with beautiful exhibits and interests of all kinds, including the now well-known Atomium. An educational holiday with night cuddles thrown in!

What a great idea it would be to become a Guide myself I concluded, during the journey back. Bluffing my way, "how" I shall never know, I was given the responsibility of a coach full of knowledgeable tourists. I had never set foot on a coach before the Brussels trip and my acquaintance with geography was non-existent! It was a rather tedious journey and my commentaries were practically "nil"! Oh! I did point out an interesting building or a lovely tree, perhaps even a panoramic view, but too late! We'd already passed by! The rest of the time I spent standing up mutely by the door!

Not all that far from our destination I caught sight of a vast area of bluish water. The excitement and relief got the better of me. "La Côte d'Azur" I thought! So, facing my audience and grinning from ear to ear, I proclaimed for all to hear, 'At last, on your right, you can now see', I took a deep breath, 'La Mer Mediterranée!' An explosive pandemonium ensued. Shifting from one buttock to the other and arms gesticulating in the air, passengers wanted to be heard too! 'That's not the sea, of course it's not,' some agreed. 'How do you know? You can't tell from that far,' were saying the first-timers. 'I should know, I've been twice,' someone shouted and, to me, 'You should know better.' Like "Alice in Wonderland" I felt myself shrinking! It lasted until they were all convinced to be the only one correct! Most of them were! I definitely was not! It turned out to be salt marshes! Gradually I returned to my former height! If compared with the bedlam of our journey's end, this had only been a minor mishap.

Kilometres away, at last we arrived at our destination; la Côte d'Azur. Nice to be presized! On leaving the coach people were issued with a sheet of paper giving details of their booked accommodation. Within minutes it became evident that dreadful mistakes had been made. Couples were not best pleased to find out that they had been separated and booked to share with a complete stranger. Some singletons had not only been allocated the sharing of a double room but also the double bed! It was so very funny, only to me of course, but when things heated up and the vociferous pack charged towards the hotel's door, I took my bag and literally vanished into the sunset. I returned to Paris by another coach. The coach company never asked me again. I wonder why?

Meanwhile, My-Ellen's and my financial situation were worsening. Occasionally my stepmother sent me a small note. My "Sundays birdwatcher friend" René Bonet had also become a mutual friend of My-Ellen and sometimes helped with buying our coal, but those were hard times.

I was not entirely aware of the impasse facing our future. My-Ellen was deeply concerned for both of us and, in a last desperate thought, she conjectured my learning a second language. She was fully competent in English and I had always wanted to learn it. English it was to be!

An unbelievable quirk of fate cemented our decision. I was on the commuter train one day when I met an ex-fellow commuter. As we conversed I mentioned my wish to learn English, to which he enthused. His English mother-in-law in Surrey was looking for an "au pair" and would I be interested? Would I, indeed! Telephone numbers and addresses were exchanged and I hastened more than usual to My-Ellen. That mid-November day was to be yet my third change of destiny. My-Ellen and Mrs. Page, my future employer, took great care of that!

At the Gare du Nord on the damp and misty morning of January the 29th, 1959, My-Ellen stood alone on the platform. I was leaning out of the carriage window of the London train. Both of us with hope in our minds and sadness in our hearts. Our goodbyes were resigned and irrevocable. A few blown kisses, waving of hands, then the unknown. My contract was for one year. Could this be Adieu La France? Only time would tell ....

PART TWO

ENGLAND

As an "au pair" under a one-year legal contract, she arrived in England. The year? 1959. Her age? Twenty-seven. Her assets? A five pound note and a dribble of small change! A year on, homeless and destitute, the authoress tells us of the many difficulties, but also glorifies "Englishness". She never lived again in her native France. We are told about her visits there and the consequences they brought! In England there were more than twelve moves. Three times destitute, over fourteen jobs, her baby girl and many genuine friends, also the authoress known as Rainbow to these days, plus her tenacity eventually made her British life simple but successful. Never dull!... Every step. Her lifelong yearning to find her real mother became plausible. The readers will be able to join the saga of the search one, and search two loaded by unexpected results.

Chapter Thirty-Four

THE TWO FACES OF MRS PAGE

The journey was an unexpected ordeal. Glass, china, personal belongings, debris strewn everywhere. Seasick travellers were stretched out anyhow, anywhere, amongst their lidless sick-bowls. I spent my time freezing on the deck or inside curled up by the door.

My English was practically non-existent. It took a while to find someone to understand that I wanted to catch the train... I wanted to go to "Vaterrrlo"! On arrival at Waterloo I wondered why we had stopped next to rows of cars! Had we gone off the rails? The taxi rank being in the station itself in those days. Is it not often the case that strangers and newcomers almost infallibly find each other? Mrs. Page, her son and I did immediately. My new employer drove us in her Rover to her house and well-groomed garden on the outskirts of Weybridge, Surrey. England is no longer the paradise of forty years ago, but I still think of it as heaven on earth... well nearly!

Mrs. Page, in her low-heeled shoes, was medium height, well proportioned, always immaculately attired. She had smiling eyes and her facial expression often showed wry amusement. She could be stern, yet one knew that it was only superficial.

"Fernside", her home after her widowhood, had been converted into two dwellings. A retired G.P. and his wife lived on the ground floor and Mrs. Page occupied the top. The only other employee was Hampton the gardener, who, on cold mornings, lit the sitting room fire and filled up the wood basket and copper coal scuttle. In company with his feathered friend, a robin, that perched on the edge of his plate, he ate his lunch, which I prepared and took down to him and which they shared sitting in the garage. Hampton sat on a low wooden chair using a wooden stool as a table, or, should I say, "their table"! I was only allowed to give him cheddar, all other kinds of cheese being strictly assigned to upstairs.

Mrs. Page was a connoisseur of cheese with a penchant for camembert! She and I took our main meals in the dining room but every morning I served her breakfast in bed.

After the midday washing-up I was free until it was time to wheel the tea trolley into the sitting room where she would assume the role of hostess. She was an excellent teacher in most fields of English life and taught me a great deal including the do's and don'ts of etiquette. A well travelled woman, she took me with her everywhere she went and on those occasions I became her "dame de compagnie".

Eight months into my employment we went for a three week French holiday to Nice. I had precious little to do. I was even given a week off to go and see My-Ellen. Fantastic! A pleasant change from being in attendance twenty-four hours a day, except from lunchtime on "early closing day"! For example, at eleven p.m. one evening, I was called out of bed to catch a Daddy-longlegs in her bedroom; the poor woman was terribly frightened of them!

Back in England my free time was resumed and I was also given one evening off to attend an English course in town.

One day, when I was on the bus, I met an elderly couple; a retired bank manager and his wife. They befriended me and sometimes I visited them in the afternoons where I was warmly welcomed by them and their dog, their "canine child". While we were drinking tea and eating cakes, the wife would hold a lump of sugar above the dog's nose insisting that he should ask for it! The dog would wait, head up and all in a quiver, but remain silent. 'Say please', ordered the owner. The dog would open his mouth slightly and a vague faraway gurgle was heard. 'No, properly', the voice persisted. 'Grrrr'! Voice, 'Properly or else'!

At last dog would respond with a reluctant 'whoof', the lump of sugar was put on the moist black nose, swallowed in an instant and the whole pantomime would be repeated! It would be to these friends that I would turn when I was made homeless.

In advance of my coming to England, it had been agreed, by telephone and letter between My-Ellen and Mrs. Page, that I commit myself to work for her a full year, afterward I would decide whether or not to continue working there for a second year.

Nearly at the end of my first year, at the suggestion of another English Class student, I had applied for a ward orderly job at the Holloway Sanatorium, a psychiatric hospital at Virginia Water. I was due to arrive the day after my full year at Mrs. Page had elapsed. I told her two months in advance, emphatically promising my commitment to complete the whole year. Upon hearing my future plans she was most displeased and told me to leave at the end of that week. I had two days to sort myself out! Very unlikely!

So, suitcase in hand, handbag on shoulder and fifteen shillings (75p) in my pocket, I walked away from Fernside's gravelled drive for the last time.

Homeless and destitute I turned right at the gate, holding my head high and once again relishing the taste of freedom.

I called at my friends and "doggie" and, unlike the dog, said 'please' properly.

In spite of the fact that, not yet being a British citizen I still had to report to the Police Station, the thought of leaving England never crossed my mind.

My dog owners, and only friends, rescued me.

Outraged by the situation they took me in without further ado. They negotiated on my behalf with the Sanatorium Matron, who advanced my starting date of work, and then took me there the following Monday.

From the huge stone flight of steps I watched the car disappearing away at the end of the long drive. That was it, I was on my own. Holloway Psychiatric Hospital, the sister building to the Royal Holloway College, was at Virginia Water and its entrance hall was imposing. A tall, thin, grey haired woman was coming downstairs, shuffling her feet on each stair. She looked straight ahead of her at nothing in particular. Over her blue-grey dress and cardigan she wore a cotton floral overgarment. Violet, whose name I was soon to learn, was holding both arms tightly against her waist. Her fists were clenched together except for her left index finger with which she touched, rhythmically and continuously, the other fist. That was my first encounter with a psychiatric patient.

To the left of the beautiful double doors there was a reception desk where I announced my arrival and was given instructions on how to make my way to my room. As I turned towards the stairs Violet was pacing to and fro from one step to another.

I was about to start my search for the attic room when a young woman, wearing spectacles, short hair and black trousers, appeared. She stopped as we crossed on the same level and, with a sunshine smile, said, 'Do you play table tennis'? It was friendship at first sight! and yes, as it happened, table tennis had been a passion of mine. Anne, a German girl, and I met on the 29th November, 1959, and we are still in contact. She was the first member of staff I met, like me a ward orderly and with whom I was to share a room. We had both come to England to learn the language and to work, and work we did, very hard indeed, for forty-eight hours a week.

Some months later we were granted promotion to Assistant Nurse and we had the opportunity to move to new accommodation.

A quarter of a mile from the hospital there was an old country house, Lynne Place. A modest building in its own grounds with a tennis court, wooded areas and a lake. The first floor was occupied by the housekeeper. Anne and I, and two newly promoted German girls, were given the four bedrooms on the top floor. Our private living quarters, one might say! It was wonderful!

Six months later a "Preparatory Training Group" was to start. I sat for the entrance test, an essay, and was accepted. My lifelong enthusiasm must have seeped between the lines! At long last I was learning all about the human mind and body and looking after the patients on the wards one day a week; it was simply magic. However, it was not to last.

It was when I was on ward duty that I first set eyes on Giovani. A young hospital porter, wearing a brown overall and pushing his large laundry basket, emerged from the lift. He had short, wavy, dark hair; his slightly tanned face was beautifully proportioned with fractionally protruding cheek bones. As he wheeled his basket towards me his brown eyes looked straight into mine, stayed there and his sensual mouth answered my smile. We were in love! So we both thought!

Spring and summer 1960 were warm and sunny, so was my heart. Giovani and I saw each other every single evening. We met away from it all, here and there, field, woods and even the Lynne House boathouse. On the night of St. Giovani's Day, the 24th June, 1960, and under a full moon our minds and bodies united.

Chapter Thirty-Five

ARRIVEDERCI GIOVANI

WELCOME ERICA

Morning sickness soon confirmed it. I was with child.

My first reaction was that of panic, Giovani was all smiles.

One evening, with Anne's moral support, I had a failed attempt to straighten my predicament. Anne and I were so naïve in those sorts of doings that, in retrospect, the trial was bound to fail and thank goodness it did. Deep in my heart I wanted that baby and would have carried the guilty grief to this day. I was so pleased when the pile of bath towels was still unused at the end of that experimental and frightening evening. The love child had won. Three months later I rented a self-contained flat in Staines and there Giovani and I set up home. The train journey only took twenty minutes. We lived on the middle floor of a large house. There were four flats in all and the landlady-cum-agent lived in one of them.

We had been living together for four months when I noticed that Giovani began to write letters. This, I thought, was out of character. The letters became more frequent and one day I queried the importance of that correspondence. Half jokingly, half seriously, he said that he was writing to his girlfriend in Italy. On several occasions he chuckled, saying that he would marry her but I did not believe him. All was fine between us, we were, so I thought, settled and we did talk much about our expected baby. However, the latter was always referred to as "his" baby, never "our" baby.

Christmas 1960 came and went. There were no presents, no celebration, no cards, we both worked as much as possible making the most of overtime. On New Year's Eve he telephoned Italy. I did not object, thinking that it would go in my favour. It was on the second of January, 1961, that, having just finished our most affectionate love making, Giovani, still holding me in his arms and looking at me tenderly, asked me, 'Was it enjoyable?' My answer was in the affirmative. Then, with sad eyes and near to tears, he declared, 'It is better like that because in the morning I am leaving for Italy never to return.' I was astounded. Turning my back to him I stared at the wall, my brain and heart were in pain but I was unable to move, speak or weep.

I went with Giovani to the airport, it was cold and the sun was shining, for me it was not. Holding my belly I did not have the strength to wave when I saw the Alitalia plane taking off. Homelessness and destitution were looming once more only this time there was a baby to be considered. On returning to the flat I found only three shillings in the money drawer.

I went to see Matron who, although illegally, demoted me back to an assistant nurse. Nevertheless, she was kind enough to allow me to go back to Lynne Place until I went on maternity leave. Once more I had been rescued, but it was only a temporary situation.

Giovani had a cousin who had been in this country for longer than he and with whom we used to associate. Rosario, his Irish wife Margaret, and their two boys aged under two took our flat over. In green uniform instead of my blue one I returned to my old room, put books away and bought knitting needles, wool and patterns! My sole thought was the welfare of that budding human being that was "mine". Someone to love implicitly.

When I went back to full time work I was put on one of the heaviest psychogeriatric wards which entailed a lot of heavy lifting. This brought about a false alarm and I was rushed to the hospital's sick bay. There I spent ten days bathing in luxury.

Mrs Nailor our deputy matron wearing her burgundy uniform and lacy hat came to visit me professionally. I was not allowed up and for once relished having everything done for me. There was excitement among the other nurses, I had many visitors who were all in a quiver when they listened to my baby's heartbeat through the auditory device.

All the same, there were anxious times. Where to go? What to do? How to live before and after my baby arrived? Even if My-Ellen had had the financial means and wish to help, I would have refused, as England would, I hoped, become my country of adoption. I felt I belonged here and, having found it, I was going to struggle to deserve staying.

Via my doctor the Welfare Services advised me to go to the "Unmarried Mother and Child Council".This I did on a sombre, drizzly day. It was at Slough and difficult to locate.The very large house door was dark brown, the surroundings unwelcoming. Apprehensively I rang the bell. A short, hard-looking woman opened the door and said abruptly, 'This way.' I followed her along the dimly lit corridor, there were a few closed doors lining each side of that dismal passage. Half way, a dishevelled woman, holding a baby, came out of a room. Her clothes were unkempt and she was dragging her feet in threadbare slippers. She seemed to look aimlessly ahead of her, in other words she epitomised hopelessness. In that instance my mind was made up,no baby of mine was to start life in such a pitiful place.

The interview, conducted in a gloomy room, was not only useless, to me at any rate, but cruel.The walls, tables, floor and chairs were bare wood. I sat facing the interrogator, a condemning and condescending woman who asked, 'Where is the father of your baby?' She said I could only stay there for the length of my maternity leave. 'Then, what next?' she asked. 'There are only two answers.You go back to France or, and this is the "best", have the baby adopted.' Relentlessly she continued, 'What kind of life do you think you could give the infant?' and so on and so forth. The word "love" never came up and how about my emotional trauma? That was not part of the equation either.

I do agree with the saying "beggars cannot be choosers", nevertheless, in that instance, a modicum of humanity would have been appropriate. I left, more determined than ever to fight on my own. No one was to take my baby away from me and that was that.

When, on my way back, I called upon Margaret and Rosario it was agreed I should move in with them in my old flat. It was better than the street! By no means was it ideal, but they rescued me and for that I shall remain indebted.

Nothing had changed in the flat, with its tiny kitchenette and minute bathroom and their family of four slept in the only bedroom. In a corner of the sitting room, by the open fireplace, there was a narrow, wooden-framed, lumpy sofa where I slept, knit and read. Margaret became a very good friend and I hers. Her husband was hot tempered and was verbally and physically violent. The worst of which I saw was when Rosario came out of the bedroom holding his toddler at arms length. The boy's face was bloody, so was his pyjama top. Margaret took the child from her husband and I silently determined to go to the Police Station. Unfortunately, I could not take the risk either of being thrown out on the street or of being battered too, so I didn't go. Later, when Margaret and I were alone by the fire, we sympathised with each other's situations, though she was suffering enough for me to keep from her the fact that her husband was making advances to me. Still I stayed there with great anticipation to the birth. I had made a dressing gown for myself, a bed was booked at Windsor Hospital and the layette ready.

Under the stairs there was an enclosed space with a window overlooking the garden and also, against one of its walls, was a very small kitchen dresser. Then luck came my way when one day I noticed our landlady coming out of the door under the stairs and went to speak to her. Afterwards I thought of nothing else and asked her about the potential of my living there. In a matter of days it was my abode. Dear Mrs. Augur, a golden-hearted landlady, had also put a bed and a drop-leaf table in there. It was going to be my heaven!

In the outside shed I had my motorised bicycle which I sold to buy a two-ringed gas cooker. Two orange boxes, with two little curtains matching those at the window, and I was ready to move in. On the pavement, the day before, I had found, amongst the refuse, a raffia carrycot which I made useable. All that was needed was a gas cylinder. It was delivered and installed early on the morning of March 22, 1961. Owing to the lack of space I had to move it from my "nest" to the hall. I felt a twinge inside me. I went up to see Margaret who, late afternoon, called for an ambulance.

My daughter, Erica, was born at eleven-fifty that evening. It was wonderful. A tiny creature to love, respect and care for without impunity.

I may have had to lose some of my life long dreams but that one of having a baby had been the strongest and she made it happen.

She had stiff standing thick black hair, I called her my flue brush*. She was going to be named Eric, so I immediately substituted the missing anatomical features for the first letter of the alphabet. What better letter for such a new beginning! Erica she IS.

* see fig 36, page 182.

Chapter Thirty-Six

BACK ON MY FEET

It was with joy that I saw Margaret come onto the ward to collect us, for my week there had been rather traumatic. For example, at the first visiting time after Erica was born, I thought I would not have any visitors, but, when I saw a wave of men, most of them carrying flowers and making their way to their progenies' cots, my resolution not to cry went out of the window. I hid under the blanket and sobbed! I had no one to show my baby to, especially not her father…. Oh! I had visitors! First, the following day, my Weybridge benefactress, the dog owner, to whom I had telephoned the news, came.

Disinterestedly, she glanced at my daughter and to me, without a vestige of a smile, said, 'My! We are both most disappointed in you, we never thought you could be like that.' My throat ached from holding the tears away. I could not understand why they had withdrawn their friendship. She left a small brown paper bag and a plastic carrier-bag on my bed, said goodbye and left. There was a bunch of grapes in the brown bag, the other held two worn out garments. This was our last encounter. Yet the second visit later that day was indeed unexpected and heart-warming; two nursing colleagues stayed the full visiting hour. Talking and laughing, they told me everyone at our hospital wanted to see the baby and sent best wishes to both of us. That was much better received. Erica was given a soft toy duckling with a hanging red ribbon and, even more meaningful, it was new! It is still nearly so today. The flowers were most welcome too.

Back home, in my under-stairs abode, it felt a little as if people were walking all over us, which, figuratively speaking, they were, of course, but it took only a few days for my ego to adjust.

Margaret, her children, Erica and I spent a lot of time together. However, I kept my independence. Erica's nappies were boiled on the gas ring, the rest of my washing was washed outside and rinsed at the garden pump, which supplied all my water. During the day Erica lay in her cot on my bed and at night they rested securely on the table with one of its drop leaves extended over my bed, all cosy and happy, if not a little cramped! But things were brightening up, even the weather.

On Easter morning, kind Mrs. Augur gently knocked at my door and handed me a saucer containing two coloured boiled eggs. 'I thought, as it is Easter, you might like these for your breakfast?' I was choked by her kindly gesture, dear Mrs. Augur, she was such a good woman, I owe her unlimited thanks. When soon a ground floor flat became vacant she offered it to me. I was, needless to say, over the moon. There were to be good times ahead, difficult ones, but the best yet.

As I was not yet a British citizen I still had to report to the police every fortnight, and later, once monthly. Apart from my maternity leave allowance I was not eligible for any State help for myself. Even so, Erica was allocated a place at a State-run nursery, together with transport, and I paid a shilling (5p) a week. Back at Holloway Hospital I requested to be given a job in the occupational therapy department and matron agreed. It entailed machine sewing and helping the patients make teddy bears! I was thankful, as my working hours coincided, almost, with Erica's nursery care. Anyway, it was with reluctance that, at 7.30 a.m. each weekday, I handed over my small bundle to the nurse, but there was no alternative.

There were two rooms in our new home but one of them was too cold, damp and dark to live in. The bedroom/sitting room was an ideal space where, each evening before cot-time, Erica and I played together. It could be quickly heated by an open fire. I used to return home just before Erica. Only once the train had been late and, when I opened my door, I found baby and basket left on the spare bed ... quietly Erica was looking around sucking her thumb for the first time! We were now secure, settled and happy.

Half way up the hill there was a British Rail coal depot from which I was permitted a free supply. This I fetched with cardboard boxes which, one by one, I carted back home on the pushchair. Although I kept the flat aired and warm Erica developed bronchial infections, which became almost continuous.

Yes, there were some moments of sadness. For example, when, in response to my letter announcing to him the birth of his daughter, Giovani stated that he was going to take the baby but did not want anything more to do with me. In spite of that, he offered to send a few shillings a month. My solicitor was outraged and said that if I did accept even a penny from Giovani he would officially have rights over his child. This frightening statement was enough, I did not respond to his letter. I plodded on and faced the difficulties, but I kept my daughter.

What still infuriates me today is that, in spite of the times Erica's father and I had lived and loved together, I still had to declare her father "unknown"!

To continue with our story, Erica and I, like everybody, had our ups and downs but we were able to live as most people did. I worked, Erica played and together we socialised.

So far, so good! So far, too good ….

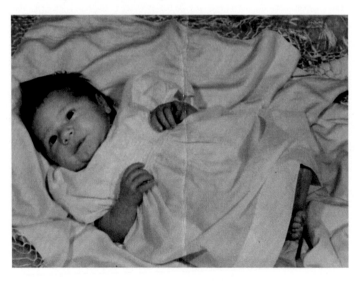

Fig: 36: My "flue brush" Erica, a few weeks old.

Chapter Thirty-Seven

FROM JOY TO SADNESS

Having every evening and weekends off was lovely. Erica and I had good times with Margaret and her children, also visiting or even staying with friends. We travelled by train in the luggage van, it was so simple and easy then. The guard would help lift the big pram, with Erica in it, into the van and there we stayed. For long distances we left the pram in the van and settled in the wonderfully comfortable compartments, where one was able to adjust the blinds and individual lights to one's requirements!

All the while, since I had left My-Ellen, she had continued to write long and frequent letters. She suggested books for me to read, and, now that the dust of the past tumultuous months had settled, I could concentrate on reading avidly again. My-Ellen had informed my stepmother of Erica's arrival, and her response was of disapproval, anguish and concern; see fig. 37 showing her authoritarianism in her writing. From time to time, she sent a very small amount of money and a short note, although not often, though she had sent two beautiful hand-knitted baby dresses, but it did not last.

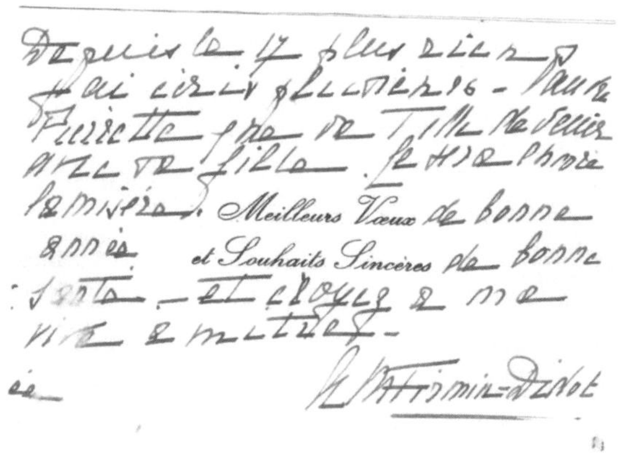
Depuis le 17 plus rien [illegible]
[illegible]
[illegible]
[illegible]
[illegible] Meilleurs Vœux de bonne
année et Souhaits Sincères de bonne
santé [illegible]
[illegible]

Fig 37.

It was a brilliant spring and a glorious summer, autumn was colourful in every way and winter, bright and cheerful. Happy, happy days .... I savoured my happiness with unreserved gratitude and my fondness for England strengthened. Then, in early February 1962, calamity struck.

Very regretfully, I was sure, dear Mrs. Augur called on all the tenants. Her difficult task was to give us two-and-a-half weeks' notice. The proprietor, British Rail, was putting the house on the market. This, to me, was "the calm before the storm" in the reverse order! Margaret and her family moved to Esher, but her absence was compensated for by the presence of my friend, May Mole, who lived on the top floor. May was a school teacher who was waiting to meet "Mr. Right". She later became Mrs. Griffith and our friendship lasted a long while.

Meanwhile, the storm was imminent. I had to find shelter and, as I wished to pursue my nursing studies, I wrote to the five nearest psychiatric hospitals, applying for the position of student nurse. I only had one answer but my interview was successful. I started on March 4th. It would have been marvellous, except that, unfortunately, my eleven month old Erica had to go to foster parents, as there was no other way until I was able to find accommodation away from the nurses' home. The Social Services were supposed to keep an eye on her. They had designated the foster home, so, by taxi, amongst all our worldly goods, we left our home. When I entered the foster home, with my daughter in my arms, the woman said coldly, 'So, this is Erica. She will be alright here.'

Keeping a tight grip on my emotions, I put Erica in the playpen and rushed back to the taxi, which took me to the nurses' quarters. In a forceful and unfeeling voice the foster woman had told me not to visit my little girl, as she would settle down better that way. This belief still exists today, but I still disagree.

Bereft of my most precious "raison de vivre", I restarted my studies. This softened the pain a little, but, despite the warning, I did visit Erica and was told that she was not doing very well. I was worried when I left. A week later the foster mother informed me that the doctor had been called, Erica was most unhappy and losing weight. I called on him and he went straight to the point - Erica's life was in danger. Owing to her first parting from me, and also missing other children's company, it was obviously too much for her and the social worker was looking for a residential nursery to have her.

I understood, long afterwards, that Erica had not been adequately cared for.

Things were going from bad to worse. At the hospital I had already made some friends. I thrived on my lessons and learned eagerly, but the residential nursery was miles away. From the hospital, there and back, it took five hours and, because of short visiting hours, I only had time to see Erica once a week, but she began to respond to my demonstrative affections again.

I always arrived, not by choice, after the children's lunch. There were no staff to be seen and I went straight upstairs to Erica. Each time it was a pitiful tableau; two little girls, standing at the foot of their cots, were sobbing at each other and trying to touch each other's hands. Alas, to no avail, the space between the cots being a few inches too far apart. It was the children's afternoon rest-time, evidently not for these two little girls. The beautiful black-faced child always had thick green mucus running from her nose and the white one, my Erica, was soaked with tears.

I used to take my child, in my arms, into the garden, and wished I could have taken the other one too, but I had to leave her alone with her sorrow in that curtained room.

It was indeed a lamentable state of affairs. Each journey back, tears rolled down my cheeks until I entered the nurses' home. Nonetheless, unbeknown to me, the sun was about to shine again ....

Chapter Thirty-Eight

CLIMBING UP THE HILL

It came in the shape of Noëlle, a French Ward Sister, who, unannounced, knocked at my door one evening.

Having visited Erica that day, I had been sitting on my bed, tristful and disconsolate, pondering over my situation.

'Come in,' I answered to the knock.

'You are French?' enquired Noëlle, in a cheerful voice.

'Yes,' said I. 'Vous aussi?'

'Oh! Ah!'

'Ah! Ah!'

Noëlle had seen me at a distance and had been told I was the French newcomer. I suspect that her curiosity got the better of her! We spoke in French. In a short space of time I had opened my heart to her, divulging the secret that nobody at the hospital knew. Noëlle made up her mind there and then. Could we not, both of us, take care of Erica? I was speechless, had I heard correctly or misunderstood? I had not. So, with rising, but somewhat doubtful, hope, I agreed.

We decided not to mention Erica for fear it would jeopardise our getting a flat. However, I intended to have her with me as soon as it might be possible.

Twelve days later, we had taken possession of our flat in Purley, only a few miles from Coulsdon, where we worked. Higher Drive is the longest and steepest in Purley. It was lined on both sides by large houses. Our house was about two-thirds of the way up the hill, its attic had been converted into a flat and had extensive views, but the only access into it was a small attic door.

A home-made partition divided the space into two; Noëlle made her bedroom in the larger part which also was, at times, a sitting room. The entrance room was where I slept, and in a corner was a small kitchenette. Albeit, there was room for a table and a chest of drawers. The owner/occupiers were lovely. Mary and Maurice Wenstock had four children, all boys. John, the youngest, was four years old. It was a wonderful family, open, friendly, always cheerfully smiling. We saw them, one way or another, every day.

With Noëlle's quick, frequent and amusing repartee, it became evident that, to the pleasure of the whole Wenstock family downstairs, the attic had become an additional source of gaiety. I was not the most animated, for my little girl was on my mind more often than not, and I had to wait for the most propitious time to broach the subject with Mary. But, after a few weeks, one morning I knocked on Mary's door.

My voice faltered, I blathered, I beat about the bush, I was so afraid of Mary's reaction. I was sure that she would refuse me, she was going to tell me that I could not have Erica with me.

I was not doing her justice, but I knew no better at the time. Instead of my dread, Mary answered, 'I have had four of my own, eight years of nappies. I don't want anything to do with babies anymore, but, if you are able to look after her and do not ask me to do so, you may have your little girl with you.' How could I possibly hold back my tears …? The next day happened to be my day off and I visited Erica for the last time. I gave notice that I would be removing my daughter the following week. I told Erica too, but how could she understand? She still cried when we parted, but it was to be my first tearless return journey. The next and last one would be with Erica.

Chapter Thirty-Nine

NOËLLE NOËLLE

The wheel of fortune had turned my way. Most of the time Noëlle exuded joviality mixed with, 'I know it all' attitude and her way of accepting her being wrong or having lost her authority was to curtail her laugh, lit up a cigarette and to utter a disbelieving m. m. m. An engaging young woman in her early thirties, with waist long auburn hair and almond shaped green eyes, Noëlle intended to be like the wild fauna of Africa, where she had lived as a French forces' child and could never have been completely tamed. She was never without make-up, especially thick mascara and enveloped herself in cigarette smoke! She consumed forty a day, smoked the last one before falling asleep and before opening her eyes in the morning, she reached out for the packet and lighter. She was open about her lost sense of smell but the trauma of its cause, together with those of her childhood in Morocco, were well guarded secrets. However, between us we had but a few.

Erica was thirteen months and not yet on her feet when at last, I was able to retrieve her, I hoped for good. It took two weeks for neglected and loveless "crawler" my Erica to become a walking smiling toddler (figs 38 and 39). Her arriving at our flat provoked cheerful acclaim all round

Fig 38: Neglected crawler.

Fig 39: Happy smiling toddler.

and without my full approval, became immediately Noëlle's living doll.

It was not to be easy to share my daughter and my life with someone so openly better-off financially than I. Noëlle bought clothes and shoes that I could not afford as well as toys and treats.

Noëlle and I had more or less managed to be working on opposite shifts, interestingly enough, we never worked on the same ward! Overlapping hours, such as travelling and hand overs, had to be arranged.

Mary, our landlady recommended Maggie, a registered child minder, who most conveniently, lived down the hill and on the route to our bus stop! She agreed to look after Erica even though the irregular hours could sometimes start at six a.m. And at other times ended at nine-thirty p.m. Perfect! No longer neglected and receiving ample loving care and attention Erica blossomed. She took to her feet and was potty trained within two weeks. Now my toddler had bright eyes, short hair and was at long last her own little person, another traumatic page turned.

Whether I liked it or not, the great majority of all things concerning my daughter were one way or another under Noëlle's dictation and at times Noëlle's interjections were aimed at me, for instance, when returning from shopping one day she threw a plastic bag on my bed saying 'Take this I've had enough seeing you wearing your old rags'! My thanks were not heard, instead she dressed Erica ready to take her down stairs to be admired! Hard as it was, I was the beggar, Noëlle the chooser and it had to be so. Apart from that we lived in harmony, laughed a lot and indulged in our passion for playing cards. We usually played a two person patience appropriately called 'Spite-and-Malice'! (credit must be given to Noëlle, who behind her "couldn't care less" pretence and make up, was an honest and faithful friend)

In February 1963, less than a year with Noëlle, Joyce, a nursing colleague and I were making beds we were talking about this and that, when suddenly, she looked at me and said pensively

'You should meet our best friend. '

'Yes'?

My husband, Roy, and he joined the Royal Navy on the same day in 1948, they are still best friends.'

'What's his name?' I asked vaguely interested.

'Ronald'. She continued smoothing the sheets.

'Yes?' I repeated.

'He has recently been promoted to an officer' she smiled.

The words 'Officier de Marine' carries high prestige in France, my curiosity awoke! So, when I was invited to join Joyce, Roy and Ronald for an evening meal, I accepted without hesitation.

As usual my fertile imagination flared up, the remnants of my stepmother's inculcation was telling me that no 'Officier de Marine' would ever be interested in insignificant me! Yet all the same my somewhat apprehensive excitement was building up by the day! My exuberance had spilt around the whole household. The great evening was there! I wore a straight tight white fitting dress with white shoes, a gold pendant and looked radiant! The bell rang, the downstairs family held their breath whilst Mary opened the door, I poised at the top of our stairs looking down. Joyce entered followed by a man wearing a gabardine and a trilby hat! My heart sank! Why, I immediately assumed, had Ronald's father come instead of 'he?' At the end of the evening all was well, Ron, for it had been 'he' and not his father, was a polished gentleman.

A few days later he went to sea for six weeks and we wrote to each other more and more. Ronald was not tall, dark and handsome but his voice was most agreeable, his speech monotonous yet his conversation and letters were interesting enough. He had a narrow face, slightly protruding teeth, his nose was noticeable his hair line receding. My-Ellen, in years to come, qualified all this a 'most attractive ugliness.' When he returned after the six weeks he visited the flat and met Erica and Noëlle

Then followed brief alternate periods when he would work at sea or ashore and whenever possible, we saw each other. He wooed me assiduously, respectfully and, to my scrupulous delight, proposed marriage. Little me, I felt, a Naval Officer's wife? Surely there must be a mistake somewhere? Not before our introductory friends took Ron and I for an evening meal, and announced, for all to hear, that we had just become engaged that I finally believed it.

In May I went with Erica to meet my future parents-in-law. It was a very long train journey and Erica behaved perfectly at all times, except for the following anecdote. She began fidgeting, thinking that it was time to have some refreshment, I turned away from her towards our food bag but, when I turned back to her, she had taken her potty out and was comfortably using it in the corridor! Well! What could one expect, a little girl had to do what a little girl had to do! To the amusement of passengers! We stayed two days at Ron's parents during which he gave me an eternity ring. Later, full of happiness and alone with Ron's mother I showed it to her, she looked at me most kindly and said in her Devonshire accent, 'Pret (Pierrette) Twill not last dear' I did not believe her of course. Where ever I went I was floating on a cloud rather than on the earth.

On the last day of that month, only a matter of weeks before my nursing finals, I gave my notice to the hospital and the day of my thirty second birthday, I left Noëlle to share my life with my 'Officier de Marine' in Plymouth.

Another page had been turned and the freedom of a brand new one glittered ahead ... Would it really be so?

Chapter Forty

MAN AND WIFE

On reflection, it is now clear that, had my fiancé been considerate enough about my own nursing career, he would have encouraged me to take my finals. Instead he had rented a flat in Plymouth. I too, of course, should have known better but the sparkling image of a secure family life was too magnetic to resist. Like a moth around the lamp I couldn't let go. All this should have been a warning, it was not! I have no regrets, never had in my life any thought to waste on the word "if".

Erica and I settled down with "Daddy" in the bottom flat of a large house facing a small park with swings. The flat was spacious, its furnishing upmarket, it had tall ceilings and long brocade curtains, also central heating and an open fire.

We bought a car, an old Ford Popular with which we went shopping, took Ron's parents for drives and drove to our naval social gatherings. I was allowed to drive on my International Driving Licence, but later I passed the English Test.

My-Ellen and I were still writing regularly to each other. During the first festive season at Holloway Sanatorium, I had spent Christmas at My-Ellen's. I had stopped smoking for four months and with the savings bought my flight to Paris. The idea of flying for the first time and on my own had been immensely exciting and took place on a "Caravelle"! Sitting by a window, agog, eagle-eyed and nose in the air I thought I looked self-assured! It certainly did not fool the man who came to sit by me! We talked at length during the journey, he was a business man. I was a nurse, he would like to see me again... What was my phone number? My tenacious lack of self-esteem was still rife then. That "English Gentleman" wanting to see me again went to my head and full of eagerness to tell My-Ellen about it, I left my suitcase in the taxi's boot! Luckily, in spite of my panicked annoyance the taxi driver returned it. The following day the "English Gentleman" telephoned and My-Ellen left me to it.

"I told you I would call back", he began.

"Oh?" I enquired.

"You told me that you were a nurse, no?"

"Yes" I confirmed.

"I would like to ask you for a helpful favour", he continued.

"Yes"

"How are you?" He went on.

"Very well, thank you, and yourself?" I retorted.

"I have a problem" he said tentatively.

My ego began to swell.

"Yes, yes I am. I said eagerly.

"I would like you to come over and give me an enema, you know about these things", he asserted.

I could not believe my luck! To be nursing a private patient. Hardly able to contain myself, I asked the man to wait and rushed full of pride to My-Ellen to announce "the good news!" Upon which she, raising and gesticulating both her arms in the air, she said in a strong dismissive tone, — "Darling, go and put the phone down quickly." " But he said . . . . ," She interrupted firmly, "go now, and put the phone back, the man is a pervert," then she explained. Such a level of gullibility and lack of discernment in a twenty-eight-year old woman now seems untrue, but it was so. There had not been much improvement by the time Ron and I got married. This brings me back to the point from which I diverted to tell the relevant anecdote of the so-called "English Gentleman."

On August 17th 1963 Ron and I married (fig 40). My-Ellen and our birdwatcher friend René, who had arrived from France the evening before, came to fetch me at the flat from where, at eleven o'clock, friends including Noëlle, family and my sailor groom were waiting. The marriage was at Plympton Registry Office, the reception took place aboard H.M.S. Urchin (fig. 41) courtesy of Captain Geoff Duffy. The buffet and cake were perfect and the party carefully well attended by the steward. Noëlle and

Fig 40: Man and wife.

René being there was most agreeable but My-Ellen's presence crowned the day's happiness. Ronald and I left the ship walking under the archway of swords and the confetti shower at the bottom of the gangway. Erica stayed with some friends and we drove away.

It is almost legendary that, on

Fig 41: H.M.S. Urchin.

wedding days, something would go wrong. Ours was a minor mishap and fortunately I was wearing stockings, "Stockings?" I hear you say, one of them made a splendid replacement for the car's broken fan belt. The car radiator began to boil. We had lost the fan belt and naturally had no spare, a small detail really, one of my stockings did the job admirably.

It is strange to relate that although since we had met five months since we had not yet known each other biblically yet at any opportunity we had shared the same bed we had remained celibate (to all intense and purposes) with each other. Straightforward embraces and passionate kisses were as far as we went. It had been Ron's determination to prove his respect for me.

My experiences in that field, as described in previous chapters, had always been so horrendous that, strange as it was, I enjoyed and respected his respect.

Wedding nights are supposed to be "the night". Permissible, lawful and almost obligatory to "perform" officially the sexual act. I thought of all the people who knew of us, and I made sure that all their assumptions would be wrong! When we arrived at Llangmmach Wells, it was raining. Ron had booked the best en suite double room but much to his sadness (Ron showed more chagrin than anger), we were given the only free room, a single room, with a single bed, not large enough to swing a cat! There was a noisy lavatory cistern in the adjacent room, the one alongside our bed! Nevertheless, it was a room with a delightful view. The weather brightened, the food and service were acceptable. We went for walks and enjoyed beautiful drives around glorious Wales. Further more we became man and wife. It was to be the most successful aspect of our married life.

THREE CHANGES OF DESTINY

Chapter Forty-One

SNUG AND SMUG

Ronald, Erica and I were, now a family unit, a small one at that, but Erica was most loved by Grandma and Granddad, Ronald's parents.

Ronald and I missed each other when he was at sea but we enjoyed his time ashore tremendously… Alas, something was lurking.

After five months Ronald, whose personality was by no means flamboyant at the best of times, became more and more lethargic. He fell asleep in his chair as soon as he returned from work and again, immediately after his meal. He looked unwell by the day but would not admit it. Something had to done, so unknown to him I called on his captain who understood and kindly took the matter in hand.

My husband, who previously had had testicular tuberculosis and one infected kidney removed, was diagnosed with having a secondary infection; this time the tuberculosis resumed between the ribs. He was admitted to the naval hospital in Portsmouth (Hasler), before being transferred to the Sanatorium for Officers in Midhurst.

As soon as the date for his transfer had been fixed, I rented naval quarters as near to the sanatorium as possible. I kept quiet about it and on the eve of the transfer my car was tucked up on packed to bursting point with essential belongings and the rest put in store. In the front, next to me, Erica was tucked up on piles of cushions, and food, drink and of course, the potty, were at hand.

We set off at ten o'clock and arrived at Yeovil five hours later! There we stayed at a bed-and-breakfast and the next night was spent at Midhurst in a hotel, from where, in the morning, we drove to Liphook and took possession of a new home. To Ronald's amazement we visited him on his first evening of his arrival in Midhurst!

We lived there for six months, in a fair-sized house with lawns back and front.

Ironically enough, the Liphook times were very happy, except for the first few weeks when Erica, having recently grown used to a daddy was suddenly only permitted to see him on the balcony of his bedroom.

We had friendly neighbours, and by good fortune, they had a little girl of Erica's age, so the mother looked after Erica when I visited Ronald. Erica was never allowed inside the sanatorium but, when I was on my own, I was permitted to do so.

Soon a beautiful Spring, and later, the Summer, enabled the three of us to be together outdoors and it was as beautiful as the weather itself. After four months, Ronald came home every weekend and then two months later he was discharged. However, It took several more months after convalescing, before he was completely recovered.

Curious as it may seem, the past months had been extraordinarily happy. My parents-in-law came to stay, Noëlle spent some time with us and, delight of delights, Myellen and René came over for ten days holiday. To my mind, as a whole and all round it had been six months of affectionate togetherness and warm contentment.

We left Liphook on a glorious mellow September day in 1946, for our new home in Yealmpton, Devon. At first sight of the cottage I was overwhelmed. Tor Bridge Cottage was an old beamed building; it had seven rooms, of which three of the upstairs ones were bedrooms and bathroom. The whole place was split-level and it had large gardens front and back, the latter overlooking fields.

Now we were to live at the bottom of a short but steep hill alongside the river Yealm. What an enchantment it was going to be!

At the top of the slope the Plymouth to Woodbridge road ran through the village, passing 'Old Mother Hubbard's Cottage'. There were no tourists there when I first went to see it, and who would believed it, when I opened the door of the very cupboard, the dog was still there, a man-made puppy with a pitiful expression, begging for a penny or two.

We all enjoyed real country life and both the garden and greenhouse benefited from our caring attention. My husband had been posted ashore, as the radio-radar officer of H.M.S. Cambridge Gunnery School, half an hour away, and so was able to return home each evening. The snug and smug winter was uneventful, a sort of taken for granted routine set in. Erica learned her first card game, called 'Sympathy', renamed by us, 'Grandma's Patience'. We played all sorts of games and I was never short of domestic help from her eager little hands!

It was so enjoyable and altogether I was fully content to be a wifely mother at home. Every Sunday, whether or not we had gone for a drive, we had high tea with Ronald's parents. Ronald was also the catering officer, which meant that at evening functions the two of us served behind the bar and luckily I had an excellent baby-sitter who lived immediately opposite us. These parties were incredibly entertaining and at the end we were all at various stages of modest inebriation. I having to dispense the drinks and to drive us home, was more sober than most.

Mean while, My-Ellen, having kept in mind my need, and her ambition to improve my minimal schooling in my native tongue, had enrolled me in a correspondence course in O-Level French, this to start on the next academic year. Erica, too, started her pre-schooling at a private school in Newton Ferres, and for both of us, learning was bliss.

Chapter Forty-Two

BY THE RIVER YEALM

Although very good qualities, my husband's loyalty and integrity were almost obsessional and were blinded by his narrowness of mind. For example, my, so to speak opening his eyes to birdwatching, launched him into recording pages of elaborate statistics. There was also the time when having checked his tomato seedlings that day, he returned to the greenhouse, torch in hand, at past midnight, presumably to ensure their welfare.

These pastimes, together with Scrabble and Philately, I had brought into his life, and that was that! Optimism or vivacity were not of Ronald's making, he had gone to seed at puberty. I was still at the age of adolescence! A combination hardly conducive to a lasting union.

We were now at the age of thirty-four and thirty-five respectively, when one day Ronald stated assuredly; 'we couldn't possibly do this at OUR age darling!' So help me! I thought, need I say more. He showed no interest or encouragement in my studies whatsoever.

Only a matter of weeks later, I was sitting at the desk facing the front bay window when I heard the garden gate it was the telegram boy… My-Ellen was dead! There my memory fails me, I did not weep, this I do know, the pain was too intense, the sorrow too deep. I received no understanding, no comfort, and forty eight hours later; alone, I arrived at My-Ellen's house in France.

Birdwatcher René, and the undertakers, were there. 'We waited for you before closing the coffin', someone said. Two steps forward I walked, said nothing, touched nothing, reversed, and saw her no more.

My-Ellen had, at her request, a secular interment. I was one of five mourners, three of whom left us as soon as the coffin had been lowered. René took me for a meal at the nearby bistro and, to my disconcertment, no sooner had he eaten, said goodbye and left me. I, forsaken, as the protagonist of that living nightmare, tearless in the darkness of the daylight, went back to My-Ellen's house alone. To everyone who new her I had been her daughter, and I had lost my spiritual mother.

Except for the house, she had left me all her worldly goods.

The same afternoon I sold, by telephone, her two knitting machines, and packed her jewellery and silver in my bag. The new owner of the house, an unscrupulous antique dealer had persuaded My-Ellen to will him her property and he had unlawfully ordered it to be sealed within thirty hours. I worked till the early hours gathering and sorting my old and new belongings. By the end of the day, and exhausted, I curled up in the very sheets and bed where My-Ellen had taken her last breath. In the morning a discourteous man nearly knocked the front door down, and, without exordium, practically threw me out. I was told that I would be contacted as to when the seals were to be removed.

On returning home, it was as if nothing at all had happened. Erica had been happy with Grandma, Ronald listened to the few things that I was able to say and no more questions were asked. The routine went on but my silent and single hearted bereavement was hard to bear. Suffice to say that, one evening I happened to mention missing My-Ellen, 'Huh, I can't see why, you have me,' my husband said huffily. No comment!

Along the length of our garden, on the other side of the fence, there was a large area of bare ground belonging to the County Council, beyond flowed the River Yealm. At the far end a long wooden gate led to the pastures and meadows. To the right of the unkempt land there was a large corrugated building and attached to it a very large lean-to shed.

The metal building where John Maxwell Saunders lived in penury was his castle (fig 42), albeit a rather primitive one! Inside the uneven earth floor was filled with cars and carts, together with all sorts of bits and pieces of wood and metal. The three-sided work bench to the right of the door and surrounded by windows was where J.M.S. earned his 'breadline' keep. At the top of his 'castle', accessible by a precarious wooden flight of stairs, there was a storage floor, it took up most of the space. Finally above the working area and with a view over the countryside was his postage stamp

Fig 42: J.M.S.'s castle!

sized bedroom.

Since his divorce some years earlier he had lived a semi-recluse and frugal life. The fruits of his labour as a mechanical engineer and also as a designer and painter of public house signs, supplied his meagre income. He could make anything out of anything. Necessity literally was the mother of his inventions and there was never any shortage of them.

Between J.M.S.'s lean-to and the road, a good part of the barren ground was an occasional car park and from day one at Yealmpton, Ronald and I had parked our cars there. We had met J.M.S. and in a short space of time had become better acquainted. His gait and gestures were elegant and in spite of his 'fallen out of a dust cart' accoutrements he was a distinguished figure. Despite his toothlessness his speech was clear, his accent educated and his conversation erudite.

As time went by J.M.S. was made welcome by us three at Torbridge Cottage, where he talked at length on many subjects, including the salmon and otters of the River Yealm.

Chapter Forty-Three

J.M.S.

This nonconformist had been a close friend of Doctor Gordon St John-Ives, a fellow Oxford graduate who was Modbury's GP, but when J.M.S's marriage had broken up, the protocol had smothered that long standing amity. Gordon too, was a gentle and highly intelligent man and a rebel, but lived it in secret: He was never divorced… So, 'my dear', he remained respectable! He will be given more lines later in this narrative.

J.M.S.'s company was pleasurable, entertaining and interesting at all times. He, like I, had an unquenchable curiosity and when, for some reason or another, I started calling on him, I discovered how much we understood and complemented each other.

J.M.S. was very nearly the masculine equivalent of My-Ellen, in as much as his sentiments towards me were appreciatively inspired by my real-self; whereas, Ronald's mawkish way of thinking was based on his wrong wish for me to be what I was not.

As My-Ellen had done, J.M.S. recognised and encouraged me to discover my potential. For about two years we enjoyed many wonderful hours together, some sad, others jolly, some alone or with Erica and also with dear acquaintances in pubs. An alcoholic who was inebriated every evening, J.M.S. was too dignified to be completely drunk.

When Erica had started school all day, he and I saw each other every day. At home the lack of intellectual stimulation, joyful anticipations of any kind, let alone an occasional laugh had become more than I could stand. I had at last discovered another world, a world of creativity, cerebral enrichment and mutual harmony, furthermore it was on my doorstep.

My first and only mentor and I shared our respectful admiration of the world of nature. We would enthuse about everything from a blade of grass to grey seals' 'whiskers'. But his whiskers and goatee beard, poor things, never had much of a rest, for he kept twiddling, twisting and smoothing them far more than necessary! To his true friends it was one of his charms.

Each time I called on J.M.S. he delighted in awakening and explaining the avalanche of questions I put to him. He would often illustrate them by drawing on any flat surface available with a fragment of pencil picked up from the floor or, if need be, used a finger oily from his work!

What a breath of fresh air all this was. Such a contrast to my mind-atrophying life with Ronald, and slowly but surely, he was receding into insignificance, so I decided to rent a caravan. It was parked in the grounds of a country hotel, a few miles from Mothercombe beach and about half an hour by car from Torbridge Cottage.

I had been occupied and preoccupied with making it a clean, homely and cheerful place to live in for Erica and myself. Openly I had prepared some bits and pieces and made small-size curtains for it, which, a couple of weeks before Erica's birthday, I was ironing in the sitting room. Ronald was reading the paper and Erica was in bed. I paused.

"I have something to tell you", I began.

"Yes?" queried my husband, keeping his nose in his paper.

"I am going to leave you", I carried on, still ironing.

... Silence ... nose in paper ...

"I'll wait till Erica's birthday, then I will go."

... Silence ... nose in paper ...

"Erica's birthday is on the twenty-second, we'll leave on the second of April". Still ironing, I waited.

Ronald, holding up his paper, turned his face towards me and impassively said:

"If that's the way you feel", ... Then returned to his reading!

I might have had a tiny speck of guilt before, now I had none! Nothing changed in the everyday routine.

J.M.S. had not been personally involved in my decision but was not surprised when I asked him to store some of my belongings in his attic. When the fixed day arrived, Erica went to school, Ronald went to work and I left him. Later that day I telephoned him to give him my address, a must for Erica's sake.

Now being completely free, J.M.S. and we spent most of each day together, except at night, for we never were lovers. He was a good conversationalist in congenial company.

After leaving Yealmpton, ten years were to elapse before Erica and I holidaying in the South called on him. As soon as we arrived, J.M.S. went to see his closest acquaintance, nicknamed the hairy Mexican, who lived across the river facing his shack (home) – would he, his friend, be agreeable for Erica and I to spend the night in his garden's caravan? The answer was affirmative. So the three of us enjoyed 24 hours of enchanting happiness (fig 43).

Not suffering fools gladly, he had many acquaintances but few true friends. Erica and he always got on very well and as she grew older, she became extremely fond of him and as time went by she remained the apple of his eye.

Only a few things are still to be said about J.M.S. The man who, simply being who he was, brought so much richness to our lives and to the few who befriended him. One of them, the hairy Mexican, fourteen years from then was to write to Erica telling her of J.M.S's demise. His ashes were scattered on the street by his fellow companions in drink, between their two favourite pubs. Rightly the best way to wish him 'Goodbye'.

Erica and I shall carry his memory faithfully, alas he will never know how much he gave us.

Fig 43: J.M.S. and Erica in the caravan.

Chapter Forty-Four

MATRIMONIAL RETRY

Erica and I had been in the caravan six months. Out of those Erica attended the school at Nethercombe where she, aged four, went by coach.

After a while Ronald had called a few times and we talked more and more seriously. But Erica was at school and I thought it better that he did not see her, so as not to confuse the child. Although she, J.M.S. and I had been individually happy, I became aware that, she not being with her 'daddy' was taking its toll. Ronald and I had summarised our situation and decided to give our marriage another try.

As a reunited family we were allocated a large three-bedroom house in Plymstock. We were the last but one of the street, and part of a naval married quarters estate. Ron was given a new commission on the Ark Royal based at Portsmouth, he came home weekends and the trial went so well, that after Ronald returned from the Suez crisis (the three days war) I bought a house at Ivybridge, Devon.

Before the deed was completed I attended My-Ellen's succession. This as usual, without help, advice or support, emotional or otherwise. On arrival in France, I was completely bewildered and disconsolate. My-Ellen's house had been unsealed and violated. Its contents, my inheritance, was being appropriated by the recipient of the property who, together with removal men had arrived earlier. I was greeted by being shouted at and ordered to pack up and be gone by the morrow. It was terrible, in equal state of bereavement and fear I was packing all I could, but around me the men were turning the place inside out. They totally ignored me, calling to each other and throwing my, so precious new possessions to each other — Do you want that? How about this? It was cruel, hopeless, lamentable.

Fortunately large transport wood containers, ordered for that date, were delivered and also in mid-afternoon, the vultures left.

It was not that easy to compose myself, however, now on my own, I peacefully meandered from attic to the last cupboard. It was an Aladdin cave. Shelves, nooks and crannies full of four generations' memorabilia; having no time, no space and no money I was able to keep but a few. When I reached the ground floor that had been my living space an additional discovery came to light. The boxes of most cherished things dating from my early childhood and since were no longer there. Antique items, stamp collection, Myellen's dolls and dolls' house and much more all gone, stolen.

The house was abundantly furnished. Late afternoon the transport people collected the comparatively tiny load, and not knowing any better, but painfully reluctant said 'au revoir' to My-Ellen and like a zombie I went to René in Paris.

At René the next day, again ill advised, I was conned by an antique book dealer and made the worst irrevocable financial mistake of my life.

When I was still married to my first husband, my stepmother had given me a collection of books which for some reason was the only item left in the Grand Château. She wanted me to have them. They were piled up in the Bishop's bed alcove. When I left France, René had taken care of them for me. Allow one to justify my elaborating at such length about mere books. This was no ordinary library.

My ancestors as I have said before can be traced back to 1689. The first one to become famous was Editor/Printer called François Didot. His son François-Amboise Didot (1730–1804) was the inventor of the typographic system of dots, he also was the inventor of the single stroke printing press. The two most sought after are his 64-volume work (collection d'Artois) and "les classic Français", 26 x 29 cm thick twenty-one volumes ordered by Louis XVI for the education of 'Le Dauphin' whom at the age of seventeen disappeared, never to be seen again.

For seventeen years these very books were mine too. They were magnificent, green leather -bound embossed with the royal seal, all immaculate and complete. Turning and reading the French Classic from the Dauphin's own collection brought a feeling of respect, grandeur, humbleness.

It had been in 1950, five years after the war had ended that, roaming around the skeletal Grand Château, Charles my fiancé had discovered the one and only material thing there. In the Bishop's quarters, on the floor in the alcove were four piles of large heavy books. The royal edition of French classics! No less! By whose hands? From where? How and why had it returned home will remain a mystery. Where is it now? I frequently ask myself, for no longer do I have them.

At René on the morning after I had been dispossessed of My-Ellen's legacy, yet another antique dealer persuaded me that my books were not the Royal edition, alas their authenticity became known to me too late! The ongoing project to buy a house at home in England was calling for extra finance. I sold that priceless and irreplaceable library for the derisory cash sum of 3000 francs. The book dealer lost his life in a car accident a few weeks later, perhaps there is some justice after all at times.

I flew back home with 3000 francs literally squashed loose in my handbag and the next day I went to the village tiny bank office, stood at the desk facing the manager and casually emptied my handbag throwing notes from my height in front of him! His face changed colour, tried to compose himself and still sitting (I suspect his legs had weakened) he grabbed the telephone.

Allo! I, I there is ... He blurted out. 3000 francs have just fallen on my desk, what shall I do with it? Unperturbed and smiling, I sat waiting for the outcome. Having regained his composure the bank manager picking up the scattered notes from his desk said 'it will be collected this morning, then he gave me the receipt of my irreparable mistake!

No sooner I had access to MY money, one-third was spent on household goods, two-thirds on securing our house mortgage, a revelant point noted in chapters to follow. Pestered the estate agent so much that, I suppose, to get me off his back, he hurried the proceedings! From my first enquiry to moving in took less than five weeks!

We had left Plymstock for Ivybridge upon Ronald's return and enjoyed what every house buyer wrongly names 'Our House'! Totally ignoring the fact that it will not be owned before it is PAID FOR! Ours had been described by the Estate Agent by the pretentious adjective of 'chalet bungalow', in other words a way of describing a building which is neither house nor bungalow.

I had named the house 'Tufted Marly'. Tufted because of its sloping pointed roof, Marly after 'Marly-Le-Roi', the historic little town where My-Ellen had spent all her life. This Anglo-French appellation caused much confusion to both writers and readers, not the least the flummoxed postmen and women for, a neverending variation on the theme. A 'Tufted Mary', a 'Tufted Pairly', a 'Tuften Morby' and more, all passed through our letter box! Indeed the mind boggled!

Erica was at school at Ermington, Ron had been commissioned on H.M.S. Albion and awaiting the date when the Aircraft Carrier was to sail to the East. Based at Singapore and joining other ships on exercise.

Erica and I flew in a VC10 two months later to join him. Albion's Commander Bigden and Ron became closely acquainted and his wife and I ended up inseparable friends. We lived life to the full day and night between the Officers Mess, the American ships and the inland night clubs — A life of leisure if ever there was one. There were holidays in Malaysia, New Year in Hong Kong, etc, etc. Yet it was good to be back home again.

Alas the same predictable day after day, week after week, month after month all too familiar spark-less routine set in again. The lack of laughter, the well-being sense of joie de vivre were never present. One day I expressed the possibility to something quite ordinary, I have forgotten what, and certainly nothing outrageous, my husband age forty at the time said, quote: oh, we couldn't possibly do that AT OUR AGE! unquote, enough said.

Sadly the hibernating worm in the apple had started eating once more and that time the fruits of all my efforts never ripened. There was never a mention by my husband about our evidently growing apart.

It was early April 1971. My fortieth birthday was shortly to be. On a particular Sunday, indeed as most Sundays we, seven of us crammed in Ron's parents' sitting room, were watching the television, through cigarette smoke. I worked my way around legs and feet to go to the 'scullery' for

a glass of water. Once there a frequent need to scream and put aside thoughts resurged. Already on my wedding day and on many occasions since, I had been embarrassed, alienated, out of context as it were. On reopening the sitting room door the uncongenial brain and body smoked tableau hit me in the face. The voice within me screamed: what are you doing here? The answers were twofold. Either to be annihilated slowly by the embrace of the aforementioned conceptual anvil or, to regain my id. Lest I suffocate I opted for the latter. My mind was made up there and then. Freedom! The priority! To follow the adage. Life begins at forty... It did.
　　Vive la Liberty!

Chapter Forty-Five

THE LAUNCH

Contradictorily, it is not easy to leave one's husband/partner. There is an established misconception that the one leaving is always the culprit, it could not be more erroneous.

It took me several years of cogitating before resolving the situation. On the first occasion, one may remember, I had told Ron face to face and his reaction had been, quote: 'if it is the way you feel,'... followed by a total non-attempt to mention my statement again! On the second and last time, I simply drove away (in my own car) and with essential belongings, went to a friend from where I phoned him to let him know. His only sentence was 'You might have told me'. I said that I would 'phone later. I went to collect Erica from school and drove to my relatively new friend Helen Dallow. Later she called herself 'Fossil' and was to have immensely important influence over my life during several decades to come.

When we first met at work she was already Doctor Gordon St. John-Ives mistress.

One day at Moorhaven Psychiatric Hospital, near Ivybridge, Devon, it was the nurses' morning break. I was at the kitchen door when I saw a lively little thing in blue uniform, big matching blue eyes, she was skipping seemingly five inches above the floor towards me. In the kitchen where other nurses waited for the water to boil, she skipped even higher, jumped and twirled, uttering in muffled excitement "He's here! He is here!". Who was there? Evidently 'the' Doctor! She and I being females could not 'fraternise', so we 'sisterised' immediately. She had just qualified as a S.R.N. (M), I was a S.E.N. (M). We saw each other at work and, at any possible time at the drop of a hat.

Helen was short, blond haired and thin. She had a glowing personality, we shared the same sense of humour and the zest for life, although more often than not Helen was tense in body and intense in mind.

When I returned from Singapore and went back to work, Helen told me about Gordon away in Biafra. He had volunteered to go to look after the wounded of the disaster of 1968/69. Meanwhile she had developed the urge to go to Australia to see her emigrated family.

As we had rekindled our friendship, she had asked me to look after her belongings. I asked her to be my babysitter. I was not too pleased one early morning, after a social evening on board, to find Helen in my spare bedroom bed with an unknown man! He fled out of the back door. She, as usual finding the situation most amusing, explained. He panicked for he was a sailor who had taken advantage of an officer's home! Helen was in hysterics, her forte was to laugh at anyone's discomfiture. To shock and debase with contempt and satirical irony everyone's point of view and feelings.

She was, she announced, getting married to Alan the sailor who played the guitar and was bound for Australia very soon. As a married naval wife she would qualify for a charter return flight paid for by her husband. Her plans materialised and away she went and worked as a nurse whilst over there. When she returned our friendship went on.

We shared mischief and misdemeanours. Played cards and Scrabble, going to junk places and generally enjoyed our young lives. Gordon and she one way, J.M.S. and I with or without Erica elsewhere. Then obviously, one track minded Ron still saw Erica and I. So when I left Ron it was to Helen's flat that we went.

Via Gordon I knew the name of Ivybridge's biggest estate owner. It facilitated my renting one of their lodges. A dear tiny damp darkish cottage (fig 44), once again by the river. A lovely small dwelling which burst at the seams with all my books, heavy furniture etc.

On the evening of my leaving home, I recall so vividly to be at Helen's on a mattress in her room when overwhelmed I flung both arms in the air and screamed: "I am free, free!"

Now, for me things settled down happily. Living on the breadline, for all the money I had from the 'royal books' and the joint struggle to pay a

Fig 44: The Cottage, Eastern Lodge.

mortgage I was left £900 out of £3000! Need I say more?

As I had done when I had returned from abroad, Helen too on returning from Australia some months from being there with divorce in mind, having left her unfortunate sailor-husband, went back to work.

Gordon was back in England; soon it was going to be Helen (and Gordon)'s turn to cogitate… For she was bearing his child. He arrived on February 1971 and was registered as Tantalus Spike Fitz-Gordon St. John-Ives, known as Tan. My daughter was ten years old at the time. I was nearly forty, Helen was in her twenties? Both our children were without a shadow of doubt 'Love Children.'

Helen moved to a flat close to my cottage less than two miles from Ermington where Erica went to school; it meant that every day, after dropping her I went to Helen, we spent most of the time of most days together. Erica and Tan, close to being brought up as sister and brother.

In January 1972 arriving at Helen's residence, I saw a letter on the table at the bottom of the stairs, the white envelope said "Helen", that was all. I took it up and found her collapsed in tears in her armchair, a woman (social worker) was looking after her. I gave her the letter, it had been written by Gordon's hand; Explaining why, when she read his lines, she and their baby would never see him again. Gordon was no more. The evening before, he had passed my door to call on the last hope from his assumed friend my landlord who, like the other few people who had been called upon for help, had refused to give it. It had been evidently too cruel to cope with.

In a deserted lane, in the early hours he committed suicide. He was found in his car no longer asleep, why he did not knock at my door as he used to? Perhaps because it would have weakened the courage of his decision. It was one month before his baby's first birthday.

Now Helen and I were both single mothers. After a difficult period of time during which Helen had a psychiatric breakdown. I looked after Tan awhile, then the hospital asked for her to take him back. I had double pneumonia. Eventually Helen and I recovered. I executed completely on my own with my car Helen's move from her flat to a two bedroom council house, plus at times looking after Tan as well as my Erica of course, etc. etc. and thanks to our dynamic optimism and inborn 'joie de vivre' we left behind the trauma and trials and launched ourselves onto the ocean of hope.

Chapter Forty-Six

NEW HORIZON

In Eastern Lodge (my cottage in Ivybridge) it was a struggle to make ends meet. I worked as kitchen assistant-washing up staff. This corresponded well with Erica's school attendance.

The launch also sealed an extended future of friendship between Helen and I. Many a year of great fun, of sharing good and hard times now and in the future, from close range and from far apart.

At one point Erica became involved with the local riding school and worked there too. A pony called Beacon came up for sale and she asked me to purchase it. Together we went to look at him. He was at a distance in a field. I thought that it would benefit Erica and broaden her everyday life. I sold a few things and bought the quadruped and as soon as possible I went to fetch him. I cannot recall how it was arranged for me to pay and take him with me but what will never leave my memory was that, I had no advice, no help and certainly not the foggiest idea about horses!

I had taken with me an orange rope no thicker than my middle finger and no longer than an adult size skipping rope which I secured to his head collar, thus equipped I led him along the country road! All the way out of my wits with fear and saying whoa! whoa! Gently, whoa! His ears went flat back from time to time; for reasons known only to himself, rather than common sense on my part I got him safely to the cottage. There was a very small three-sided woodshed in the back garden, where I supposed the pony would stay until I asked Erica what to do. The pony to my surprise was not happy about the shed so when he was half in, half out I tied the rope to a large nail already at the end of the shed and waited for Erica to come home. Her awareness and riding school knowledge egged by my line of action, I walked up the hill to the big house to see our landlord who was somewhat displeased at the news but very kindly stopped being angry and provided that we had the pony wormed the next day, Erica was welcome to keep him in the same field with their daughter's horse.

Two years on, our way of life was still quiet, pleasurable, routineer. Varied in subjects repetitive in action. In other words too insular. Stimulation of intellect was needed.

Poor Erica at twelve years of age had already changed school (including a spell in as a boarder) five times and Ivybridge left lots to be desired in various fields. The want to educate myself was as strong as always. So far I had had an attempt at selling the Encyclopaedia Britannica, surveyed people in the street for a food company, and now my job in the school kitchen was less than educational, except perhaps in psychology!

The time had come to go forth… Bravely Erica and I pinpointed our new horizon! We pointed a pencil on the map of England, it fell on Lancaster, so Lancaster it was to be. Luck would have it that a removal man I knew of was due to go North in three weeks time. His van would not be full so he was very happy to take my things, if I were prepared to wait, upon my request he also accepted to store my belongings until his main job's day. A week later I had sold many things, including Beacon the pony.

We left Devon on a beautiful sunny morning, the three cats were secured in their cosy prepared cardboard boxes. As soon as the removal van left we loaded the car and went to the road where we used to live. We had four cats, a green-eyed white puss called Moon-Moon kept returning to where she used to spend a lot of her time, in and around our all-purpose outer building. Many a time I had been to fetch her, but though she was purring and evidently pleased to see us, each time she went back across a football pitch, then crossed the M5 construction work or there about and a built up estate, before reaching her habitual corner. On the morning of our departure, we went and called for her. She came, I took her in the car and we made a fuss of her but although she was responsive and purred abundantly, after a very short time she meowed and asked to be let out. I had enquired several times about her and had been told that she was well fed and sheltered, so sadly I thought it kinder to leave her where she had chosen.

Finally we called on Helen and Tan. A cup of coffee… A hug… But no tears… We were on our way to an unknown new horizon.

Chapter Forty-Seven

MIND-ENRICHING HARDSHIP

At the first sighting of road sign LANCASTER we continued on the A6 road but slowly towards evidently the town centre. At the approach of the first roundabout, at the end of Scotforth Road we saw two houses with 'B&B' at their window. The last one, next to a park had a vacancy. We spent the night there, in a pale mauve scheme room and everything to match, hideous! Breakfast was greasy less than appetising bacon and eggs etc. The landlady was heavily made up, her coiffure raven-black and stiff, and her shoes too high, but she was pleasant enough. She told us where to find the housing agencies.

Still with my supportive daughter in tow I went to town, stopped people in the street, called at the theatre (the Duke Play House) and by late afternoon, settled down in a very large double room for one month rental. We smuggled our cats in and they behaved quietly and silently. No complaint came.

There were only three weeks ahead before our belongings were to arrive. Early each morning we set off 'home-hunting' stopping all post people, milk floats, touring and asking at shops plus twice, sometimes three times a day calling at the agency. One of them was expecting a vacancy for a ground floor flat, the agent promised me the first refusal, but the date was not yet certain.

Our temporary accommodation was jolly good, a three star hotel standard, a spacious kitchen shared by a few other tenants. The large house at Dolphinhome was in its own grounds in the heart of the green and peaceful countryside.

It was very lucky that the Scotforth Road flat became vacant on time. I was given the keys only a few days ahead of the removal van arriving. Helen and Tan arrived too from Ivybridge on the same day.

I had but a few pieces of furniture. An old Cyprus pine long haberdashery cupboard, waist high and three sets of drawers and a shelved space with doors each end, price of purchase £3.50! A large bookcase, a piano and cooker were the lot. The remainder were dozens of cardboard boxes.

The first night, the children used a small mattress brought in the car, Helen and I slept in a blanket on the kitchen floor. The cats chose the airing cupboard. The next day Helen left.

Suddenly it was the city. Streets of shops with lit up counters. Cars, buses, the hustle and bustle and the dusk lights, lights everywhere, all almost too much to take in, extremely exciting.

A five-minute walk from our place there was a secondary school, Greaves School, where Erica soon went.

The Northerners have the reputation to be friendly, helpful and jovial, I can vouch for that. Their welcoming, their bonhomie and repartees also brought unexpected colours to my life.

I began by visiting the theatre's restaurant. At Lancaster college I joined a music course and spent many evenings going to Folk Clubs. But not before Erica had made new friends where she could stay at someone's house.

Greaves School was not an establishment which I wanted for my daughter, Erica herself was not that impressed by it either. Ronald, my estranged husband, agreed to pay for a private school. At George Fox Erica finished her schooling before going to Morecambe and Lancaster College.

While still at Greaves Erica had come home with a newly acquainted school girl, within a matter of days one of her brothers called as well, the girls 'friendship' ended quickly but before I realised it my flat turned into a drop-in centre for teenagers. Adolescence is my favourite age group. A few of them called now and again others more frequently but three boys in particular a set of twins and their best friend.

Jonathan and Peter, and Graham known as dizzy! The twins almost lived with us. There were card games, drawing games, all sorts of amusements (fig 45) to music but rarely in the sitting room, more in Erica's room, but

Fig 45: Peter and I playing chess.

we had no carpet and some card games were rather noisy. In addition with the piano my flat was by no matter of means a 'silent' place. There was constant comings and goings we even celebrated Christmas the continental way by having our meal at midnight! All to the fury of the elderly couple living in the flat above! Thirty years on, having nearly reached the age they were then, I understand their furious exasperation, however this does not, by any means justify the bedevilled way they nastily marred our lives.

It began before I took possession on first viewing day. No sooner had we shut the front door there was a thundering knock. I opened the door and a ferocious eyed little old man, without introduction blatantly said: "is there any mail for us?" And before I had time to open my mouth to answer — "We live upstairs, your key fits our door." Without time for me to compose myself, he took the key from my door and went up the outside access steps to his flat, returning down instantly he asserted: —"We shall have to have the locks changed!"

"Certainly," I replied.

Mr and Mrs, Clare and Bill, Hutton spent a good part of their time sitting and looking out of the window, their other occupations were watching television, arguing and having sex!

Once we were finding our feet in our new environment the harassment went from bad to worse. The first complaint was: tell your daughter not to stare at us as she walks the front path, then - would that child of yours close the gate, as she 'always' leaves it open.

Then there was an unexpected visit by someone from the 'Health Department' wanting to check a complaint that my flat smelt of cats! The inspector was satisfied to the contrary.

On a quiet day, only three people talking, and a huge bang at the door made us jump. We were making too much noise and could I keep my cats under control!

All the aforementioned occurred during the first month. Unfortunately the offensive verbiage and physical menaces did not stop there. The Huttons were after us constantly. For example, should we be playing darts in the back garden (which was our garden, the front being the top flat's) Mr H. would march in and holding his fist towards one of the boys, shouted: "Here you! IT WAS YOU . . . The child: "What was?" Mr H: "You left the gate open".

Then another visit that of the RSPCA. It had been reported that my cats had been left alone in the house for a week. It was yet another waste of time for the inspector as my cats were left alone for three days under the vet's advice. They had been fed and looked after by my next-door neighbour.

For years we were spied on day and night, openly or from behind the curtains. Each time I came back from shopping one of the two watchers came on the garden path and slowly paced up and down along the flowerbed. In the morning after I had come back in the early hours Mrs H. had been waiting and I heard her waking up her husband by shouting at him and at the start of the day she stopped me nearly grabbing my arm and shouted: "Do you mind being more quiet when you come back in the middle of the night and pointing at my window! What have you got in there? What kind of woman are you? We know what's going on in there." It was becoming intolerable, we started to live in fear of the next caller.

At one point Mr H. asked one lad for his address and went to see his father to forbid his son the use of the garden path! It was the same lad whom Mr H, a few weeks later, chased with garden shears and intending to harm.

On and on I was insulted — this was a respectable house before you came and I had exhibitionists at my party and strippers! Also "You'll suffer! And you will pay for that!" We were often petrified by the banging at our door, and on the calling simultaneously at any time day or night. It could be 3pm or 5am. I was told not to use my lavatory as much!! And, quote: "We will get you out of here!" Unquote.

There were three years of endless calumny, it went as far as having the drugs squad calling to verify the allegation that we were drug users. Indeed on the day, joss sticks were being used as they often were. I was livid as my feelings were so strongly against such practice.

Mr and Mrs Hutton were the only source of recurring nightmare during my Lancastrian stay. Five years, the longest happy lapse of time I had ever known.

Some of that happiness I would like to share with anyone interested. It had many forms, came and went and varied in length and intensity and all because of British northern altruistic humanity.

The first two years, or there about, I still had my car and used it quite a lot, Within no time at all I had many new acquaintances who soon became friends. That part of Lancashire so near to the Lake District brought a cornucopia of natural world marvels! From Leighton Moss bird reserve to sheep and blue butterflies on the heath. The dales and salt marshes and all so near to all that which a city life has to offer. Financially it was real hardship, I tried to buy bread and oranges wrapped in tissue paper but that did not supply to our need and newspaper had to do!

My daughter and I never once bought new clothes, it all came either from jumble sales or in the case of two skirts and her school uniform I knitted or sewed them, her shoes were the only new things she wore. I for three years was ninety-nine per cent of the time bare-footed but this was by choice, not necessity for second hand shops had footwear.

I had been in Lancaster fifteen months when I was lucky to have made enough friends to contribute to my having a birthday party in my home. I had by then camped at the foot of Langdale alone and once taken a group of teenagers, including my daughter for a camping weekend (fig 46). Lots of fun, lots of laughter, lots of singing. It was too lavish! The car had to go!

Fig 46: Langdale, 1976.

Fortunately I took on a job as a manageress of a tiny dry cleaners/laundry depository and collection shop, and on early closing day I attended a music appreciation course at the local college. From time to time I sang and twice some of 'my' youngsters did as well in my usual folk club. The above illustrates that even living on the breadline, there is always one way or another to smile and survive.

Living to the full, very happy albeit on a shoestring was not enough for my brain. Helen and I were still very much in contact, visiting each other, by car at first, then by endless coach journeys — our letter exchanges were constant — that was all very well, but constant too were my late childhood unfulfilled hopes: to study both biology and human biology, naturally, but not the least to find my own mother.

Towards the latter I started by writing to the Salvation Army and the

Red Cross. As for the former I acted upon and enrolled at the Lancaster and Morecambe College of Further Education. A two-year course in Human Biology, French, Art and English 'O' Level. I was infinitely grateful and over the moon to be given a grant as a mature student.

No matter how hard I could try, no words could convey to anyone the so long awaited beatitude to be taught and learn scholarly four subjects. Encouraged by passing them all I went on to A-levels.

During my scholastic break I followed courses of field study, this included archaeology, evolution etc. All of these cumulated my being accepted for the job of planning technician at Lancaster County Council. As one of a team of four I contributed to an in-depth detailed ecological survey of the entire county. It was fascinating, revealing, enormously satisfying. This was a temporary post created by the Manpower commission. It lasted one year. It was by then five years since my daughter and I had arrived at Lancaster, she was approaching her eighteenth birthday and I felt that as well as the constant heavy grey sky above us, there must have been more to life that (no offence!) Lancaster had to offer. Perhaps a city such as Cambridge or another large place or Norwich might give both of us some opportunities. Also I have to admit that I was not best pleased by the company my daughter was keeping and the temptations to be nearer to Helen, both decided me.

It took much diplomacy to persuade Erica to come with me and I could not say now whether or not I should have guided her in that direction, only she can answer that.

After a couple of days reconnoitring in Norwich and Cambridge, the latter won the toast. It took less than a week of hard work to secure a rented dismal bedsit at the top of a dismal house and to put myself on the waiting list of a local housing association.

On departure day, some friends gave a hand, others ruefully watched.

Erica and I, the cats in their baskets travelled in the front of the van. We drove to turn back at the close by roundabout and passing the place of so many memories, waved for the last time to our friends and Lancaster.

I still have a fond attachment for that historic old city and have been back several times since, when I call on acquaintances and friends. Two families which will always be very special are still there. All the relations of 'my' twin youngsters group as well as their parents of now twenty-seven and twenty-six years old women, the last I was introduced to 'before she was born!' To Lancaster and its people I remain thankful.

THREE CHANGES OF DESTINY

Chapter Forty-Eight

TAXING TIMES

During my five years in the north Helen and her son had moved twice, they were now in Cambridge. With the endless varieties of interests bursting out in all directions, this vibrant city had already started to stimulate Helen's zest for life, so now I too joined in. I became a landlady to foreign students. The three bedrooms were occupied by: a French violinist, a Japanese cellist and a Saudi-Arabian appreciater! All were there merely to learn English, this they did, but as for Cambridge itself, except for viewing the colleges and on the Cam, they learnt little, the reason being that my house was a home to them all.

In the evening we had an 'almost!' cordon-bleu, three-course dinner, then we held long discussions or played at the table, parlour and card games. We had music-playing evenings and sometimes entertained.

It was hard work to keep up with the food supply bought from over a mile away. Overloaded baskets at the back of my bicycle, four large plastic bags each side of the handle-bars, was arduous, but enjoyable.

Helen and I saw each other frequently. Erica started her independent life by taking up my bedsit and soon settled down in a large house shared with other young girls. And so the first year flew by.

To my mind Cambridge had a lot to offer but gave little. A city of mostly transient people and few 'somebody's', teeming with aspirants to grand things with only a tiny percentage of fortunates become achievers.

At the mention of Cambridge the prestigious word 'accomplishment' springs to peoples mind. Success! fame! glory! none of these, being arbitrary, did not impress me.

Of the twenty places I have lived at, Cambridge was the most alienating. People meet people, so-called friends meet so-called friends, work colleagues meet work colleagues; it is all rather superficial and without continuity. Unlike where ever I inhabited, it took nearly two years to find but a few friends. One in particular became a long standing one.

We had been regularly passing each other along the pavement towards the local shop. One day we stopped and she said "Hello, we meet again", to our surprise we found that we were both working nurses. Jan was her name (fig 47), she was bringing up two young daughters on her own, called Louise and Sophie, as I had too brought up Erica. She loved cats, I did too and as days passed, our friendship never ebbed. Jan was warm-hearted, extraordinarily well-read, she shone

Fig 47: Jan.

at knitting as well as being an excellent raconteuse (fig 48).

Amongst my Cambridge years there was to be one when I would have been alone at Christmas, Jan invited me to share the day. The ambience, the home-prepared food, the comforting simplicity were all shared and as my pen writes these lines, I cannot help somehow being a trifle melancholic;

Fig 48: Jan recounting in my sitting room.

225

for, the very table on which we ate is now my writing desk. We remained good friends for many years, I called on her, she called on me

Dear Jan was not an awfully healthy woman, in her later years she suffered and fought the 'big C' but lost. My sadness was made worse as I too was ill at the time making it impossible to join the mourners.

She had travelled a lot and never once did she return without a present for me, I still have them, see some almost every day. Often say 'thank you Jan'.

Seventeen months into being a landlady the owner of my home needed the house for his son and consequently I had to go. I had been on the list of Granta Housing Association for over eighteen months and was the third one down at the top of the waiting list. Because of my official notice to quit I was most beholden to Granta to list me as a priority. As I planned to pursue my role of landlady I was allocated a two bedroom flat.

Grassmere Gardens is a semicircle row of two-storey buildings with pleasant external wooden stairs giving access to middle and top floor balconies. The back of the flats overlooked the green and the trees of a small garden called Alexandra Garden. The front was gravelled and looked over a lawn dotted by bushes from a flowerbed, all in all it is an agreeable complex at a walking distance of the city centre, a few minutes from the river along Jesus Green. This new development had just been completed, not all dwellings were lived in as yet. I was the very first inhabitant of no. 28 and what an amazing sensation it was to make a place one's own for 'its' first time. I painted, had it carpeted and connected to the telephone.

Shortly my first lodger a young German male student arrived and settled in the main bedroom. I used the small one, we shared the sitting room.

On a particular afternoon as I was passing the Grassmere news board, I felt a sudden urge to look at it. A vacancy was advertised for the position of clerical work at the D.V.L.O. (District Vehicle Licensing Office). Just my cup of tea! I thought. There was only a few hours left before the closing date, it was lucky that the employment office was almost next to our boundary wall. I collected an application form, filled it in and like a demented 'Frog!' I bicycled to the government office where in the nick of time I delivered my envelope by hand. I got the post. Since then I often wonder if my answer to one of the interviewing panel: "Why do you think you should be given the job?" "Because I like anything to do with sorting out and classification," I said, "but especially, because of my enthusiasm for" (here I put on my pompous voice, uttering) "minutiae".

To Helen I went full speed, we laughed as we always laughed together and toasted the event with a cup of coffee and cigarettes!

I loved the work. It consisted of opening the mail, checking road tax applications, issuing the disks on the machine and from time to time working at the customer counter. We were a jovial and happy group of workers. I enjoyed every working day there and was sad when it closed down, but I was fortunate enough to be transferred, at my own request, to the tax office next door, a very different concern altogether and to my mind positively loathsome.

I started in a vast room. The entire length of one of its sides and at right angles to the windows was occupied by a single row of small tables, and at one of these, there I sat ticking off small squares on top of reference cards according to a number from another reference card. My training lasted twenty minutes. The supervisor, breathing down my neck from his important height explained, something in the line of: 'This is the yellow card' ... A yellow card being put in front of me and the same was applied to the blue card.

"Yes?" I was asked.

"Yes" I replied reverently and holding back a sarcastic 'sir.'

"If a number between 0-to-10 has been circled on the blue card you have to tick the top square on the yellow card. Will you do a few while I watch?"

Dutifully I was ticking or not ticking, when the male voice resounded with "Well done!" How lovely it would have been to throw the cards all across the desk and walk out, but I didn't!

One day I was sent to return some files to the file archive cellar. When I entered the very large room I was faced with such an unexpected shambles, it defeated the imagination. Files littered the floor, I had to wade across an ocean of individual ones and mountains of awaiting ones to be classified. This appealed to my penchant to categorising anything under the sun! I requested the possibility to be given the job of Sorting out the Archives. Without a moment of hesitation and to everyone's incomprehension my wish was granted and I disappeared into the bowels of Cambridge government offices!

The task lasted several months as there were thousands of files but I relished every working day. It also involved fetching and replacing files to and from the offices. There I met Alan, a handsome young man of my daughter's age, but in our (to put it mildly) erratic and erotic friendship, this, instead of being an obstacle was an added magnetism. His immediate maturity and irrational behaviour was to put me through hell, but the wonderful hours on end of child-like bickering, card games and shared sense of humour amply made up for the suffering, for suffering there certainly was on my part. Alan was clever, an outstanding wasted actor (member of the Cambridge Player theatre group). His inability to come to terms with his 'id' and to control his confused emotions was his curse. I called him 'my smile' and even now the thinking of him brings a smile to my face. Our amorous friendship lasted fifteen years and yet in some ways it shall never end…

It was June 1981, two years in Cambridge where I had enjoyed cycling every which way, in and out of town, any time of day or night. Helen and I saw each other all the time, sharing laughter as we had done over the past twelve years. However I was missing my professional work, the urge to return to nursing surfaced stronger than ever and on the twenty first of June of that year I resumed duty at Fulbourn Psychiatric Hospital where I nursed for three marvellous years. I worked in various wards and was fortunate enough to be asked to join the pioneering team for a special unit. This was run in conjunction with the hospital but headed by Professor Roth, later Sir Roth. Therefore, the single outbuilding was named the professorial unit.

I last worked for Fulbourn in the adolescent unit, a kind and understanding place where youngsters were given comfort and rehabilitation. In most context adolescents have always been my favourite age group. Presumably because fully adult people tell them not to act like children and yet they are too young to say, do and act in an adult fashion. Adolescents are labelled as 'problem' individuals, whilst the truth is the other way round. In our unit there was a girl who was not only physically abused at the age of four by her stepfather, but had also been thrown into his maggot tank! And a thirteen-year-old boy who had endured pederasty abuse since the age of seven! Need I say more. I was extremely fond of them all and they demonstrated, one way or another, that they were of me too. We were sad when I left, but pastures new were calling…

Chapter Forty-Nine

A FEMINIST JURY!

Between my arriving in Cambridge, the second town Helen and I shared, (Ivybridge, Devon, having been the first one), Helen had lived at St Neots where by various means she started looking for and sampling male companionship. Quote: 'I can't manage financially, I'll have to find a man.' Unquote! On the third trial she became entangled with a man from Cambridge University, a maintenance engineer named Mike, in a love affair of a sort and moved to Cambridge with him. To start with they occupied a small, damp and miserable hovel. There a despondent and disconcerted Helen awaited for a house being made habitable by Mike's own work. They lived in it only a few years and finally took possession of a rural property at Smailwell near Newmarket and where at this point of my tale, and in order to understand the pages to follow, a pause concerning Helen is called for.

In my opinion, in modern times, the word friend has become, too lavishly used, commonly misused and flagrantly unmeant.

Reflecting on the distant past, I see now that the main sentiment which drew Helen and I to each other was more of an affectionate association rather than an equitable friendship. However, as with people who are close at heart, our togetherness was a loving one, yet more often than not it was spiritually and emotionally one-sided. All her acquaintances, friends and family, to each of which in so many ways I partook, succumbed under the weight of her elocutionary skill. Situations, discussions and conclusions inevitably ended in accordance with Helen's undiluting suggestions, she was an expert inveigler! Many a time I responded in words and/or actions against my principles and felt dishonest and blameworthy.

Our care for one another was deep and genuine, but our motives were poles apart. She thrived on her successes to make me fail my upbringing and moral standards. I, although with reluctant guilt plunged myself into the sea of laughter and the 'non-you' freedom.

Helen was excessive in all her emotions from the pleasure of the flesh (so she used to claim!) to paranoia.

Drawing, painting and letter-writing (of which I have scores) were a few of her gifts. We shared our unbridled love of the natural world, but above all she loved life and had the uncontrollable ability to satirise everyone! I was perpetually the subject of her amusement and laughed with her. It was not unknown for us to be still talking and laughing at 7.30am having done so since our children's bedtime the evening before.

When my marriage ended it was at Helen' flat that Erica and I stayed (as written before) for a couple of weeks. Similarly when Gordon St. John-Ives took his own life, it was at my cottage that during a few days with me, Helen and their baby boy (Tan) found solace.

Spring 1984, the present time in my story, when I was still in Cambridge and working as a 'play worker' at the C.W.A. (Cambridge Women's Aid): the refuge for battered women. These were taxing months too. I enjoyed tremendously being with the women and their children and they always responded favourably towards me, not so all but one of the other workers! My attitude to the residents was that of understanding and equality, I respected them and should they show or express the wish for my caring help or point of view I gave it unreservedly. This apparently seemed the opposite to rules and regulations by which the refuge was run. The women, I felt, had to comply to the staff's subordination. Admittedly they ended up being rehoused one way or another, then their allowance book was returned to them. Alas in spite of the setting up of the play group, from a disused basement to a gaily painted place with toys and games and where a colleague worker, mothers and children played together, and my affinity with the residents, I was called to a disciplinary hearing. In no uncertain terms I was accused of failing to work collectively to encourage one-to-one relationships, and other untruths verging on the accusers' paranoia.

I had been ordered to attend a special meeting at the head of the workers house, where I duly went. When I arrived and unbeknown to me, the entire refuge's work force, seated in a large circle was awaiting. Silence.

Then I was asked to sit on the only vacant chair and then an avalanche of questions and accusations, were hurled against me. There was no arbitrator, and if any of those present were on my side, they would not have dared saying so. Alone and defenceless I kept quiet; the verdict given, furious and baffled I left the room and made my exit and went to see Helen (who was now back in Cambridge) and as usual together we laughed at such a self-elected criminal court!

When I received the dismissive letter of accusatory judgement, my resignation was already posted and also read my views on the women's pitiful glorification, I never set foot at C.W.A. again!

Chapter Fifty

HELEN AND ENTOURAGE

Helen and entourage did not live at Snailwell all that long but it was then that shortly after the birth of her 'female' infant, her personality started undergoing drastic changes that, ultimately, led to dire consequences.

An up-to-date fully equipped women's resources centre had opened in Cambridge and Helen's always avid reading interests had switched from her many subjects to exclusively that of feminism. As to be predicted, everything, everywhere and everyone was to have or to be meant to understand. Helen's attitude on the matter stretched from the ancient knowledge of wise women (i.e. witches and not malevolent females) to Emily Pankhurst and W.A.M.T. (Women Against Nuclear Threat). The male gender ceased to exist (except if desperately needed in any which way!) A conviction later to include her son.

I, Helen's poodle, as I often was, joined in feminist political and antiwar movements and as usual, albeit directly or indirectly Erica was infected by the situation but not personally involved.

These were also times of general concern and I did not need Helen's voice to join the CND. In 1982 when thousands of women held each other's hands to make a human chain around Greenham Common American Air Base, I was one of the links. Many remember as 'Embrace the Base Day' (fig 49). At other times I made spider webs

Fig 49: Embracing the Base.

Fig 50: Part of our peaceful protest.

with wool in the wood (fig 50) along the peripheral wire fence and sang during the night's vigil; Helen was there too. All the same without Helen, I participated in many other occasions for the cause, such as 'Plant-a-Tree-in-1983' day at Molesworth CND Gathering.

At Midsummer Cottage, Helen's family home at Snailwell, it was getting more difficult to appreciate and also to cope with her increasing irrationalisations of her troubled thoughts and behaviour. At each of our encounters, which were quite frequent, there were imperceptible yet noticeable new or added dimensions to her irrationality. It is odd to relate, that as time went by, the ongoing misconstruing, misperception and Helen's misgiving troubled mind put an end to the country living, Midsummer Cottage was sold for another abode in Cambridge.

Helen and I were nearer to one another once more, in presence certainly, but no longer in complete association. Midsummer Cottage will be remembered by a few, for some delightful days, particularly with the children go-karting and sledging. Bonfire night and strolls to the brook. Also a children's Art Exhibition held in the garden on Githa's fourth birthday party.

Back in town Helen again had to struggle and make do with all the adversities and discomfort of an unfinished dwelling, but at least the women's liberation movement and its followers, as well as the politically involved were at hand.

We did resume some of our long-standing habits with great enthusiasm and laughter; for example when it was dark, torch in hand and head first we rummaged in skips and rubbish heaps. Junk shops, jumble sales, church bazaars were all favourites of ours. This lasted a little while but my attendance and partaking of her increasing women involvement gradually subsided. Even though she still wrote specific dates in my 'Women's Liberation Diary 1983'! Without my knowing. I was no longer being dictated by her orders.

I left Cambridge in October 1984 and continued to call on Helen who by then had separated from Mike. She went to a flat, then to a house and finally settled at walking distance to where she had left. As time went by our visits to each other became (I felt) rather strenuous, marred by Helens sombre aloofness. Several years back when her efforts to intimidate me to her 'overboard feminism' had been successful, she said, with relief one day, quote: 'I thought I had lost you', unquote. Now she was lost to me and to the ones nearest to her and the saddest thing of all, she had lost herself.

Things went from bad to worse. Be as it may there were few events shared at my new home as I was, in 1984 living at Mildenhall, Suffolk. For example a birthday party for Helen, a Christmas with Erica, Robin (her partner) and Helen's family and irregular visits between Helen and I: none of all this was really successful and Helen's laughter was out of tune! After two years all contact had stopped. Mike and Helen's son came on their own once or twice.

Once in the past Helen had telephoned late in the day and laughingly let me know about all of us going to the Notting Hill Carnival, I was to be ready early in the morning. I was and it had been a fairly amicable day.

The last time but one that I was to hear Helen's voice was also on the telephone but oh, so different a call. "Rainbow you must come over, as soon as possible", I was told. "Mike is on his way to collect you now," a somewhat afraid voice ordered. There was no explanation to be got. It was about 9.40 when Mike deposited me, after a thirteen-mile journey in the fog in his unheated van.

Helen had summoned other women we both knew and half a dozen or thereabout were in her sitting room when I arrived. The uncanny silence begged for the same. I walked across to Helen's chair, and bending down cupped my hands gently around her face and quietly said "We have been through so many things together". Her face reddened, her eyes moistened, her expression showed uncontrolled fear. "'Keep away from me" she screeched, "don't come near me!" she insisted. I seem to remember that most women stayed until the early hours, two of them responsive to Helen's 'asked for needs'. It was an almost wordless dramatic night, painful to all but, assuredly worse for Helen whose discordant, disjointed and disassociated bizarre comportment called the tune. At 5.30am I went to the lightless kitchen, made sure I used a lower seat than Helen's one and I put my hand on her arm… "Helen", said I, in a low soft voice "that was too much from me". "Go! I want you to go NOW!" Helen commanded. So I did and was never to see her again.

Some while later at night… Would I please come over? At that time my yet uncontrolled heart condition was incapacitating and my declining was genuine. Now I was never to hear her voice again either!

Still, occasionally one of our ex-acquaintances or friends would give me news of her, one way or another. Alas! As years went by those increasingly made the deplorable and sorriest of hearing.

It was a catalogue of outrageous events. Ignominious mental treatment to her merciless but now violent actions towards her son, deceits, spiteful wrong accusations to and enticement to murder. No violence came from Helen except the ones inflicted on herself! Including the multiplicity of subjects troubling Helen's thoughts, fright was certainly ending up being the most powerful and eventually reached ultimate proportions. She attempted suicide three times in the course of the six years following her last 'phone call on that often remembered dark long evening.

In 1993 I left Suffolk for Wiltshire, where I still am. In spring of the following year, a woman I know telephoned me to say that, Helen who had always feared water and could not swim, finally had chosen that specific medium to end her life. This irrevocably ended any vestige of our lengthy association, or was it a friendship after all? Brave would be the one speculating on such a complexity…

And what of Helen's children one might ask? Although over the years since, I have been the listening outlet of their traumatic past, I believe that it would not be appropriate for me to expand on Tan's and Githa's personal lives. These lines relate to my own story and therefore I will respect theirs. Yet credit must be given where it is due. In spite, or perhaps because of dissimilar circumstances, both children could not have received a better motherly upbringing in every way, cruelly for them it vanished too soon.

Gradually, all of us involved at one time or another with Helen's saga, managed to pick up the loose ends of the strings and fastened them again to a family like ring.

Chapter Fifty-One

THE SEARCH (TAKE ONE)

When I was still a temporary Cantabrigian, and about a year before leaving for Suffolk in late 1984, the ever-smouldering wish of finding my own mother resurged once again. I had not forgotten My-Ellen's unsuccessful efforts on the subject two years previous to my coming to England. Neither had faded the memory of the extraordinary and unexpected course of events which in the fullness of time led to the last search. This I am about to relate.

Since the "Shattering Revelations" (Chapter 10), I had always heard, that in addition to my sister Louisette mentioned in my childhood chapters, there were other ones. The eldest, Solange, it was known had worked on the land when leaving school, then worked in a sugar works in Nassandres and not all that far from Chandai. That was all. As an adult I had found no understanding or help from anyone, neither had I been given any sympathy from either of both my ex-husbands.

Where to start? What to do? And who to contact? It was in September 1975 that I wrote to the Red Cross and to the Salvation Army, over the years I had acquired by writing to various archives, a few documents concerning my mother but for the time being I hoped that the above organisations might help, but no affirmative responses were forthcoming. Meanwhile I attempted to reach my elder sister, my letter was wrongly addressed and it was lucky that she still lived where I heard decades ago. Nassandres then had few inhabitants, everyone knew everybody. Solange received my letter and answered by return post, this was to be the fore runner of many such emotional discoveries.

The following year I went with Helen, Mike and Tan to see her. Thus it was that having found each other, by post as it were, we then met and spoke to each other for the first time. She espied my having changed, I did not recognise her, she having been seven years of age, and I six months old when we were separated!

On that first encounter I had learnt nothing about our mother. Solange didn't want to know. She was bitter and hated our mother and said she had no wish to remember or know anything about her. 'After all, she (our mother) had abandoned her children... Solange had given me a photograph of our mother and a young adolescent girl, she also gave me the address of our second eldest sister named Marcelle. By summer 1978 she and I were also exchanging letters but still I was no more advanced as regard to our mother's whereabouts. Nevertheless I had become better acquainted with two siblings and was an aunt to five nephews and nieces.

Both my sisters came to England and I visited them a few times during which I was making notes of any possible small information. Also gathering by post official documents, birth certificates which in France bears full details of all marriages, divorces etc. This helped my search greatly. Now, I had met my two sisters who had given me fragmented information, yet precise dates of events. So gradually I built an embryonic dossier but strange as it may seem, eight years had to go by before it was put to use... The reasons were twofold: firstly I was still slightly reticent about engaging in upon detective work around the Lush Oasis area, my old fear of Hubert's retaliation and the malevolent reactions of everyone from the distant past (I know now that it had been justified, but that is another story!) Secondly, I had no financial means and no personal transport.

It is why, not before 1983, when at long last I had saved three hundred pounds I made up my mind, once and for all to find my mother. By then I know that she was still alive. I also had acquired a tremendously useful document stating details of her long-ago incarceration and the age at that time of her three children. There had been occasional mentions of our mother's offspring but no one knew how many all together, neither of which gender those were. There was not much to go on but I was ready to pursue my quest. On approaching a private detective who was asking one hundred pounds a week, or was it a day, I cannot remember which ever it was, I promptly and politely escorted him to the door!

My decision was taken there and then, I would do the job myself. I made over twenty telephone calls to France that day and about the same the following day and wrote many letters to hospital, prison, register offices etc.

Then an idea jumped to mind, perhaps a French detective could advise? To that effect I tried to telephone Charles, my French ex-husband's son! That French ex-husband of mine was already a divorcee when we wed and had an eleven year old son. Fortunately thirty years on he was now in the telephone directory, so were two out of three half brothers from my ex-husband's third matrimony.

A man answered my 'phone call… "Richard?" I asked. "Non Madame" went the voice. "I am his brother".

We exchanged a few words, then in all innocence I explained that I had been, as he probably knew Pelo, his father 'the middle wife!' Oh

dear! The poor man had no idea about 'the middle wife' but his astonishment was good humour, he took my telephone number for Richard and that was that… Not quite however. Before I had time to make a cup of coffee, the 'phone rang… It was… No not Richard but my ex-husband! (Pelo is one of my many nicknames) "Pelo? It's Charles" (fig 51) he began, then "how wonderful it is to hear you! And where are you??" etc. etc. His voice and words were spontaneous in the line of… "'As I was telling you yesterday!"… The conversation with his wife Françoise (about whom I have written in the war chapters), was equally warm and jovial. The past three decades lapse

Fig 51: Still Charles.

evaporated in an instant, and accepting their invitation I went to stay at their Paris flat. We reminisced a lot and laughed even more. To prime the search for my mother by driving and stopping, driving and stopping at many villages around Chandai. I enquired at cafés, at diminutive town halls, which consist of one or two rooms with the national flag above the front door. La Mairie-cum-register office and open only now and again, when or how long for is anyone's guess, the café knows! I asked the few elderly in sight and showed my mother's photo, some had heard the name but none knew anymore. The beautiful sunny afternoon was drawing on when we stopped the car to ask an old man who indicated the way to Madame Mession's cottage who, "you know" "knew about something", "you know?" We found two cottages on their own, I knocked at the first but, naturally it was the wrong one.

Madame Mession, indeed had known my mother and all about her…"you know," but had no idea where she might be, and besides "you know," had no wish to hear anything whatsoever about that woman. On the other hand my mother's sister, Madame Mession beamed at the thought, always spent her summer holidays here with us "you know"… No I did not know! It was news to me to hear that I had an aunt, Tante Louise, to be precise, whose name, address and 'phone number might help the search, "you know", Madame Mession hoped "you know!'"

I hoped so too then…

THREE CHANGES OF DESTINY

Chapter Fifty-Two

THE SEARCH (TAKE TWO)

My hope proved ill-founded. Aunt Louise lived quite a distance away from Paris, the journey by car, train, taxi etc took two hours each way. It was amazing to anticipate an encounter with my real mother's sister. Surely the search would soon bring success?

I was greeted with the warmest of welcomes. Our conversing was fluid, Aunt Louise showed me photograph albums, she was understanding about the search and willing to help. To that effect she told me about yet another of my sisters I had never heard about! Better still she knew her fairly well and she gave me "Jeannine's" name and address.

I was delighted, but what about my Mother?

"I understand very well your wish to find her", Aunt Louise accepted. "She is your Mother, it is normal that you want to meet her" she acquisced. Unfortunately, she, Aunt Louise herself, did not know anything, did not wish to hear about the woman who once had been her sister. All that Aunt was able to tell me was that Mother had been a woman of ill repute, so the gossip went. I was, it seemed, back to square one.

Before my detective few days with Charles and Françoise I had spent three days with my second-eldest sister, Marcelle, there had been some hope there too. I had been given the use of a motorcar, a most generous offer indeed from a friend of the family, but already there, two long days of investigations had brought nothing. However, my sister Marcelle had mentioned Versailles as she vaguely remembered where out Grandmother once lived. Also Pontoise I knew was the place where she was to have been known and only I knew through official documents that she had been seen (in prison!). With this in mind, after I left Marcelle and returned to Paris I was taken to Versailles. I found my grandmother's last abode. Yes indeed the other tenants confirmed, but she had died there a long time ago… And did she have a daughter living with her? I queried, yet again no one knew!

Charles, Françoise and I took a day of rest, then we went to Pontoise, the only certainty I had about that area was that my mother had been incarcerated there. Alas there was nothing to be had there either. Frouville had also been mentioned at some point by someone; this prompted us to go and search thereabouts. Frouville is a tiny village, again I knocked at doors, asked around, Françoise came with me along a little lane that went no further than a farm house hidden by trees and guarded by ferocious canines. La fermière came to the gate first. "Looking for something?" she asked. "Yes ,sorry to trouble you but, etc etc", I answered, showing the photo. "Ah yes" she affirmed, "we (le fermier had joined us by now) remember them both very well, don't we?" She continued looking at her husband "Oui", said he "they both worked here during the harvest."

Still standing at the gate I was told why, so many decades ago, my mother had been arrested and sent to prison. She had been Monsieur Fournier's accomplice in the theft of a golden chalice from a village church tabernacle. My informants were civil enough but they did not know what had happened next, except that Frouville villagers might know more. There was a spark of hope at the approach of Trouville.

The Mayor sent us to a nearby farm where a Monsieur Fournier and his wife had worked on the land from 1948 to 1951 (the year of their incarceration). The man had been a farm worker, my mother was also a ploughwoman. The farmer's wife had not forgotten the three Fournier childen, my siblings, as it were. Still it would be better for me to call at Madame's house (the largest in the village evidently!) but Madame had no idea and why could I not try Monsieur B, who ran the farm, she pointed out in the direction? She could help… Monsieur B had employed M. Fournier, it was a long time ago and he had heard nought since!

At that point of the search proper, I had written twenty-three letters, travelled kilometre after kilometre, made over 60 telephone calls. I knocked at doors, showed my Mother's photo and talked to anyone, all of these, countlessly. Names, addresses, information had piled up in my dossier. To my surprise I (and Erica of course) was part of an increasing family, nieces, nephews, sisters and brother gradually sprouted and the plot was thickening by the day. It was all very interesting, many people had either known or knew Madame Fournier but no one could or would enlarge on her mysterious fate. Nevertheless, I was not – NO – NEVER, going to stop the search. Mother! Where were you?

Chapter Fifty-Three

THE LAST GLIMMER OF HOPE

By a strange coincidence I had discovered that my mother's birthplace at Verneuill-sur-Havre had been within a few hundred metres from where I had spent my married life with Charles!

Now my holiday and time off in lieu was almost over but there was still time for one more attempt. I hoped that one of my yet unknown sisters or brother could solve the mystery. Madame Jeannine Dubois was the sister I was looking for. There were a few Dubois in the telephone directory but as I was ignorant as to her husband's initial, Françoise, Charles and I made our way to the area indicated by Aunt Louise.

To the first café we went. "Ah – I think there is some Dubois that way" mumbled the disinterested garçon. Now an old woman with a stick hobbled past. Her answer to the name Dubois was "hoooo!" dunoo! There's a Monsieur Dubois that way but... 'e lives tout seul… "you know." So we were no better informed. Then the familiar adage came true, our third port of call was lucky. A sister never heard of before a few weeks since, materialised on her doorstep. "Madame Dubois?" "C'est moi, why?" I showed the photo I had of her and from then the emotional "hahs", "ahs" and "ohs" filled the air of her rather primitive but warm and welcoming kitchen.

My younger sister by eighteen months, Jeannine was the mother of eight, one of these was a daughter. She had never seen our mother either and adamantly had no wish ever to do so, having been given for adoption at birth. So much perplexity, so much resentment, such a confusion of joy and sadness, that first meeting of many between Jeannine and I ignited further curiosity. Jeannine had heard of sisters of hers, so had they of her and myself, but neither of us two had met the others. Soon I introduced each to each other and now we were four (fig 52).

Fig 52: Four sisters.

All of us had been told by diverse mouths that we had siblings and that by-the-by the rumour was that one sister lived at Mante-la-Jolie not far from Paris? Her name being Fouque.

I knew that there was still some hope if only I could find the missing three.

Time was up, I had to be on duty the day after the morrow. I returned to England leaving behind three sisters and twenty-seven cousins, nieces etc. Quite a find, but no Mother!

Sunday, sixth of November 1983, the day after my return from France. I had the one and final lead to explore. It had been impossible for me to fit everything in.

I was anxious, apprehensive, it was my last hope... and not a promising one at that ... Poised at my table with a cup of coffee and an ashtray within reach, I lit up a cigarette and rang international Directory Enquiries. There were some Fouques at Mante-la-Jolie, there were some at Flins-sur-Seine. The former was fruitless, the second call attempt at the latter went thus.

"I am sorry to disturb you, I am trying to locate my mother, called Marthe Fournier."

"It can't be true!" shouted the woman at the other end of the telephone – "Vous êtes ma soeur?"

So the conversation started. that sister was one of three of us children I was still to find. She too was called Solange! From that day I referred to her as Solange 2, the first one naturally became Solange 1!

Solange 2 explained that our Mother lived with, quote: her daughter Jeannette, to neither of whom, she, Solange, would never speak again! Still she was willing to give me Jeannette's telephone number. Was it the end of the search? I wondered.

Restraining mounting euphoria, calmly I made another cup of coffee and of course lit up yet another cigarette, then I rang Jeannette.

"Sorry to, etc etc, do you know where etc etc"

"Our Mother is with me."

There was a pause as Jeannette and I were unable to speak, so strong was our emotional shock. Hers for having found me, mine needed no explanation. A hasty and simultaneous agreement was made to telephone again in half an hour.

Having recovered a modicum of equilibrium, I rang back, to be told that our mother lived at Jeannette's, but at present was in hospital. Jeannettte would be so happy to meet me, and I her, and so on.

Indeed the search was over, at last I had found my elusive Mother, naturally she was in France and now I was back home in England. There was no time to lose, after all she had had a heart attack…

Chapter Fifty-Four

THERE SHE WAS

In all my working days, only twice did I lie to my employer. Both of them by telephone. The first time I pretended to be unwell and unable to work. I spent the Bank Holiday weekend at an alternative three-day fair. Guilt plagued me for months! The second time was on the very day when, at long last, I found my own Mother. Instead of trying to explain the lengthy saga of the search, I thought it simpler and more straightforward to say that my mother had died and please could I have some compassionate leave. In that instance I felt no guilt, I knew that, contrary to his name, Mr Savage, my nursing officer, was a kind and understanding man and had there been time enough to elaborate on all the details, he also would have granted leave.

I still think that my option was forgiveable. I still think also of what a disharmonious necessity it had been to say that the elderly bedridden woman, who fifty years ago had given me life, had supposedly to be dead before it was too late for us to meet! A quirk of fate.

Having at long last located my Mother I was not prepared to wait, that very night I sailed back to France. Gare du Nord where Jeannette most kindly was waiting with a car. It was bewildering to lunch at my newly found sister.

It was soon to be the hospital visiting time, I followed Jeannette to a small landing and across the threshold of a small room. Jeannette walked between two beds, stopped, bent down to the old woman on her left saying "Maman…." Evidently there she was! (fig 53) The occupier of so many dreams, of so many years of so many questions, so many emotions.

Jeannetle asked her to name her children to which with a pensive, puzzled look Mother obligingly began.

"There was Solange."

"Oui said Jeannette.

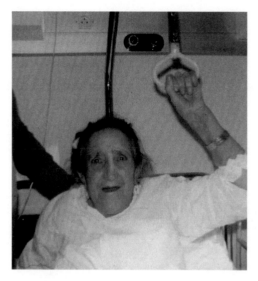

Fig 53: At last! There she was. In hospital.

"After that Marcelle", came on Mother's lips.

"That's it," Jeannette approved.

"Then Louisette", pursued Mother.

"Oui, continue" prompted Jeannette, "Go on".

"There was la petite Pierrette" Mother obliged.

"That's it!" agreed Jeannette – "Well, there she is!"

My mother looked at me, cupped her hands around my face and, pulling me gently to her, kissed me repeatedly on the same spot, on one cheek then the other. When she let go of me she gave me a sad, deep, intense regard and meaningfully said.

"Oh! My little one…."

That was more than I had anticipated. Short and fragmented tittle-tattle went on, when out of the blue Jeannette asked our mother, quote:

"Mamam, did you lay with Monsieur Didot?" Unquote.

Instantaneously mother looked positively petrified, but putting her finger on her mouth she nodded

Jeannetle then asked, quote: "Did you like it?" Unquote.

A timid smile came on Mother's lips and again she nodded. That cancelled any infinitesimal doubt I might have had about my paternity.

Too soon, visiting hour was over.

In answer to the news, my own "little one" (now aged twenty-two!) arrived at Jeannette's thirty-six hours later.

I dare say that Erica meeting her only blood-related grandmother for the first time was bound to be somewhat emotional. It was so. A calm, unsophisticated, gentle and of a few words encounter. There were no dry eyes amongst us. It certainly would have been even more emotional, had we known, then, that these few short moments were to be the only ones. Erica never saw her real grandmother again…

For the time being Jeannette put Erica and I up for three more days, and most garrulous and gregarious days these were! They were also, to say the least, amazing times. My newly found family was increasing by the day! Jeannette's family on her father's side also figured in the snowballing affair. My mother's current and active lover, the son of her ex-one, was also living at Jeannette's. Throughout the developing ebullient events he kept a low profile and was mostly mute. The fact that each time he uttered a word he was stopped in no uncertain terms by Jeannette or others (quote: "No one's asking you for your opinion!" or – "To begin with you have no right to speak ever – shut your face!") might have had something to do with it…

The French being French and on their own territory meant that food and drink as well as argufying and gesticulating were profuse! I was befogged in a whirl of activities including, on Erica's first full day, a visit to Marcelle. Solange our eldest of all was there too, suddenly we were four sisters together.

Phone calls and forty-eight hours later, organised and offered by Jeannine, was a celebratory meal. Seated at the table the entire length of Jeannine's small cottage twenty-two guests feasted for two hours. All adult siblings, spouses and cousins, many meeting each other for the first time, better still our mother's six out of nine children. Solange "the second" was unable to attend. "La petite Louisette" had died of poverty years since, and one of us had died at a few days old. However, our only brother, Jean (John) was there, so four of us met him for the first time too.

It was not the delicious food or the variety of drink which made that unique twelfth of October, 1983, an extraordinary one. It was that, up until then, of the five sisters (fig 54) and one brother all between the age of forty-four and fifty -nine, not one of them had ever seen all of us.

    a)   the two eldest knew each other well, but me vaguely (we

Fig 54:The sisters' first and last encounter.

had met briefly eight years since)

      b)   One knew none, but knew of some

      c)   Three knew each other and of some others

      d)   Apart from our brief encounter with the eldest I knew no one either but knew of all the others

      e)   Solange, the second one of the c), knew two, had heard of some others.

    The truth is difficult to believe at times. All of us since birth had lived no further than two hours, as the crow flies, from each other, and had it not been for my lifelong wish of finding my Mother nothing would have changed. I was the enzyme that made this remarkable catalyst happen.

    No thanks were needed as the catalyst had been my exaltation which is just as well as not even a soupçon of acknowledgement was ever expressed by anyone concerned!

Chapter Fifty-Five

SHORT & SWEET

On the day that followed the family gathering Erica and I spent a few hours with Françoise and Charles in Paris. A most friendly first, and probably the last of such encounters for Erica.

Between then and July 1984, there were regular letters and telephone calls amongst the newly constructed family. On the 12th of that month, nine months to the day of the feast, I left for a six-week holiday in France. I had given up my job and had bought a 50cc moped, with which, loaded at both its ends and from footrest to footrest, I rode to Le Havre to arrive in the early hours of Bastille Day!

In the afternoon Jeannette and I went to see Mother who was in hospital following one of her heart attacks, but that holiday was to be a memorable one. I stayed for unlimited amount of days at each of my sisters, spent a day at my brother's home and visited acquaintances of life long past.

I rode up and down the Normandy hills where the cows stopped grazing in surprise on hearing the put-put of my two-stroke engine, and all the while entirely alone I went across kilometres of Forêt Royale being showered with clouds of all sizes of many brown and orange butterflies. It was magic. My moped and I covered nine hundred kilometres in all, for the extravagant sum of £10.00 including oil!

My last stop on the way back to Le Havre was to see my Mother. She had returned to Jeannette, but now was back in hospital after yet another heart attack. How I wished to have been told and see her up and about at home. Still it was lovely to see her on her own and to be able to record her voice as we spoke. Our embraces were warm, our kisses meant. Jeannette had told me several times, and still does, that throughout her own life our Mother often used to mention my name and this comforting thought helped as I sailed away from her on the 23rd August 1984.

Jeannette's telegram arrived on the 31st. My Mother was dead.

MOTHER DEAR MOTHER

Mother dear Mother
It was the other mother
Who told me about you.
She, my step-mother
Who said "I'm not your mother-
your mother deserted you"

Mother dear Mother
At six months old, not older
She snatched me away from you,
And she, the other mother
Owned me forever
Having slammed her door on you.

Mother dear Mother
Fifty years later
When I was a mother too
My search drew nearer
Ill in bed, Mother,
My own Mother, I found you !

Mother dear Mother
We hugged each other
But the hours were too short and few
It was all over
No card, no flower
You were gone – but I had known you.

EPILOGUE

For us mere mortals the velocity of our life is startling…
A blink of an eye in fact.

Days, years, time, are all human conventions. The butterfly
I saw this morning kissing the rose will be dead tomorrow,
yet the bicentenary Oaks beside my garden might still sway
for another several hundred years.

This brings me to thinking of my last fifty years passing by.
A half century gone! How? Where? A wee fluff in the
history of time.

And so following the conventions, albeit mostly in my
case following them not, led me to write the major
circumstantial memoirs.

A TRIBUTE TO ENGLAND

Though you are not my native land
I respect you, royal England.
From France I came, lone and lonely;
You held a hand, showed me the way.
I was naïve, young and lost then;
You offered me a safe haven.
I slaved at work – I'd no option –
My reward was my adoption.
I cherish still that great honour
And remain your loving daughter.
And, when I do grow very old,
Happy I'll die, if in England;
And with my ashes soft and cold
I'll feed your soil of Golden Land.

This book is dedicated to my daughter, Erica Firmin-Didot.

ACKNOWLEDGMENTS

My deeply heart felt gratitude to L.A. without whom this work could never have been completed.
Jonathan Inigo Aucken deserves my thanks for his help with some typing and his excellent reading aloud.
My everlasting thanks to Sandra Andrews for understanding and invaluable help over the past ten years, and for her execution of my idea for the cover.
Barbara Hammond
Deanna Bennett
Becky Mason
Sara Smith
to whom I owe much and always will.

Photograph on p.115 by kind permission of June 1944 Museum, L'Aigle battle (publisher Macon)

ISBN 978-0-9564597-0-1

Printed in England by thinkink, Ipswich

Published by Memory Press, 4 Seagry Hill, Sutton Benger, Chippenham SN15 4SA.